Law and Soc

Volume 5

Chinese Legal Theory and Human Rights

Rearticulating Marxism, Liberalism, and the Classical Legal Tradition

Volume 1
Criminological Theory. Just the Basics
Robert Heiner

Volume 2
Is Legal Reasoning Irrational? An Introduction to the Epistemology of Law
John Woods

Volume 3
The Law's Flaws. Rethinking Trials and Errors?
Larry Laudan

Volume 4
Logical Concepts in Legal Positivism. Legal Norms from a Philosophical Perspective
Juliele Maria Sievers

Volume 5
Chinese Legal Theory and Human Rights. Rearticulating Marxism, Liberalism, and the Classical Legal Tradition =
Elena Consiglio

Law and Society Series Editors
Robert L. Heiner   rheiner@plymouth.edu
John Woods   john.woods@ubc.ca

Chinese Legal Theory and Human Rights

Rearticulating Marxism, Liberalism, and the Classical Legal Tradition

Elena Consiglio

ISBN 978-1-84890-308-1

College Publications
Scientific Director: Dov Gabbay
Managing Director: Jane Spurr

http://www.collegepublications.co.uk

Original cover design by Laraine Welch
The image (© the author) on the front represents Xie Zhi: a legendary
animal dispenser of justice, and the symbol of law in contemporary
China

to my Teachers, to Igor and Lucia,
with awe and love.

TABLE OF CONTENTS

Acknowledgments

I would like to thank Professor Angelo Rinella, Professor Francesco Viola, and Professor Michael Palmer for their invaluable academic guidance, for their support throughout the long gestation of this work, and for their commitment to making young scholars flourish. My gratitude also goes to Professor Xu, Professor Chen, Professor Qi, Porfessor Pu, Professor Miao, Professor Zhang, Professor Jiang and Professor Yan for their precious help with my fieldwork, and to Chen, Deng, Li, Yong, Lee, for their valuable assistance with the research. I would also like to thank Clelia Bartoli, Bruno Celano, Igor Cherstich, Pierluigi Chiassoni, Lucia Corso, Giorgio Maniaci, Eva Pils, Albert Chen, Isabel Trujillo, Giovanni Sartor, Aldo Schiavello, Russell Wilcox and Francesco Zanetti, who either read earlier versions of the manuscript, or discussed their arguments with me, always providing valuable insights and comments. The following Institutions have also greatly contributed to this work, either by providing research grants or by facilitating the fieldwork: University of Palermo (particularly the coordinators of the course 'Human Rights: Evolution, Protection, and Limits'); the Bingham Centre for the Rule of Law, the British Institute of International and Comparative Law; Chongqing University; South West University of Political Science and Law; Xiamen University; University of Hong Kong and the School of Oriental and African Studies; University College London. Finally, I would like to acknowledge the love, encouragement, and patience of my husband and my parents.

CHAPTER ONE

Introduction: Critical Engagements

'I hold the firm conviction that in spite of the huge challenges before us, if we draw extensively on the best of cultural, spiritual and institutional creations that humankind has hitherto contributed, and at the same time embrace and give new expression to our classical discourses, then our extrication from our predicament will not be as distant as we may imagine.'

He Weifang[1]

In Western discourses, it is generally assumed that the concept of human rights, and perhaps even the idea of subjective rights, do not have a close equivalent in the Chinese legal tradition.[2] However, citizens' rights are now enshrined in the Constitution of the People's Republic of China ('PRC' or 'China'), and with the 2004 amendment the Chinese government has officially made a commitment to protect human rights at the domestic level, proclaiming that 'the state respects and protects human rights' (Constitution of the PRC, Article 33). Furthermore, having signed a number of treaties on human rights,[3] the Chinese government is bound[4] to respect relevant international standards on these matters. The third 'Human Rights Action Plan' released in August 2016 by the Information Office of the State

---

[1] He Weifang (2012) *In the Name of Justice: Striving for the Rule of Law in China* Brookings Institution Press at 59.

[2] See, among others: Svensson, M (2002) *Debating Human Rights in China: A Conceptual and Political History* Rowman and Littlefield; Cheng Liaoyuan and Wang Renbo (2014) *Quanli Lun* [On Rights] Guilin Shi Guangxi shi fan da xue chu ban she at 147-150; Angle, SC (2002) *Human Rights and Chinese Thought: A Cross-Cultural Inquiry* Cambridge University Press.

[3] The PRC signed and ratified the International Covenant on Economic, Social and Cultural Rights. The PRC signed the International Covenant on Civil and Political Rights (ICCPR) on 5 October 1998, but has not ratified it as yet, notwithstanding internal and external pressures from Chinese citizens, scholars, lawyers and journalists who signed a petition urging the National People's Congress to ratify the ICCPR and international NGOs such as Human Rights Watch.

[4] According to Chinese Law, norms contained in international documents ratified by China are not directly applicable by Chinese judges, being China a monist system. In order to be enforced, they need to be transposed into law.

Council for the period 2016-2020,[5] defines this as a 'decisive time' for the development of human rights. The document mentions the problems, some which qualify as 'serious', in the actual realisation of human rights for all, and commits to their 'steady and sustainable development'. The question to be asked, therefore, is not whether China has traditionally developed the notion of human rights or not. Rather, one needs to ask how this notion is understood, articulated and discussed in the Chinese context.

Chinese authorities have often declared that their interpretation of human rights differs from that of European liberal discourses.[6] On the one hand, liberal discourses on human rights have been described by the Chinese authorities as morally flawed because, at least from the official ideological perspective, they foster individualism. On the other hand, they have been rejected as inherently Western constructions based on values that have nothing to do with Chinese culture. In distancing itself from these discourses, the Chinese government has proposed alternative views of human rights that—they claim—are compatible with Chinese culture, and that can be relevant for countries that share some of China's cultural values (Socialism, Confucian heritage etc.). When faced with these claims one wonders whether this position only represents a façade to justify limitations on civil liberties and rights by the Chinese authoritarian regime. It is important to clarify, however, that the Chinese discussion on human rights goes beyond the official views of the government.

In his article 'Conditions for an Unforced Consensus on Human Rights', Charles Taylor poses the question whether an

---

[5] Information Office of the State Council of the PRC (2016) 'National Human Rights Plan of China (2016-2020)' available at <http://english.gov.cn/archive/publications/2016/09/29/content_281475454482622.htm>.
[6] The Final Declaration of the Regional Meeting for Asia of the World Conference on Human Rights, released in 1993, also called the Bangkok Declaration, at paragraph 8, reaffirms the universal nature of human rights and states that 'they must be considered in the context of a dynamic and evolving process of international norm-setting, bearing in mind the significance of national and regional particularities and various historical, cultural and religious backgrounds' UN World Conference on Human Rights (1993) 'Final Declaration of the Regional Meeting for Asia of the World Conference on Human Rights' (1993) available at: <https://www.ru.nl/ publish/pages/688605/bangkok-eng.pdf>.

agreement on specific human rights norms can be reached globally.[7] Taylor refers to the well-known intuition by Jacques Maritain that a consensus on human rights norms that governments are obliged to enforce can be reached on some norms, provided that we ignore the question of *why* we agree on these norms. In this theoretical perspective, the global consensus on human rights norms can only be reached at the practical level, leaving out the reason(s) why we agree on the specific norms. In other words, although agreeing on some principles and on some norms that demand protection for human rights is possible, different cultures and societies would still disagree on the justification for these norms.[8] In any given society, the human rights norms 'would have to repose on some widely acknowledged philosophical justification' to be accepted and, 'to be enforced, they would have to find expression in legal mechanisms'.[9] If Jacques Maritain and Charles Taylor are right, the justification of human rights must necessarily arise from and thrive within a specific legal and philosophical tradition, including non-liberal traditions, and must resonate with broader social norms and cultural codes in order to be successfully established.

In this perspective, the problem arises of whether and in what ways a non-liberal philosophical and legal tradition such as the Chinese one can accept and justify human rights. Taylor hints at different moves that can work. In particular, these moves could be either changes in the underlying philosophical justifications or changes in the legal forms in which the norms on human rights are expressed. In both cases, the change must take place within a specific culture, and should be based on justifications internal to the culture, because only in this way can the human rights norms be widely accepted, observed, and upheld in the face of their violation by the whole society and its institutions. In the case of China, where shall one look in the attempt to find the justification of human rights?

As already mentioned, the official discourse claims to offer a new idea and justification of human rights alternative to the liberal one and which stands in opposition to the liberal one. However, this

---

[7] Taylor, C (1999) 'Conditions for an Unforced Consensus on Human Rights' in Bell, D and Bauer, JR (ed) (1999) *The East Asian Challenge for Human Rights* Cambridge University Press 124 at 129.

[8] Charles Taylor defines this consensus as an 'overlapping consensus', referring to the famous theorisation by John Rawls. Rawls, J (1993) *Political Liberalism* Columbia University Press, at 133-168.

[9] Taylor, C 'Conditions for an Unforced Consensus' supra note 7 at 129.

claim does not appear to be solid or supported by sound arguments. Indeed, a more nuanced analysis of the Chinese discourse and practice of human rights shows at least three different layers of this discourse: the already mentioned 'official one' sponsored by the government, the one of activists who fight for rights on the ground, and the intellectual one of scholars who theorise about rights. Up to the first decade of the 21st century, activism has generated a certain effervescence in the Chinese perception of rights. Chinese activists have been increasingly vocal in their fight against abuses, corruption, and violations of basic human rights, and their actions have sometimes been connected with human rights litigation in Chinese courts.[10] Chinese human rights lawyers as well have courageously taken cases to court and some of them are activists.[11] The success of their action, it has been argued,

---

[10] The judicial interpretation of rights, however, is limited. The most important limitations are due to the fact that the courts are prohibited from applying constitutional provisions directly. In addition, the judiciary suffers from its relatively weak institutional position within the state architecture, vis-à-vis the powerful government and bureaucratic administration. Analysis of the position and role of the judiciary in the fight for rights is not the main goal of this book. For a broad and up-to-date overview of the judiciary after the reform see Balme, S (2016) *Chine, le visages de la justice ordinaire. Entre faits et droit* Les Presses de Sciences Po. On the role of the courts in vindicating rights and the limitations on their action by political and administrative powers see Silverstain, G (2003) Globalization and the Rule of Law: 'A machine that runs of itself?' (1-3) *ICON* 427; and Palmer, M; Fu, H, and Zhang X (eds) (2019) *Transparency Challenges Facing China* Wildy, Simmonds and Hill Publishing.

[11] A prominent figure is that of Teng Biao, a human rights defender and activist. On 14 January 2016, Human Rights Watch reported that Chinese police had rounded up approximately 300 rights lawyers, legal assistants, including Falun Gong defenders, and activists across the country, between July and September 2015. Six months after the start of the crackdown, eleven were formally arrested, three had been released on bail, and twenty-four remained unaccounted for. Those officially arrested faced a high likelihood of prosecution and conviction. Amnesty International reports that plainclothes police officers have continued to launch raids on the homes of those suspected of having such a connection to Falun Gong. Of those who are currently detained, reports have additionally surfaced that some are not receiving the medical care and attention that they need. The prominent human rights lawyer Wang Quanzhang was held in police custody on dubitable grounds and awaiting trial. In November 2017 the human rights lawyer Jiang Tianyong was convicted for the crime of 'inciting subversion of state power'. The assimilation of the lawyers into the regime ranks or their annihilation through repressive means is documented by

was one of the reasons for their crude repression and persecution since the beginning of the new millennium.[12] This level of the discourse is entangled with the actual practice of human rights. Enquiries on this level have demonstrated the extent to which the public authorities offer human rights recognition and protection, the limited efficacy of the legal remedies when citizens' rights are violated, and the curtailment of rights protection whenever the stability of party rule is threatened. In addition, it has also been persuasively shown how rights are trumped when action based on rights threatens local and/or national stability, understood by the elite in power in a rigid fashion.[13] The justifications of the practice of human rights, however, even at the practical level of the fight for rights, are to be found in the philosophical premises that underpin the conception of rights at the theoretical level.

Indeed, the fight for human rights has also taken place within academic discourses, at the theoretical level, and it is this specific dimension—often neglected by Western observers—that this book aims at exploring. Since the beginning of the 19th century, Chinese scholars have contributed to the debate on human rights by providing specific theoretical arguments. The effects of these intellectual debates may not be as evident as those of street protests. Nevertheless, the efforts of Chinese legal scholars constitute a long-lasting attempt to change the Chinese legal system from within, in particular when they formulate their ideas in ways that resonate profoundly with the core beliefs of Chinese society at large. Indeed, some ideas formulated by intellectuals are eventually picked up by Chinese social movements. This happened for instance in the case of Wei Jingsheng's theories of human rights, which were voiced through the magazine *Tansuo* (Exploration). Wei's thesis on human rights informed the battles for rights in the 20th century. Students had grasped and shared the human rights thesis held by Wei, and they brought those ideas to Tian an' Men square. Wei's ideas are also significant for today's rights speculation: according to Steven Angle, the contemporary theorisations on rights follow in some aspects the blueprint of Wei's

---

Eva Pils in Pils, E (2015) *China's Human Rights Lawyers: Advocacy and Resistance* Routledge.
[12] Pils, E (2008) 'China's Troubled Legal Profession' *Far Eastern Economic Review* available at: < https://ssrn.com/abstract=1563922 >.
[13] Biddulph, S (2015) *The Stability Imperative: Human Rights and Law in China* UBC Press. See also Pils, E (2018) *Human Rights in China. A Social Practice in the Shadows of Authoritarianism* Wiley.

former theorisations and, also at this level, his theorisations had the potential to become a powerful internal factor of change. [14]

The argument of the return to a 'Chinese identity' is promoted by the official propaganda as part of the 'Chinese dream' of a great nation, whose influence is geopolitically strong but peaceful, to justify the party's actions and policies. It is perhaps right to ask whether the literati, those who have for millennia been respected and rewarded by the Chinese people as the holders and keepers of Chinese wisdom, and who are now scholars, academics, professors, thinkers and intellectuals, in fact hold a different position towards the use of identitarian claims from the official discourse. This book explores the level of justification given by legal scholars in the attempt to illuminate a different path to the recognition of human rights. Without ignoring the consistent limitations placed by the Chinese Communist Party on free philosophical exchange, this book wishes to acknowledge the different voices which are indeed minoritarian, but still present and meaningful in the internal debate, because they offer different justifications for human rights.

It is for the reason just mentioned that the present investigation focuses on the scholarly discourse only. The core question is how rights are explained, how rights are defined and what justification is given for their recognition and protection within the internal doctrinal debate in China. Discussions about the nature, justification and hierarchy of rights have taken place at the academic level. But what are the main justifications for the recognition of rights according to Chinese legal scholars? Are those justifications different from the official discourse put forward by the government? If so, in what ways? Also, are those justifications different from the prevailing ones offered by the liberal discourse? Do Chinese intellectuals agree upon a list and a certain hierarchy of rights? Is this list and hierarchy compatible with the claims made by the official doctrine presented by the party? Or are the claims different because they are based on different justifications and theoretical presuppositions? This book aims at answering those questions, exploring how much this scholarly discourse is converging with or diverging from the official one of the

---

[14] Angle, SC *Human Rights and Chinese Thought* supra note 2.

regime, whose agenda is openly and markedly against some human rights such as freedom of speech. The conceptualisations of human rights and subjective rights by Chinese scholars offer a plurality of theoretical justifications for their recognition and protection within the Chinese legal system and for their acceptance by the broader society. This book elaborates on the philosophical underpinnings of the different theoretical standpoints on human rights and subjective rights.

The main argument I propose is that Chinese theoreticians of human rights have made use of concepts from pre-existing traditions, but in a creative manner. These intellectuals took into account elements from three main discourses: Marxism (as interpreted in the Leninist-Maoist approach, but also in their original interpretation of Marx's thought), liberalism, and Chinese traditional thought. However, Chinese scholars also critically engage with these elements, combining and re-elaborating them in order to create theorisations which are unprecedented within China. The power of intellectual syntheses has not escaped the eyes of the censors. The elite in power is fully aware of the potential political change brought about by rights theorisation. For this reason the regime has recently strongly silenced the new voices coming from academia. The sophisticated process of creative theorisation was undoubtedly constrained by limitations imposed by the Chinese regime. The space of limited academic freedom has recently been tightened in the new phase of 'authoritarian resilience' that China is experiencing at present.[15] Although since the opening up of China to the West in the early 1980s the debate about human rights has been effervescent, drawing resources for debates from Western theories as well, in 2015 the government banned the use of Western resources, especially in the field of jurisprudential theorisation. [16] The indication is to use the Marxist doctrine of dialectical materialism as the basic tool for any theoretical

---

[15] The thesis of China's future development as authoritarian resilience is held by Nathan, who observed that 'Under conditions that elsewhere have led to democratic transition, China has made a transition instead from totalitarianism to a classic authoritarian regime, and one that appears increasingly stable'. Nathan, AJ (2003) 'China's Changing of the Guard. Authoritarian Resilience' (14) *Journal of Democracy* 1 at 17. See also Walder, A (2004) 'The Party Elite and China's Trajectory of Change' (2, 2) *China: An International Journal* 189 at 197; Perry, EJ (2007) 'Studying Chinese Politics: Farewell to Revolution?' (57) *The China Journal* 1.

[16] In January 2015, the CCP issued guidelines mandating higher education institution to adhere to the official ideology and the Xi Jinping thought. Available at: <http://www.xinhuanet.com//2015-01/19/c_1114051345.htm>.

endeavour.[17] Nonetheless, this book argues, the Chinese intellectuals' attitude of critical engagement that has dominated the discussion on human rights in the recent past represented an important development, not only within Chinese legal thought but also within Chinese consciousness at large.

Chinese Consciousness in Crisis

Since the early 1990s, Chinese legal theorists have tried new ways to justify human rights within the Chinese internal categories, a move that is particularly important in light of the historical relationship between China and the West. In the recent past, China has witnessed attempts to modernise its legal system in order to meet the challenge posed by Western culture. The fall of the last imperial dynasty and the growing influence of colonial powers have contributed to this phenomenon. As a consequence, not so long ago, Chinese scholars perceived their culture as inferior when compared with Western ideas. As we will see, this phenomenon was characterised by a strong intellectual rejection of all that was Chinese, including traditional legal and political doctrines. In the light of this contextualisation, it is possible to argue that Chinese academia has recently tried to overcome its crisis by (among other endeavours) formulating creative syntheses on human rights. This process is what this book seeks to capture and describe.

The introduction of the idea of human rights in the Chinese intellectual environment must be framed in the broader context of the meeting between Western and Chinese culture at the end of the 19th century: a confrontation that ended with the defeat of China and with the imposition of the so-called 'humiliating treaties'.[18] The encounter

---

[17] Ibid.

[18] The Opium War and its aftermath have been used in CCP rhetoric as a 'very deliberate celebration of a national insecurity. The insistence on the commemoration of China's national humiliation, the victimization and the induction of a feeling of defeat generated a feeling of revenge and redemption towards the Western powers. The strategy of victimization serves the purposes of the CCP of nurturing a nationalist feeling, and gaining support from the citizens. China's nationalism has been built up through celebrating the glories of Chinese civilization but also commemorating China's weakness. This negative image comes out most directly in the discourse of China's Century of National Humiliation (*Bainian guochi*)',

with the West generated the awareness that changes were needed to prevent China from being overcome by Western powers. This phenomenon, which is referred to as the crisis of Chinese consciousness, [19] was accompanied by an outspoken sense of inferiority and inadequacy, so that elements once perceived as constituting the Chinese identity, were contested and rejected by Chinese authors and intellectuals. [20] At this crossroads, Chinese intellectuals elaborated three different intellectual responses.

A first group of scholars argued for full Westernisation. A second group of scholars was convinced of the technical superiority of the Western powers, but attributed a moral superiority to Chinese civilisation. In the light of this view, this group of intellectuals advanced the theory of Chinese ends by Western means: the Chinese 'essence'—the social values of the Chinese tradition—had to be preserved and realised by using the powerful material and conceptual means provided by the West. Finally, a third group of scholars reframed the opposition between the West and China into a different opposition between past and future, backwardness and progress, and argued for the necessity to renovate Chinese thought and praxis. [21]

Callahan, WA (2004) 'National insecurities: Humiliation, salvation, and Chinese nationalism' (29, 2) *Alternatives* 199 at 202. Humiliation symbolises both the insecurities in the technological and economic field and the moral insecurities. The leverage of humiliation is used to activate a positive reaction. 'In other words, the narrative of national salvation depends upon national humiliation; the narrative of national security depends upon national insecurity.' (Ibid at 202) Therefore, the use of historiography that heavily stresses episodes of humiliation serves the purpose of building public adherence to potentially contestable policies such as the determination of the CCP to recover lost territories (Taiwan and Tibet, for instance), and to build confidence in and support for CCP governance itself by showing its capacity to guide economic development, unlike previous corrupt governments. As the view of narrative approach to history explains, the historical memory of humiliation shapes both domestic and international policy.

[19] Lin Yu-Sheng (1979) *The Crisis of Chinese Consciousness: Radical Antitraditionalism in the May Fourth Era* University of Wisconsin Press at 152. In this expression the Chinese intellectuals are represented, in traditional terms, as the 'consciousness' of the country.

[20] Ibid at 152.

[21] The Chinese philosopher Fung Yulan wrote 'Some people say that Western culture is a motor car culture … But motor cars did not exist in the West originally [and only came into existence at a certain point in history]. Having motor cars and not having motor cars is a distinction between the ancient and the modern, and not a distinction between China and the West' Chen, AHY (2006) 'Conclusion: Comparative Reflections on Human Rights in Asia' in Peerenboom, R; Petersen, CJ and Chen, AHY (eds) (2006) *Human Rights in Asia. A Comparative Legal Study of*

These discourses affected Chinese legal culture between the end of the 19th century and the beginning of the 20th century. Some Chinese intellectuals started to use Western legal ideas to critically evaluate their own tradition.[22] Others[23] put forward the notion that a degree of Westernisation (for instance the modernisation of law) could be combined with the maintenance of some 'traditional' concepts and values (eg Confucian notions such as respect for parents expressed through the virtue of filial piety). Generally speaking, however, legal backwardness was identified as one of the causes of the Chinese defeats by the West. The Chinese legal system was seen as unable to address fairly the disputes between Westerners and Chinese because of its supposedly irrational provisions.[24]

In this context, at the beginning of 20th century, the Qing dynasty initiated a process of 'modernisation', which also affected

---

Twelve Asian Jurisdictions, France and the USA Routledge 487. According to Chen, human rights are an invention of modernity. Chen describes the rise and globalisation of human rights as 'a sign of humanity's moral progress, a quantum leap in the moral consciousness of humankind' (Ibid at 488). In the book, the theory and practice of human rights in various Asian jurisdictions including China are compared and contrasted, and they are further compared and contrasted with those in France, the EU and USA, considered as representative Western jurisdictions.

[22] Lin Yu-Sheng *The Crisis of Chinese Consciousness* supra note 19 at 153. For a study of the early Chinese discourse about rights and human rights see Svensson, M *Debating Human Rights in China* supra note 2; Angle, SC (2000) 'Should We All Be More English? Liang Qichao, Rudolf von Jhering, and Rights' (61) *J. of the History of Ideas* 241; Angle, SC and Weatherley, R (2000) 'Review of the Discourse of Human Rights in China: Historical and Ideological Perspectives' (59) *The Journal of Asian Studies* 719; Angle, SC and Svensson, M (eds) (2001) *The Chinese Human Rights Reader: Documents and Commentary 1900-2000* Routledge; Weatherley, R (1999) *The Discourse of Human Rights in China. Historical and Ideological Perspectives* Palgrave Macmillan.

[23] See Scarpari, M (2015) *Ritorno a Confucio, La Cina di oggi tra Tradizione e Mercato* Il Mulino.

[24] This has been recently argued by scholar He Weifang (1999) 'The Judicial System and Governance in Traditional China' in The Mansfield Center for Pacific Affairs (2019) *The Rule of Law, Perspective from the Pacific Rim* The Mansfield Center for Pacific Affairs 91, a prominent Chinese legal theorist, who has been ostracised for expressing his ideas of law which conflict with those of the CCP. For an account of the legal treatment of foreigners see Edwards, RR (1980) 'Ch'ing Legal Jurisdiction Over Foreigners' in Cohen, J (et al) (eds) (1980) *Essays on China's Legal Tradition* Princeton University Press 222.

Chinese law.[25] The reform resulted in the implementation of a new civil code adopted at the very beginning of the 20th century. The code drew on Western models[26] and on the idea that some aspects of traditional Chinese culture were fundamentally unjust. The collapse of the Qing dynasty soon nullified the efforts for the new codification, but the notion of a need for modernisation and Westernisation remained part of Chinese legal debate. In particular, in 1919 this notion inspired the May Fourth movement, a significant moment in Chinese intellectual history.

The May Fourth was a radical iconoclastic movement whose scope and depth have been described as 'unique in modern history'.[27] The intellectuals of the May Fourth movement,[28] whose writings would later influence Mao Zedong's thought, rejected previous theories centred on the possibility of combining Chinese and Western concepts. The May Fourth intellectuals saw cultures as organic wholes, which could only be adopted or rejected in their entirety. In their view it was therefore impossible to integrate elements of Chinese and Western cultures into a new synthesis, since such elements were assumed to be meaningless when abstracted from the cultural framework to which they originally belonged.[29] These scholars believed that, since progress required the adoption of Western ideas, the only progressive option was the wholesale rejection of Chinese tradition and a full Westernisation of all aspects of Chinese society.[30]

The May Fourth movement managed to silence previous, more moderate approaches on law, and enjoyed a certain following. Nonetheless, it proved fundamentally ineffective. The discussion on the modernisation of the Chinese legal system, and the critical comparison of Chinese and Western legal institutions and theories, continued through the following decades when China was first torn apart by civil wars and then invaded by Japan. The contribution of the

---

[25] For recent insight on the Chinese model of modern development see generally Cao, T (ed) (2005) *The Chinese Model of Modern Development* Routledge.

[26] Mainly the German civil code through the Japanese code. Lau, AKL and Young, A (2009) *In Search of Chinese Jurisprudence: Does Chinese Legal Tradition Have a Place in China's Future?* Hong Kong Baptist University School of Business at 11.

[27] Lin Yu-Sheng *The Crisis of Chinese Consciousness* supra note 19 at 6.

[28] Gu, EX (1999) 'Cultural Intellectuals and the Politics of the Cultural Public Space in Communist China (1979-1989): A Case Study of Three Intellectual Groups' (58) *The Journal of Asian Studies* 389.

[29] Lin Yu-Sheng (1979) *The Crisis of Chinese Consciousness* supra note 19 at 153-154.

[30] Ibid at 9.

May Fourth movement to this debate came to an end with the Maoist revolution. As expected, following Mao's rise to power and the foundation of the PRC in 1949, Marxist-Leninist legal theories were adopted, and both Chinese tradition and (other) Western influences were rejected.

In many ways, the Maoist Cultural Revolution (1966-1977)[31] resembled the May Fourth movement in its quest for change and in its desire to erase the past to create a new, revolutionary 'sense of infinite possibility'.[32] However, the two did not share the same visions of progress, which were Westernisation for the first, and the realisation of communism for the second. In any case, very much like with the May Fourth movement, the Cultural Revolution proved unable to provide a distinctively Chinese response to the challenges of modernity. Moreover, it failed to eliminate those traditional practices that were judged as 'wrong' and 'unjust' by revolutionaries.

Stepping Out of the Crisis

The debate on the modernisation of the Chinese legal system was reignited towards the end of the 20th century. Significantly, it started as an academic discussion, though the input came from above, and particularly from party members who witnessed the consequences of abuse perpetrated by the party elite during the Cultural Revolution. The real impetus, however, came after China abandoned a Marxist

---

[31] See generally Cheek, T (ed) (2002) *Mao Zedong and China's Revolution: A Brief History with Documents* Palgrave Macmillan. Mao Zedong was 'hostile to both Confucianism and liberalism because he saw in liberalism and Confucianism the common trait that they both belonged to the same discredited past, not because they shared anything of genuine value.' Confucianism and liberalism had in common 'the same traits of tolerance, moderation and compromise which he attacked in his essay "Combat Liberalism".' This image of China was given to Mao by the opinion that Marx and Stalin had of China: 'hopelessly retrograde and without any capacity of its own for renewal or fundamental reform.' De Bary, WT (1983) *The Liberal Tradition in China* The Chinese University Press at 93. Maoist ideology is a synthesis between Marxism, as understood by Leninism, and Chinese culture. See Metzger, TA (1996) *Transcending the West: Mao's Vision of Socialism and the Legitimization of Teng Hsiao-ping's Modernization Program* Hoover Institution on War, Revolution and Peace, Stanford University; and Collotti Pischel, E (1979) *Le origini ideologiche della rivoluzione cinese* Einaudi.

[32] Lin Yu-Sheng *The Crisis of Chinese Consciousness* supra note 19 at 159.

economy based on state plans, and embraced the so-called socialist market economy: a quasi-capitalist system that generated impetuous economic growth. This phenomenon forced the Chinese state to re-think certain assumptions about law, and to reprise the discussion on the role of Western and Chinese legal discourses.

Marxist thought harboured a suspicious attitude toward law, generally understood as a bourgeois method of governance that, under the façade of guaranteeing freedom and dignity, fosters social inequality and class divisions. With the advent of a new economic system, however, the authorities realised that in order for the market to function, China needed a systematised legal system and a more coherent articulation of rights. Not surprisingly, the party elite began to express the need to modernise the legal framework in order to bring it in line with the new conditions in China. During this time the Chinese government also began to relax its ideological constraints on the academic debate, allowing scholars to discuss Western theories of rights. Albert Chen[33] describes this moment as an 'exciting legal revolution that raises interesting theoretical issues'.[34]

The effects on law produced by this phenomenon were enormous, and could be compared to the process of 'Confucianisation of law',[35] experienced by China during the Han Dynasty (206 BC-220 AD), for the momentous changes it brought about.[36] This new discourse of modernisation differed from previous ones in the fact that Chinese legal scholarship began to move away from the mere technicalities of particular areas of the law—a topic that had occupied scholars for quite some time—and started to reflect on the

---

[33] Albert Chen Hung-yee is professor of law at the University of Hong Kong.

[34] Chen, AHY (2004) *An introduction to the legal system of the PRC* (3rd ed) Lexis/Nexis at 228.

[35] During the ages of the empire, some of the norms that originated in the kinship system, called *li,* were gradually transposed into the positive dispositions of the imperial codes. This phenomenon is known as 'Confucianisation of the law'. See generally Tsu-Ch'u Tung (1961) *Law and society in traditional China* Mouton. Some scholars, such as Liu, challenge the generally shared assumption that the law of imperial codes was influenced by the precepts of Confucianism (Liu, Y (1998) *Origins of Chinese Law, Penal and Administrative Law in its Early Development* Oxford University Press). See also Chen, J (2015) *Chinese Law: Context and Transformation. Revised and Expanded Edition* Nijhof at 18-20. Chen defines the 'Confucianisation of law' as 'the incorporation of the spirit, and sometimes the actual practice, of Confucian teachings into legal form' which occurred in the Han period (206 BC-220 AD). Ibid at 18.

[36] Gellhorn, W (1987) 'China's Quest for Legal Modernity' (1) *Journal of Chinese Law* 1.

fundamental values of the law.[37] It is in this intellectual environment that, according to many scholars,[38] the new legal modernisation inaugurated the development of the theory and the practice of human rights. The need to recalibrate Chinese law in the light of new challenges and developments brought about by the socialist market economy is visible in the fact that, concurrent with the changes in the economy, Chinese scholars moved away from early positions on human rights based on what Chen and Nathan have defined as conservative Marxist views, and embraced more liberal theorisations.[39]

This is particularly evident when it comes to the definition of the nature of human rights. In the past, dominant Chinese definitions of human rights were characterised in a Marxist fashion by a combination of economic, historical and emancipatory connotations.[40] Early accounts on human rights made use of class analysis, stressed the unity of rights and duties, and were centred on the notion that provision varies from one Constitution to the next. These definitions were programmatic, open-ended, based on a legislation that recorded changing cultural and socio-political values, and enforced by social practice rather than through formal judicial institutions. The implementation of human rights was considered dependent upon hierarchical patterns of deference to achieve worth rather than upon popular sovereignty. With the advent of the socialist market economy Chinese scholars moved away from these Soviet-like concepts. The ways in which this happened, however, has been subject to discussion.

With the new impetus for modernisation, Chinese scholars began to recognise the relevance of some Western values, particularly the Enlightenment. Given this phenomenon, many Western observers have claimed that, in the end, the notion of 'human rights' was a

---

[37] Lesson on legal philosophy by Cheng Liaoyuan, Chongqing University Academic Year 2009/2010.

[38] Chen, AHY (2006) 'Conclusion' supra note 21 at 489.

[39] See in general Chen, AHY (1993) 'Developing Theories of Rights and Human Rights in China' in Wachs, R (ed) (1993) *Hong Kong, China and 1997: Essays in Legal Theory* Hong Kong University Press 123.

[40] Ibid at 140.

Western importation into the Chinese intellectual environment.[41] Others, however, argued that even though with modernisation Chinese theories of rights began to be intertwined with Western discourses, this intertwinement possessed a distinctively Chinese character.[42] Nathan, for instance, notes that many Chinese intellectuals of the early 20th century held that the problem in Chinese modernisation stemmed from the 'systematic overconcentration of power' and its abuse,[43] which was supported by premises stemming from Confucian legal thought.

If it is true that with the advent of the socialist market economy Chinese legal scholars discovered the Enlightenment, it is also true that they rediscovered their own philosophical tradition. With the advent of modernisation Chinese intellectuals started to put forward the idea that Chinese tradition played a positive role in motivating thinkers to develop the concepts of rights (*quanli* 权利) and human rights (*renquan* 人权). Some of these intellectuals, for instance, looked favourably at the fact that, since the early 20th century, a portion of Chinese scholarship based its idea of rights on the theoretical structure of neo-Confucian thinkers of the 14th, 15th and 16th centuries.[44] More importantly, Chinese scholarship began to elaborate on the idea that human rights are neither incompatible with nor incomparable to legal and political notions developed by Chinese classical doctrine.

This positive re-assessment of Chinese tradition questions a number of notions held by the Chinese authorities, particularly the view—often raised by Chinese leaders, including Deng Xiaoping —

---

[41] Choukroune, L (2006) 'Justiciability of Economic, Social, and Cultural Rights: The UN Committee on Economic, Social and Cultural Rights Review of China's First Periodic Report on the Implementation of the International Covenant of Economic, Social and Cultural Rights' (19) *Colum. J. Asian L.* 30; Svensson, M *Debating Human Rights in China* supra note 2; Angle, SC *Human Rights and Chinese Thought* supra note 2.

[42] Ibid at 205-249.

[43] Nathan AJ (1986) 'Sources of Chinese Rights Thinking' in Edwards, RR; Henkin, L and Natan, AJ (eds) (1986) *Human Rights in Contemporary China* Columbia University Press 125.

[44] Among them Xu Liangying, a scholar and human rights advocate, see Miller, HL (1999) 'Xu Liangying and He Zuoxiu: Divergent Responses to Physics and Politics in the Post-Mao Period' (30) *Historical Studies in the Physical and Biological Sciences* 89 at 97-103.

that human rights are part of the Western imperialist project.[45] Doubtless, the West has often used the argument of the violation of human rights as a justification to initiate hostile actions in developing countries and maintain dominance.[46] However, the thesis that demands for human rights are mainly inspired by external imperialism fails to grasp the nature of the human rights debate that originated in China, especially following the inception of the socialist market economy. The effervescence of this debate proves that Chinese scholars genuinely perceive human rights as an important component of the legal, social and political life of China.

The reflections of contemporary Chinese on human rights have not attracted much attention from comparative legal scholarship. Even so, due to their original intellectual content, these theorisations are relevant both for China and for the global debate on rights. As argued by Svensson, the study of the Chinese discourse on rights is 'valuable for the exploration of universal human dilemmas'.[47] Similarly, Angle (2002) notes that Chinese theories of human rights have distinctive elements that can enrich the global discourse on rights. This book will therefore continue the line of analysis used by these authors by furnishing an-up-to date exploration of doctrinal and jurisprudential traits of Chinese legal discourses. As argued by Taylor, in order to achieve a global consensus on human rights, every people should find their justification from within their own philosophical and legal tradition. In light of this, the theorisations by Chinese scholars acquire a new significance not only within the Chinese discourse but also at a global level, because they have the potential to bring us all closer to a global consensus on human rights. To better show how these discourses can make a contribution to the general consensus on human rights, let us further explore the relation between Western and Chinese elements in the current Chinese debate. This will also allow

---

[45] Deng's Speech of 16 March 1989. The claim that human rights are a sophisticated instrument of a new style of Western imperialism is discussed by both Chinese and Western scholars with different outcomes. See, on the Western side of the debate, Zolo, D (2004) *Globalizzazione. Una mappa dei problemi* Laterza at 89.

[46] Ibid.

[47] Svensson, M *Debating Human Rights in China* supra note 2.

us to discern the distinctive nature of Chinese legal takes on human rights.

A Perspective from Within

The distinctiveness of Chinese theories of rights is not immediately visible. A large number of contemporary Chinese legal dispositions providing citizens' rights are modelled upon the legislative texts in force in Western constitutional democracies, so that the similarity between Chinese and Western legal discourses is, as noted by Angle, remarkable.[48] This is true particularly for what concerns human rights. In Chinese legal publications human rights are described as necessary (*buke huoque* 不可或缺); common to all men (*gongshi* 共似); universal (*pubian* 普遍) and therefore linked to human nature; non-transferable (*buke zhuanrang* 不可转让); irreplaceable (*buke tidai* 不可替代); stable (*wending* 穩定); and as having a 'mother' or 'matrix' nature (*muti* 母体) as they are capable of generating other rights.[49] All these characteristics testify to the influence of the Western Renaissance and Enlightenment on Chinese legal thought.

It has been argued that, to some degree, this influence was a consequence of China's aspiration to access the World Trade Organization[50] and to attract foreign investment: a dynamic which involved the imposition by the international community of higher standards of transparency,[51] as well as the modification of local legal institutions and dispositions. However, there are some important clarifications to be made. While it is undeniable that foreign influences affect Chinese legal dispositions at the level of black letter law, the actual content of these dispositions in the practice of their implementation is determined also by other factors. As noted by Potter, when it comes to the interaction between local practices and an international normative standard there is always a process of selective

---

[48] Angle, SC *Human Rights and Chinese Thought* supra note 2 at 206, 222.

[49] Xu Xianming (2008) *Principles of Human Rights Law* China University of Political Science and Law Press at 79-81; See also Xu Xianming (2008) 'The Development of Human Rights in The World and the Progress of Human Rights in China. A Theoretical Reflection on the History of Human Rights Law' (12) Journal of the Party School of the Central Committee of the C.P.C. 30.

[50] China accessed the WTO in 2001. See Zhang, X (2005) *Implementation of the WTO Agreements in China* Wildy, Simmonds and Hill Publishing; and, more recently: Gao, HS (2018) 'The WTO transparency obligations and China' (12, 2) *Journal of Comparative Law* 329.

[51] Ibid.

adaptation.[52] In other words, local acceptance of international norms depends on their capacity to meet the needs of a local community.

This phenomenon shows that, even when legal thinking is influenced by external stimuli, it always maintains a local dimension. While human rights are recognised by legal dispositions, their justification ultimately depends upon local moral premises that implicitly underlie the legal system. Bearing this in mind, if we elaborate on the way Chinese scholars understand the idea of 'human nature' from which they derive the basic characteristics of rights we see that this concept does not coincide with the idea of 'human nature' that grounds the European and American rights thinking.

Western legal traditions see the person as endowed with some prerogatives since birth and morally deserving equal respect and protection, secured through the provision of equal rights for every human being. Conversely, in current Chinese theorisations human rights are not considered to be 'natural rights' (*ziran quanli* 自然权利). There are also other differences. In the Western liberal tradition the individual is essentially understood as a monad with original rights (life, liberty, equality) who is forced to join society in order to protect these rights—as in Hobbes's account[53] — and who agrees to make a social contract to this purpose—in Locke's and Rousseau's.[54] Contrary to this position, Chinese traditional thinking, and particularly Confucian thought, stresses the importance of society over the individual.[55]

In Chinese ancient philosophy the interest of the parts is seen as structurally subordinated to the interest of the whole. This does not mean to say, however, that the inviolability and inalienability of human rights cannot be framed starting from Chinese philosophical

---

[52] Potter, PB (2006) 'Selective adaptation and institutional capacity: Perspectives on Human Rights in China' (61, 2) *International Journal* 389.

[53] Hobbes, T (2017) [1651] *Leviathan* Penguin.

[54] Locke, J (1988) [1689] *Two Treaties on Government* Cambridge University Press; Rousseau, JJ (2012) [1762] *Of The Social Contract and Other Political Writings* Penguin.

[55] Tu Weiming (1989) *Centrality and commonality: An essay on Confucian religiousness* State University of New York Press; Bauer, JR and Bell, DA (eds) (1999) *The East Asian Challenge for Human Rights* Cambridge University Press.

premises. Though different from Western discourses, Chinese traditional culture does not necessarily diminish the fundamental importance of the individual. Rather it proposes an understanding of the person as an inherently relational being: a notion founded, amongst other things, on the Confucian idea that the wellbeing of the individual depends on that of society. This relational understanding of personhood can make important contributions to a broader global consensus on human rights: a foundation which is alternative to liberal mainstream discourses and that, in dialogue with the liberal communitarian accounts,[56] can offer an insightful understanding of human rights.

Obviously, when it comes to assessing the Chinese contribution to the general discussion of human rights, one needs to remember that terms like 'Western culture' and 'Chinese tradition' can be insidious, and inadequate.[57] Even though they can add clarity to the discussion,[58] one needs to stress that cultures are complex, fluid and ever-changing.[59] This consideration allows us to unpack the argument that mainly Western stimuli determine the current Chinese conceptions of human rights: a position which reflects a certain colonial legacy, since it denies the agency of Chinese scholars. Nevertheless, an understanding of the fluidity of culture also allows us to deconstruct supposedly 'genuine' Chinese approaches to rights.

Chinese scholars critically select both from their own tradition and from Western discourses concepts that best apply to the challenges that China is currently facing, and it is in this sense that

---

[56] Communitarian philosophers like Alasdair MacIntyre, Michael Sandel, Charles Taylor and Michael Walzer highlighted the relevance of tradition and social context in moral philosophising, and made other claims about the essentially social nature of the self, emphasising the value of community.

[57] This research does not share the ethnocentric assumptions contained in the debate initiated in the 1970s between Orientalists and Occidentalists; neither does it engage with the debate on Asian values, a discussion that has now been abandoned due to its weak theoretical foundation and to the minor relevance of its contents. See Said, EW (1978) *Orientalism* Pantheon Books; Massad, J (2015) 'Orientalism as Occidentalism' (5) *History of the Present* 83; Wang, N (1997) 'Orientalism versus Occidentalism?' (28) *New Literary History* 57.

[58] One might argue that legal developments in contemporary constitutional states (Continental Europe, Great Britain and the United States of America) constitute an area sharing a recognisable, though not completely homogenous, legal culture.

[59] An analysis of the idea of culture would lead the discussion too far away from the aims of the present study. For this reason, even though I occasionally make use of anthropological literature in the book, I invite the reader to refer to the vast body of anthropological scholarship dealing with this issue.

these theorisations on rights can be seen as distinctively Chinese. These intellectuals do not see differentiation from the West as a value in itself. Rather they only accept those Western elements that, once modified and combined—often with Marxist and traditional Chinese elements—can best fit the present conditions of China. In the light of this contextualisation (and without forgetting the political limitations imposed on academic discourses), one can appreciate that the critical engagement adopted by contemporary Chinese scholars is a manifestation of the mature state of Chinese academia. By overcoming the dichotomous contraposition between Western and Chinese discourses on human rights, Chinese scholars have overcome their crisis, and increasingly freed themselves from colonial legacies.[60]

In order to grasp these dynamics one has to make some specific methodological moves. It is important not to look at the Chinese scholarship on human rights with Western biases, but to consider, as much as possible, the point of view of Chinese scholars, assessing their work in their own terms. Rather than examining commonalities and differences between Chinese and Western legal theories, one has to consider the way in which Chinese scholars look at such commonalities and differences, and appropriate or reject elements of different legal cultures. This internal perspective is necessary in order to avoid what Hall and Ames, quoting philosopher Robert Solomon, have wisely called the 'transcendental pretence': the Western liberal 'conviction that the scientific rationality emergent at the beginnings of the sixteenth century names a universal norm for assessing the value of cultural activity everywhere on the planet'.[61] It is also necessary to avoid the risk of 'fundamentalist' reactions that are naturally triggered by 'dismissive condemnations' of Chinese the record on human rights.

The rhetorical use of identity by the official discourse on human rights links the rejection of Western ideas on human rights and

---

[60] A process that may now experience a step back due to the increasingly heavier political interferences and constraints on academic debates.
[61] Hall, DL and Ames, RT (1995) *Anticipating China: Thinking through the Narratives of Chinese and Western Culture* State University of New York Press at xi.

the rule of law to the alleged Chinese national identity. In order to justify the official position, some Chinese intellectuals, including the prominent scholar Zhu Suli, professor at Peking University, pushed for the need to articulate an authentic Chinese approach to human rights: a theoretical stance that relies on promoting the use of local concepts, or 'native (conceptual) resources' (*bentuhua* 本土化). The official discourse's wholesale rejection of Western human rights is presented as part of the reconstruction of a national identity free from undue interferences by external forces who are allegedly hostile to China. This rhetorical use of the contraposition with the West links rejection of human rights to the Chinese identity. When faced with this position, however, it is important to remember that many Chinese scholars dealing with human rights do not hold this position uncritically. On the contrary, they examine the Chinese tradition and critically reject it, in order to justify human rights on different premises. This book argues that their theories are nevertheless informed by traditional notions of the individual and society, although they combine these views with other elements in order to produce solutions that take into account the specific social, economic, and political conditions of their country.

Structuring the Argument
The book will be dedicated to illustrating the Chinese theories of rights. In terms of chronology, the analysis will concentrate on theories formulated in the past forty years that are still part of the current debate. The choice to focus on this time span was made for a number of reasons. First, it is since the 1980s that scholars have begun to move away from static Marxist interpretations favoured by the government. Secondly, this is the time when the debate has become particularly dynamic, as shown by the fact that, for instance, the view of human rights as universal—a minoritarian position back in the 1980s[62]—is now generally accepted amongst Chinese scholars.

Due to the breadth of the legal debate in China, the analysis will focus on a limited number of theorisations, which have been selected according to parameters of internal consistency, completeness and reasonableness. The main focus—with some notable exceptions— will be on scholars from mainland China who are very well known in their country, but virtually unknown outside of it. The analysis draws on the results of fieldwork activities carried out for almost a year

---

[62] Weatherley, R *The Discourse of Human Rights* supra note 22.

between 2009 and 2011 in mainland China (in Chongqing for the most part, but also Xiamen, Hong Kong, Tianjin, Shanghai, and Beijing). During this research it was possible to explore legal theories by examining original texts in Chinese, and by interacting with university lecturers, politicians, law students and legal practitioners who make constant reference to this scholarship. These experiences have allowed me to appreciate how Chinese scholars critically engage with both Chinese and Western traditions, a phenomenon whose different aspects will be explored in each specific chapter.

Chapter Two will look at the ways in which Chinese scholars relate to their own heritage. The focus will be on traditional discourses that, though ancient, still influence the current debate. In particular, the focus will be on some aspects of Confucian and Mencian thought. Conversely, Chapters Three and Four will concentrate on how scholars engage with Western concepts, particularly the notion of the Rule of Law. In China the law guarantees classic subjective rights related to the production and circulation of wealth: protection of patrimony, property, and ownership. This is mainly because these rights support the quasi-capitalist economy embraced by China. On the other side, rights such as personal freedoms—though formally recognised by the 1982 Constitution as amended—are not guaranteed to the same extent. Bearing this in mind, we will see how Chinese scholars make use of some Western concepts in order to articulate normative theories on the autonomy of law from political power. As the analysis will show, Chinese academics strive to devise a model of the Rule of Law for China, a new development which is in contrast with early Maoist views of law as a tool to attain political goals.

Scholars have argued two theses in relation to the fundamental reason to protect citizens' rights in contemporary China. The first thesis holds that the government has an interest in upholding rights to the extent that is necessary to maintain economic growth and a well-functioning market.[63] The second thesis is that the protection of rights is subordinated to the paramount goal of maintaining social order and stability.[64]

---

[63] This thesis, is held by (among others) Choukroune, L 'Justiciability' supra note 41.

[64] Biddulph, S *The Stability Imperative* supra note 13 at 243-245.

The first thesis argues that the affirmation of rights in the contemporary Chinese legal system is ultimately a consequence of the triumph of the market. The government would protect human rights to such an extent, in order to allow transactions between private and public economic actors to thrive. However, as we will see in Chapters Three and Four, others have argued that principles like equality and freedom, though introduced to support the quasi-capitalist economy, reveal an intrinsic logic. This logic would have the strength to impose itself despite the pragmatic motivations of Chinese authorities.[65] Contrary to this argument is the fact of the authoritarian resilience of the Chinese state. The patent authoritarian resilience has partially challenged this thesis and disproved the relationship that was thought to exist between economic development and democratisation.

The second thesis holds that the regime protects human rights instrumentally, to achieve the paramount goal of social stability. This thesis is partially connected to the first because the premise is that the party has promised to allow every Chinese citizen to share the benefits of the market reform, increasing the overall material wellbeing of the country, and allowing citizens to lead a 'happier and more dignified life'.[66] However, the failure of the government to fulfil this commitment generated social unrest, which represents a potential threat to the legitimacy of the party to run the country, in line with the millennial idea that power must first and foremost ensure the wellbeing of its people.[67] Biddulph analyses the responses to social unrest and grievances in the areas of labour, health care, housing, environment, petitioning, and re-education through labour. She argues that in those cases, the determination of local governments to restore social order and defend social stability is rhetorically framed in terms of the protection of the rights of aggrieved citizens by public powers. In this sense, the law and rights, rather than constituting a framework constraining the action of public authorities, remain an instrument in the hands of public authority in order to affirm the dominance of the

---

[65] This dynamic generates a plethora of interesting questions. Even after embracing capitalist economic principles, the Chinese regime has not gravitated towards democratic methods of governance. One is therefore forced to challenge the commonly held assumption that capitalism necessarily involves democracy, and that, vice versa, democracy is a function of capitalism.

[66] Ibid at 238; Also see the foreword for Information Office of the State Council of the PRC (1995) *The Progress of Human Rights in China* available at <http://www.china.org.cn/e-white/phumanrights19/index.htm>.

[67] This idea is known as Mencius's doctrine of 'people as the basis', which will be explored in more details in Chapter Three.

party, and, in practice, citizens' rights are violated in order to restore social stability. The deep relation between the idea of law and power is debated in Chapters Three and Four, within the broad and rich debate on the rule of law in China.

Chapter Five will address the significance of the academic debate for an articulation of human rights theories in China. The chapter will unpack the nature and limits of academic discourse on rights. However, it will also show that limitations imposed by the regime have not always necessarily prevented scholars from elaborating innovative theories of human rights. As will be shown, in the recent past academics have developed various strategies to affirm their positions without being censored. Their views have often been voiced in public debates on controversial issues—a dynamic that influences public opinion, at least to some extent—and on several occasions they have been incorporated within national legislation. This is visible, for instance, in the reforms implemented on the household registration system.[68] Undoubtedly, the shift to a socialist market economy has pushed academics to re-think the concept of equality that was previously dominating the debate within China, and this has in turn to some extent informed the reforms related to the right to reside and migrate within the large Chinese territory.

This chapter will also explore the conflictual relationship between the party and the intellectuals. The tension between the party control of ideas and the academic discussion is a constant trait since the foundation of the PRC. However, it went through different phases in which the relative freedom of academia widened or shrank, depending on the needs and on the changing political agenda of the elite in power. After a relatively long phase of increased freedom, from the early 1990s to the first decade of the new millennium, the freedom of academic research and discussion in the legal field has been tightened remarkably in the recent phase of authoritarian

---

[68] The household registration system regulates residence and related rights for Chinese citizens. Access to social services, for example, is linked to the place of residence (see Chapter Six for a more detailed description of the household registration system and its recent reform).

resilience under the leadership of Xi Jinping, whose institutional acme is represented by the legal and constitutional reforms of 2018.[69]

The remarkable institutional changes brought about by the fifth constitutional reform go in the direction of an authoritarian resilience and consecrate the dominance of the party under the leadership of Xi Jinping. The reform consolidates and institutionalises the concentration of power in the hands of the President of the PRC, without however modifying the prerogatives and position of the President with respect to the other constitutional organs. Most importantly, the reform consecrates the Chinese Communist Party's ('CCP' or 'the party') role of leadership and guidance. The reform added to article 1 (2) the sentence: 'The most distinctive element of socialism with Chinese characteristics is the guidance of the CCP. This is the first time since 1982 that in the core text of the Constitution explicit reference is made to the CCP that was previously mentioned only in the Preamble to the Constitution. This represents a significant ideological change because it precludes the possibility of the evolution of the Chinese political system towards a form of multiparty democracy or simply towards a more pluralist system.[70] Moreover, the amendment to article 79 (3) cancels the limit of two terms for the President and Vice-President of the PRC. The change opens the way for a perpetual presidential mandate. The reform introduced a new institutional organism: the 'Supervisory Commissions', with the task of controlling the public administrative organs at all government levels (local, provincial, national), including the judiciary. These Supervisory Commissions hold supervisory and monitoring powers, together with the power to investigate, inspect and sanction all public functionaries. In this way the party secured stronger control of the bureaucracy, in a state where control of the bureaucracy has always been one of the keys to maintain power and stability.

As well as institutional and constitutional reforms, since 2013 the elite in power has carried out a decisive nationalist policy, promoted the 'sinicisation' of all officially sanctioned religious beliefs, [71] banned 'Western' theories, resources and books from

---

[69] Cavalieri, R (2018) 'La revisione della Costituzione della Repubblica Popolare Cinese e l'istituzionalizzazione del "socialismo dalle caratteristiche cinesi per una nuova era"' (34-1) *Diritto Pubblico Comparato ed Europeo* 307.
[70] Ibid.
[71] The National Regulations on Religious Affairs promulgated in 2005 were recently amended in 2018. The amendment entered into force on 1 February 2018 and is

universities, and indicated that historical materialism is the scientific method par excellence to be used in every field of humanistic knowledge.[72] Moreover, the repression of dissenting voices became harsher, and the persecution of rights defenders, first of all the lawyers, has been intensified, together with the persecution of minorities in the autonomous regions of Tibet, Xinjiang and Mongolia. This is sufficient to conclude that the evolution of the Chinese political system is going in the direction of 'authoritarian resilience' after a relatively long phase of opening up in which a limited pluralism and debate of ideas was tolerated. All these recent evolutions have a significant impact on intellectual freedom, and academic debates have also suffered from the restriction imposed on freedom of thought.

Having examined the significance of scholarly theorisations outside academia and the spaces of relative freedom granted by the regime to intellectuals, and how these have been tightened in the recent past, Chapters Seven and Eight will analyse how scholars critically engage with the official philosophy espoused by the CCP, the Marxist-Leninist-Mao Zedong and Xi Jinping thought, and with the liberal theorisations on rights. This analysis will unpack how Chinese scholars articulate the justification for human rights, a discussion which will illuminate various aspects of contemporary Chinese legal thinking. Doubtless, the concept of rights does not coincide completely with their justification. However, the significance of the justification of rights is its normative and prescriptive dimension because the justification defines the fundamental reasons for the attribution of rights. In addition, Chapters Seven and Eight will look at how Chinese scholars define the essential, defining factor (*yaosu* 要素) of rights that grounds their attribution to individuals. In particular, Chapter Eight will show that, when it comes to the

---

highly restrictive of religious freedoms, allowing broader and more incisive ideological interference by the party and attributing to the party stronger powers to control religions.

[72] As already mentioned, in 2015 Xi Jinping banned Western texts from universities and tightened censorship in academia. This reversed the previous tendency to allow more academic freedom and the related flourishing of theories inspired by European and Anglo-Saxon authors.

26

justification of human rights, Chinese intellectuals embrace theories focused on freedom (or choice) (*ziyou shuo* 自由说) and theories focused on interest (*liyi shuo* 利益说). This will show once more how, in articulating theories of human rights, Chinese scholars critically engage not only with their own tradition, but also with Western values: a consideration which is the main contribution this book aims to achieve.

CHAPTER TWO

Beyond the Crisis of Chinese Consciousness

Introduction

It has been argued that certain fundamental differences in the evolution of Chinese and Western legal systems are linked to divergent approaches to the concept of rights and to 'the use of formal legal institutions to vindicate rights'.[73] The proponents of this line of argument point out that Chinese classical legal thinking lacks a theorisation of human rights.[74] However, it is important to remember that Chinese classical legal thought developed in pre-modern times, during the imperial period (221 BC – 1912 AD). While it is true that in this period Chinese thinkers did not theorise human rights, the same can be said for Western cultures and philosophies in the pre-modern age. More importantly, it is arguable, and it has indeed been argued, that notions of classical Chinese thought have had a deep impact on the modern and contemporary understandings of human rights.[75] This chapter will therefore explore these classical notions, establishing some key concepts that—later on in the book—will allow us to better elucidate the relation between tradition and the current understanding of human rights.

---

[73] Lubman, SB (1999) *Bird in a Cage: Legal Reform in China after Mao* Stanford University Press at 11.

[74] Lubman affirms that if we look for rights in the Chinese tradition, we encounter the most striking difference between this tradition and the Western tradition of legal thought. Western modern thought makes the individual the bearer of rights and bases rights on the fundamental dignity and equality of every human being. There were no such concepts in Chinese thought, and in the Confucian view 'identity constantly changes, varying with the context; duties and, correspondingly, rights/rites are also constantly being redefined as other actors change' (Ibid at 19). Marina Svensson argues that although it is not possible to find an idea equivalent to human rights in classical Chinese legal thought, this does not imply that the idea is incompatible with Chinese categories of legal thinking and political activism (Svensson, M *Debating Human Rights in China* supra note 2.

[75] See in general Weatherley, R *The Discourse of Human Rights* supra note 22.

In identifying the relevance of Chinese classical notions the focus will be particularly on how legal theorists critically engage with these notions. As explained in the previous chapter, it is important to look both at cultural phenomena and at the native interpretation of these phenomena. Those who belong to a certain culture constantly interpret their own culture, reshaping it and rearticulating it in a fluid manner. Bearing this in mind, this chapter will show how, in their theorisations on human rights, Chinese contemporary scholars constantly remould classical legal arguments and ideas, engaging with their own legal tradition, and rejecting or accepting some concepts, views and reasoning. In this process of critical engagement, Chinese scholars are currently shaping the elements for human rights theories, which are, as we will see, also based on their past tradition.

To support this argument, we will explore some aspects of the Chinese legal and philosophical tradition. Most of the relevant concepts considered in this chapter have been elaborated within the tradition of Confucianism. Obviously, the Confucian tradition is not the only intellectual discourse that flourished in imperial China. However, the decision to focus on Confucian thought is due to the circumstance that some of the arguments elaborated by Confucian thinkers about law, politics, society, individual morality, and power relationships are still resounding in the contemporary intellectual environment, voiced by a plurality of different authors, including non-Confucian ones.

Naturally, Confucianism is a vast, rich and highly diversified tradition. In the following analysis reference will be made only to some specific Confucian concepts, namely those pertaining to the idea of the individual; the relation between individuals and society as a generative relation made up of duties and rights; the relationship between law and morality, and the mechanisms of dispute resolution. The specific notions and their interpretation articulated here were chosen because of their potential to clarify some unarticulated premises of the Chinese discourse on human rights.[76] These ideas allow us to reconstruct, at least to some extent, the genealogy of the

---

[76] Huang, PCC (2010) *Chinese Civil Justice, Past and Present* Rowman and Littlefield; Huang, PCC and Yuan Gao (2015) "Should Social Science and Jurisprudence Imitate Natural Science?" (41-2) *Modern China* 131; Weatherley, R *The Discourse of Human Rights* supra note 22; Chan, J (1999) 'A Confucian Perspective on Human Rights for Contemporary China' in Bauer, J (1999) *The East Asian Challenge for Human Rights* Cambridge University Press 212.

distinctive intellectual context within which the current Chinese discussion on human rights is situated.

But first, a short introduction on Chinese ancient jurisprudence will follow, as it will be helpful to contextualise the analysis of classical legal and philosophical arguments. The following section shows that an idea of 'jurisprudence' can already be found in traditional Chinese culture. This fact has escaped the attention of many Western scholars who maintain that classical China lacked a separate and autonomous doctrine of law separated from other spheres of knowledge, such as ethics and broader philosophical reflection.[77]

Chinese Classical Ideas of Jurisprudence[78]

Interest in researching ideas of jurisprudence in the Chinese classical legal tradition is relatively new and constitutes part of a recent turn in jurisprudential research in Mainland China. Chinese scholars have only recently started to reflect on the relevance of their ancestors' thought on law. This turn is particularly relevant in view of two facts. Firstly, in the late 19th century and the first half of the 20th century, the ideas of Chinese legal tradition were completely abandoned in favour of Western theories.[79] Secondly, after the founding of the PRC (1949) and the flourishing of legal studies in the Universities of Political Science and Law, the progress of legal thinking suffered a forced pause for ten years during the Cultural Revolution (1966-1976), when schools of law were closed down.

---

[77] Among the most representative authors claiming that China did not develop an autonomous reflection upon law is Max Weber. Robert Marsh challenged this thesis in the light of more recent findings about Chinese classical legal tradition and practice (Marsh, Robert (2000) 'Max Weber's Misunderstanding of Traditional Chinese Law' (106) American Journal of Sociology 281).

[78] The content of this section draws on the enlightening lectures on the philosophy of law delivered by Professor Cheng Liaoyuan at Chongqing University in 2009 and 2010. See Cheng Liaoyuan (2008) 'Zhongguo jindai fa lixue, falu zhexue mingci kao shu' [The terms of Jurisprudence and Legal Philosophy in modern China] (30) *Xiandai Fashue* [Modern Law Science] 144.

[79] Consider, for example, the adoption of the Soviet theory of law after the foundation of the PRC.

30

It is only since the Chinese leadership under Hu Jintao has begun to advocate, both in official speeches and in documents, the revival of traditional ideals such as 'harmony' (*he* 和), and 'filial piety' (*xiao* 孝), one of the virtues associated with familial roles in the Confucian classics. On the one hand, this change of attitude is part of a general policy of the Chinese government to highlight the distinctiveness of Chinese law and culture. On the other hand, this re-evaluation of traditional concepts was part of a new tendency, widespread among legal scholars, to take into account the influence of classical authors on the conceptualisations regarding the nature, object, scope, purposes and limits of the philosophy of law, as well as legal science, theory of law and jurisprudence.[80]

In order to analyse this phenomenon, let us start with a conceptual-terminological analysis, in order to identify the conceptual map through which Chinese culture understands the study of the law. In the Chinese language, the two expressions indicating jurisprudence and theory of law are respectively *fali* (法理) and *falixue* (法理学). The term *fali* is the result of a combination of the character *fa* (法), which means law, and *li* (理), which means reason. The word *falixue*, in turn, is made up of *fali*, and *xue* (学), which means study. Both terms can thus be approximately translated as jurisprudence. Even though ideas about jurisprudence were not expressed in a systematic way in the classical texts, there are records of the use of both *fali* and *falixue* in ancient legal commentaries and other writings.[81]

Jurisprudence, in the sense of methodological reflection on law, is often denoted by the term *fa shu* (法术), which is made up of the character *fa*, 'law' as explained above, and the root *shu*, which means technique. The expression *fa shu zhi xue* (法术之学), which results from adding *zhi xue* ('the study of') to *fa shu*, is used to specifically denote ancient Chinese jurisprudence. Similarly, the expression *Fa lv shu zhi xue* includes 'the study of statutes' (*lv xue* 律学), and 'the study of the law' (*fa xue* 法学). In the *Han Feizi*, a book attributed to the founder of the Legalist school Han Feizi, these expressions appear in sections dealing with the reasoning about the law, which is expressed, for the most part, at the meta-legal level rather than at the level of substantive law.

---

[80] See Scarpari, M *Ritorno a Confucio supra note 23*.
[81] Cheng Liaoyuan 'The terms of Jurisprudence' supra note 78 at 144.

In classical texts, 'jurisprudence' and 'legal theory' were also referred to with the expressions *fa yi* (法意), the 'meaning of the law', and *fa li* (法理), the 'reason of the law'. In particular, in his critical appraisal of the traditional Chinese jurisprudence, contemporary scholar Cheng Liaoyuan[82] notes that the ancient Chinese dictionaries ascribe a plurality of meanings to the expression *fa yi*. These include the 'essential instances of law' (*lv li jing yi* 律例精义), 'public law' or 'public international law' (*wan guo gong fa* 万国公法) and the 'Reason and Theories of All Laws' (*wang fa jing li* 万法精理), used to translate the title of Montesquieu's *De l'esprit des lois*.[83]

Yan Fu, a prominent Chinese philosopher of the 19th century, translated the same '*De l' esprit des lois*' with another significant expression used by Chinese traditional scholars: *fa yi* (法意).[84] There are various examples of the use of this expression in Chinese classical philosophical works. In the Han Shu (Han dynasty, 206 BC), for instance, we find two expressions that may have a jurisprudential significance, though they denote a consciously distorted use of the law: *ji xiao guo cheng da qi* (积小过，成大欺)[85] and *yang fei zhu zheng ce* 养肥猪政策.[86] These two expressions have the same meaning of 'letting a small thing grow bigger', or 'ignoring a thing while it is small', and they allude to the law enforcement authorities'

---

[82] Cheng Liaoyuan, lectures at Chongqing University, School of Law, 2009 and 2010. Cheng Liaoyuan (2009) 'Zhongguo fa lixue de faxian. Zhongguo fa lixue shi zai jindai de chuangjian' ['The Discovery of Chinese Jurisprudence. The Establishment of Chinese Jurisprudence History in Modern Times] (3) *Fazhi yu shehui fazhan* [Law and Society Journal] 87.

[83] Zhang Xiangwen (trans) (1905) *Wanfa Jingli*. Shanghai: Wenming shuju.

[84] Cheng Liaoyuan considers this translation of *De l'esprit des lois* with '法意' to be creative rather than literal. As mentioned, the expression *wang fa jing li* 万法精理, has also been used to translate the title of Montesquieu's book.

[85] The meaning of this expression is that by repeated (and unpunished) misconduct a person will gradually become a big cheat.

[86] The policy to let a pig grow fat refers to the attitude of the officers who tend to ignore minor misconduct so that the criminals will get confident and commit a more serious crime, and then when the time comes, the person will be heavily punished. Literally: 'the slim pigs will not be killed but the fat ones will be'.

ability to manage social deviance by fostering criminality and favouring illicit gains.

The meaning of these expressions might seem paradoxical. However, the expression *fa yi* here appears to be connected with a widely known, and often quoted, ancient Chinese saying: 'if a man commits a petty crime the police do not correct him; when he commits a crime of great magnitude the police will catch him and put him in prison'. The concept behind these expressions thus encompasses the popular idea that at first the law enforcement authorities tolerate small crimes, in order to foster criminality, and then, when crime grows in intensity, they repress it harshly. According to popular views, the police follow the principle of, to quote another popular Chinese proverb, 'let a small pig grow and, once it becomes a big pig, kill it'. When small-scale crimes are tolerated, criminal activities of all kinds will probably increase, and when this happens the police will first arrest the criminals, and subsequently obtain lucrative bribes in exchange for letting the criminals go free.

Cheng reports a completely different usage of *fa yi* with reference to the time of the Song dynasty (960-1279). According to Cheng, the thinker Zhu Xi (朱熹) understands *fa yi* as 'a way to use the law, a method to explain the law'.[87] In his work, for instance, Zhu Xi discusses the case of a boy and a girl who had been in a relationship for three years. The law of the time instructed young couples either to marry or to part after the third year since the beginning of the relationship. Zhu Xi says that *fa yi* provides a justification for the mandatory choice between marriage and separation of the couple, which is grounded in the idea that both the country and the family need a son to support them. In this context, *fa yi* is also conceived as the basis of the rule of traditional custom, which prescribes that if a girl touches a man she must marry him.

Another example to show the early use of the term *fa yi* is the case of a person who killed a fugitive who had, in turn, murdered a number of people. The law of the time prescribed the death penalty for murder. In this case, according to the sources,[88] the judge Ma Lian (马亮) stated in his judgment that the death penalty should not be inflicted on the fugitive's killer, adducing the reason that, through his actions, the person had repaired the failure of the police to capture and

---

[87] Cheng Liaoyuan, lectures at Chongqing University, School of Law, 2009 and 2010. See also Cheng Liaoyuan 'The Discovery' supra note 82.
[88] Ibid.

kill the murderer.[89] The principle of *fa yi* in this case required the author of the murder not to be punished, even if the written law prescribed capital punishment for any person guilty of murder. The judge's explanation of the case is based on common sense. In the case at hand, therefore, *fa yi* means: 'just' or 'reasonable' or 'according to feelings' or 'according to all the people's hearts'.

Similarly, in the Qing dynasty (1644-1911), the thinker Gong Zi Zhen (龚自珍) defined *fa yi* as *yu qing* (與情) the 'common feelings and thoughts of the people'. Cheng thus concludes that the meaning of *fa yi* which emerges from the classical thinkers is that of 'spirit' or 'reason', the essence and basic purpose of law. In this sense, the concept is similar to the Western notion, embedded in Roman law, of *ratio iuris*. A very important aspect is that *fa yi* entails taking into due consideration the feelings[90] that a given situation would have presumably generated, or effectively generated, in the mind of the common people (compassion, understanding, contempt, etc).[91] It is significant that another important term appearing in the classics is *fa li* (法理), a term that is currently used to mean 'jurisprudence'.[92]

---

[89] Ibid.

[90] Desires and dislikes are considered feelings corresponding to basic social relationships, and are considered common to all human beings. See Santangelo, P. (1992) *Emozioni e desideri in Cina. La riflessione neoconfuciana dalla metà del XIV alla metà XIX secolo* Laterza 41. Santangelo points out that the Confucian starting point is that at the origin of interpersonal relationships there is an interchange of feelings which influences the relationship. In general, a relationship between two people is seen as not being on an equal footing (except for the relationship between friends and the ones that can be modelled on this kind of relationship).

[91] A further instance of the word *fa yi* is found in the text of the ancient law called *zhang du lv* (张杜律), the basic law, also known as *tai shi lv* (泰始律), the big law of the Jin dynasty. This law was promulgated in the year 267 by the emperor Wu, after it was prepared by a group of compilers, including Du Yu (杜玉).

[92] The Taiwanese Professor Han Bao interprets the characters composing the expression *'fa li'* as separable. Han Bao holds that in the historical evolution of the concept the two words maintained an autonomous meaning. Contrary to this view, Cheng Liaoyuan holds that *fa* and *li* certainly possess autonomous meanings but the expression *fa li* cannot be reduced to either of them. Instead, it possesses an autonomous meaning of its own (Cheng Liaoyuan, lectures at Chongqing University, School of Law, 2009 and 2010; see also Cheng Liaoyuan 'The Discovery' supra note 82.

Contemporary Chinese scholars have analysed the history of the use of the word *fa li*. Incidentally, according to Cheng Liaoyuan, this history pertains to the history of legal concepts, a field of interest which, in his view, is significantly different from the well-known history of Chinese law (*fa*).[93] It is interesting to note that, as noted by Cheng Liaoyuan, Han Feizi, the founder of the Legalist school (*fa jia* 法家),[94] theorised that everything in nature has its own principle or rule, and men must follow *fa li,* here understood as the principles of things. *Fa li* can also be found during the times of the Han dynasty, and in earlier texts which referred to the meaning of this word without using the same expression. For example, prior to the Han dynasty, Chunqiu discusses the notion but using different expressions.[95]

Prior to the Han dynasty, some thinkers also disputed the relation between *fa* (法) and *li* (理). One thinker, in particular, affirmed that the emperor should know what the law is (*fa*) and how to use it (*li*).[96] It is also important to remember that during the Han dynasty the emperor Han Xuan Di combined the basic tenets of the Confucian school, (*ru jia* 儒家) and the Legalist school, (*fa jia* 法家), creating a new powerful synthesis to rule the empire.[97] In the opinion of Han Xuan Di, *fa li* denotes precisely this combination of *ru jia*, which had a huge number of followers at the time, and *fa jia*.

Gao Rouzhuan and Kong Zihui also speak about *fa li*. The latter's understanding of the expression is 'common sense principle', and he indicates as an example the keeping of promises. Xu Guang, the author of the *Nan Shi*, also uses the term with this meaning, and he does so by describing the following case. After the death of his father, a man inherited 70% of the patrimony and his sister 30%, while according to the law in force the first should have inherited the whole

---

[93] Ibid.

[94] Ibid.

[95] The *Chunqui,* or Spring and Autumn Annals, is the official chronicle of the State of Lu from 722 to 481 BC. It is considered a classic Chinese text.

[96] Ibid.

[97] During the ages of the empire, some of the norms that originated within the kinship system, called *li*, were gradually transposed into the positive dispositions of the imperial codes. This phenomenon is known as 'Confucianisation of law'. See generally Tsu-Ch'u Tung *Law and Society* supra note 35. Some scholars, such as Liu, challenge the generally shared assumption that the law of imperial codes was influenced by the precepts of Confucianism (Liu, Y *Origins* supra note 35). See also Chen, J *Chinese Law* supra note 35 at 18-20). Chen defines the 'Confucianisation of law' as 'the incorporation of the spirit, and sometimes the actual practice, of Confucian teachings into legal form', which occurred in the Han period (ibid at 18).

patrimony. Xu affirms that even if the law is silent on this, this kind of decision is *fa li*, because it protects the girl too.[98] *Fa li* is therefore the act of jurisprudential thinking which, in this specific case, authorised a justified exception from the existing law, given that the law did not specifically prohibit the exception being made.

Having presented an analysis of the terminology, and having shown that, contrary to what has been argued by Western scholars, classical China had a sense of jurisprudence, let us now focus on the distinction between Westernised and traditional jurisprudence.

Another expression which nowadays carries the meaning of jurisprudence is *falixue* (法理学).[99] Significantly, this term is now broadly understood in China as referring to an approach inspired by Western influence as opposed to (*xi xue dong jian* 西学东渐): classical Chinese jurisprudence. This distinction is important given that Chinese legal scholars have extensively studied the ways in which Western jurisprudence was introduced to China. Cheng Liaoyuan, in particular, looks at this process of Westernisation by summarising the evolution of Chinese jurisprudence in Republican and Modern China.[100] In particular, Cheng notes that during the late Qing dynasty, which fell in 1911, scholars who were not professional jurists initiated

---

[98] Nan Shi (1974) *The History of the Southern Dynasties* Zhonghua shuju,

[99] The expression has attracted the attention of Shu Guoying and Zheng Yongliu, two legal scholars from Beijing, who conducted research on ancient Chinese jurisprudence. They found that the usage of this expression is related to corresponding expressions used in Japan to indicate 'jurisprudence' (with reference to the German term *Rechtslehre*, which means 'jurisprudence'). Between 1897 and 1899 the word '*falixue*', 法理学 was used by the scholar Kang You Wei during the late Qing dynasty in his work which was mostly reproducing ideas derived from Japanese and German intellectual production

[100] Cheng Liaoyuan 'The Discovery' supra note 82; see also Cheng Liaoyuan 'The terms of Jurisprudence' supra note 78 at 144. In terms of the late imperial era, Cheng deals in particular with Liu Shipei, author of 16 books of history on different subjects, including a book on legal history and one on the history of political science, both unfinished; and Liang Qichao, who discussed Chinese academic history and focused on the problems of the discipline of jurisprudence in China. Regarding Republican China, Cheng mentions Hu Shi, author of a History of Chinese Jurisprudence; and Wang Zhengxian, who wrote on the history of Chinese jurisprudence.

modern Chinese jurisprudence following the imperative of 'borrowing or importing science from the West to make sure it comes to the East'.

In contrast to this modern trend of Westernisation, Cheng Liaoyuan highlights two new trends that now characterise contemporary reflections on law. The first concerns the scholars' attitude, which is no longer oriented towards 'borrowing science from the West'. On the contrary, according to Cheng, contemporary scholars are oriented towards the development of a mature and complete system of thought which is original, peculiar and genuinely Chinese. The second momentous change concerns the professional qualifications of legal theorists, as contemporary authors of jurisprudential theories, including those on human rights, are no longer philosophers, literati or intellectuals, but scholars trained in law.

Later on, I will return to these concepts and highlight how, in my view, they contributed to the construction of Chinese theories on human rights. However, for now it is important to stress that the trajectory of the discourse on rights and jurisprudence seems to be one that takes into account the traditional past, in all its richness and diversity. Bearing this in mind, in the following sections we will demonstrate how Chinese scholars do not simply apply traditions when discussing human rights. Rather, they critically engage with those traditions.

Individual Rights Versus 'What is Constant and Does Not Change'

The discussion on the concept of a right in Chinese culture, follows the analysis made by the renowned legal scholars Cheng Liaoyuan and Wang Renbo. In their book 'On Rights', Cheng and Wang argue that there is a conflict between the idea of a right and Chinese tradition. In their view, without significant exceptions, the ancient Chinese philosophies regarded the individual 'as a servant'.[101] The structure of the social order, according to Cheng and Wang, was rigid, pre-defined, and modelled analogically on the family. The basic relationships between the emperor and the subordinates, and the relationship between the subordinates and the general public, mirrored the basic relationships between father and son, or husband and wife. Cheng and Wang hold that, in this context, the future of the individual was 'inscribed unconditionally', thus annihilating the person's

---

[101] Cheng Liaoyuan and Wang Renbo *Quan li lun* supra note 2 at 147-150.

'creativity'[102] and obliterating the space of choice which underlies the concept of a right.

In particular, Cheng and Wang focus on the opposition between traditional legal culture and the contemporary concept of 'subjective rights'. Cheng and Wang observe that this concept is expressed through the term *quanli,* a term composed of the characters *quan* 权, power, and *li* 利, interest.[103] In early and classical Chinese texts the two characters *quan* and *li* appeared separately. The character *quan* conveyed the meaning of a pondered, balanced exercise of power, while *li* meant 'personal interest'. The current use of the word *quanli* (right), appeared only towards the end of the 19th century,[104] and in the context of Chinese scholars and philosophers who were studying and translating the works of French, American, Japanese and German authors on the rights of man and the citizen in Europe and the USA. In order to translate the term 'subjective right' found in these texts, Chinese scholars used *quan* and *li*, with the meaning of a pondered choice that only takes into account the interest of the individual rights holder.

Interestingly, Cheng and Wang observe that in traditional Chinese culture, society's view of both *quan* and *li* was negative, as shown by a quotation from the Book of Tang: 'People do not like snobbery, power [quan] and interest [li]'.[105] Similarly, in the Confucian classic the Book of Changes,[106] *quan* denotes a power that can also be exercised in opposition to justice and rights, therefore it can acquire a markedly derogatory meaning.[107] Even though in Xunzi (荀子), *quan* refers to the power to make a decision on whether or not to get something after pondering and judging the advantages and disadvantages according to the circumstances,[108] there seems to be an authoritative sense in the use of the term. This is testified, for instance, by the *Lijing*, or the Book of Rites, where *quan* is used in the

---

[102] Ibid at 149.
[103] Ibid at 147-150.
[104] Svensson, M *Debating Human Rights in China* supra note 2 at 84-85.
[105] Cheng Liaoyuan and Wang Renbo *Quan li lun* supra note 2 at 147.
[106] Ibid at 147-150.
[107] Ibid.
[108] Ibid.

expression *zheng quan jie* (正权桀) with reference to the power of the emperor Jie, the last ruler of the Xia dynasty (21st-16th century BC), traditionally considered a tyrant. In a similar fashion, the 'Criminal Annals', written during the Jin and Wei dynasties, use the word *quan* to denote authority and power.[109] In the Confucian classics, therefore, *quan* and *li* seem to imply 'amoral' power, and to stand in opposition to what is moral.

For instance, in Xunzi's book 'On Learning', *quan* and *li* are explicitly defined in opposition to what is stable and constant (the Way[110]): 'This is because powers and interests cannot change it [the Way, *dao* 道], people cannot change it and the world cannot change it. Life and death is decided by it. Therefore it (the Way, *dao* 道) is called "moral practice".'[111] In another passage Xunzi writes: 'Ask him to have contact with music and girls, power and interests, hate and anger, peril and danger, then observe if he can keep his moral practice.'[112] *Quan* and *li*, therefore, may constitute impediments, distractions or obstacles in the way of moral perfection. The pursuit of personal interest and influential positions for the sake of pure power has a negative moral connotation. The *junzi,* the righteous gentleman as described in the texts, seeks social morality, justice and propriety instead.[113]

In highlighting these concepts, Cheng and Wang put forward the notion that, in Confucian thought, the individual dimension and the moral dimension are opposed to each other. According to Cheng and Wang, in the Chinese tradition individual freedom and interest stand in sharp contrast with social morality, understood as an expression of the unchanging way in which nature and society have always functioned and will always function.[114] Cheng and Wang thus identify an incompatibility between traditional ethics and the idea of

---

[109] Ibid.

[110] For an account of the notion of 'the Way' (*dao* 道), in Xunzi's thought see Cheung, LKC (2001) 'The Way of the Xunzi' (28, 3) *Journal of Chinese Philosophy* 301. In the philosophy of Xunzi, the Way refers to the right way to live. Xunzi does not attribute to the Way any supernatural character. On the contrary, the Confucian philosopher considers the Way as a human concept.

[111] Xunzi (2006) *The Great Learning and the Doctrine of the Mean* available at <http://www.indiana.edu/~p374/Daxue-Zhongyong_(Eno-2016).pdf>

[112] Xunzi (2016) 'The Way to be a Lord' in Hutton, EL (trans) (2016) *Xunzi: The Complete Text* Princeton University Press 117.

[113] Cheng Liaoyuan and Wang Renbo *Quan li lun* supra note 2 at 147.

[114] Ibid at 147-150.

human rights. These considerations show, in a very clear manner, how the authors critically engage with their own tradition.

Rites, Rights and Role-Ethics

Cheng and Wang affirm that the model of ancient and imperial society was that of a society regulated through rites: a notion which, in their view, is antithetical to the idea of rights. In ancient Chinese ritual practices, different individuals had different roles. Duties, privileges and faculties were associated with each person according to her position in relation to others within a codified and rigid ritual etiquette.[115] This framework reflected the familial roles (such as the relation between father and son) and was based on the fundamental moral standards shared by society.[116] In the authors' view, this ethics focused on the role of the individual inevitably clashes with the modern idea of rights that inherently belong to anyone regardless of their role in society. Rituals, therefore, are in opposition to rights because they are inevitably based on role-ethics. Since the concept of rights in the modern sense of the word 'has no place in ancient Chinese rituals',[117] Cheng and Wang conclude that it is derived from the Western tradition.

From a liberal perspective, which to some extent can be compared to the authors' perspective, there is also another potential contrast between rituals and role-ethics on the one side, and individual rights on the other. If the core assumption of liberalism is that the individual is able to exercise her own judgment in order to freely express her desires, rituals and role-ethics may deprive the individual of that freedom. By taking part in the rituals, Cheng argues, and by performing a fixed role, one's personal desires are tuned into the values and ideals of the ritual practice. Individual choices are thus minimised to better reflect the values of the ritual practice. Ritual practice, therefore, has the effect of modifying what can be defined as 'first level desires', ie the desires that people have when they join the practice, through the influence of 'second level desires', ie the desires

---

[115] Ibid.
[116] Ibid.
[117] Ibid.

40

that the participants should have. [118] With reference to this point, it seems that there are three possible scenarios in which this process might take place. First, this modification of 'first level desires' into 'second level desires' takes place when the person's desires remain different and in contrast with the values of the practice, and the person is not allowed to act upon them (of course this scenario has reasonable limitations, for example if the person desires to harm others). Second, this process takes place when there is no possibility of changing a person's role in the practice according to what the person wants to become, accomplish or realise in her life. In other words, the person's position is not chosen by her, but instead imposed upon her. Third, the modification of 'first level desires' happens when the person is obliged to choose something even if ex hypothesi she would have chosen the same thing freely, so that the process of choosing, in itself, does not matter. Bearing these scenarios in mind, one can also make some clarifications regarding the specific kind of freedom that is curtailed in the ritual practice.

Following the distinction drawn by Amartya Sen, the first two cases represent a curtailment of the freedom *as opportunity*, because one is being forced to do something she might want to do without giving her the opportunity to choose freely, while the latter is a curtailment of the freedom *as process*, because one is obliged to do something she would not, under any circumstances, choose to do. [119] Sen explains that the difference between the two is 'readily seen when we compare the two alternatives "choosing freely to go out" and "being forced to go out".' Unlike the former, 'the latter involves an immediate violation of the process aspect of [someone]'s freedom, since an action is being forced on her (even though it is an action she would have freely chosen also).'[120]

According to Cheng and Wang, therefore, the main issue with role-ethics is that of choice (more specifically, the opportunity to choose in the first two scenarios, and the process of choosing in the third scenario). Cheng and Wang argue that rites and roles entail duties and privileges, not choices. In the traditional understanding, the

---

[118] The distinction is based on the famous theorisation by Frankfurt (Frankfurt, H (1971) 'Freedom of the will and the concept of a person', *Journal of Philosophy*, 68, 5–20; Frankfurt, H (1999) 'On caring', in *Necessity, Volition, and Love*, Cambridge University Press, at 155–180.

[119] Sen, A (2004) 'Elements of a Theory of Human Rights' (32, 4) *Philosophy and Public Affairs* 315 at 330-332.

[120] Ibid at 331.

entitlement of the individual seems to pertain to social functions articulated according to social and familial norms, rather than to individual choices and, consequently, rights. This view appears to be in complete opposition to contemporary 'contextual' notions on human rights, where, for example, children, the elderly, women and disabled people are seen as having specific rights stemming from their specific circumstances, rather than from their role.[121]

In order to fully appreciate this criticism of role-ethics, it is also important to stress that the author's position is connected with a specific understanding of Marxist discourses. Cheng's reasoning pivots on the following quotation from Karl Marx: 'The human being is in the most literal sense a ζῶον πολιτιχόν, not merely a gregarious animal, but an animal which can individuate itself only in the midst of society.'[122] On the basis of this argument, Cheng and Wang conclude that the ideal communist society does not attribute fixed roles to individuals, but is rather a society that, according to Marx and Engels:

> where nobody has one exclusive sphere of activity but each can become accomplished in any branch he wishes, society regulates the general production and thus makes it possible for me to do one thing today and another tomorrow, to hunt in the morning, fish in the afternoon, rear cattle in the evening, criticise after dinner, just as I have a mind, without ever becoming hunter, fisherman, herdsman or critic.[123]

According to Cheng and Wang, therefore, while Confucianism does not allow space for individual freedom, Marxism does.[124]

---

[121] This view will be examined again in Chapters Seven and Eight to show how Chinese scholars have substituted the notion of 'class' with that of 'group', recognising that individuals belonging to a certain group have specific rights by virtue of their specific needs for protection.

[122] Marx, K (1973) [1857] *Grundrisse: Foundations of the Critique of Political Economy* Penguin Books at 18.

[123] Marx, K and Engels, F (1970) [1845] *The German Ideology. Part One with selections from Parts Two and Three, together with Marx's Introduction to a Critique of Political Economy* International Publishers at 53.

[124] This account of Marxism differs from mainstream interpretations within China precisely because of this emphasis on the individual. In engaging with the Marxist tradition, Cheng and Wang consciously—but in a veiled fashion—offer a reinterpretation of the Marxist tradition that emphasises the individual rather than

These are certainly very important considerations. However, contrary to what is implied by Cheng, rites and roles are not necessarily in antithesis to the individual dimension. Other legal scholars have shown that the importance of social groups and roles is not necessarily incompatible with the recognition of rights.[125] On the contrary, the notion of roles and the importance of society can be understood as involving a moral request: the necessity for rights to be exercised in a way that is responsible and sensitive to social needs. This attitude embodies a different kind of critical engagement with tradition from the one found with Cheng. Let us therefore explore this more positive take on tradition as expressed by contemporary scholars.

Human Nature as 'Achievement' and Innate Human Rights

Having demonstrated that, according to some interpretations, Confucianism has room for the individual, let us further explore the notion of personhood as found in the Confucian framework. Later on in the book, it will be argued that some of the contemporary Chinese theories of human rights are based (even if not explicitly) on a specific understanding of the person that is compatible with Confucian thought. [126] Let us therefore take a step back, and look at anthropological conceptions within a specific branch of

---

the collective. This shows how Chinese scholars critically engage not only with their own tradition, but also with non-Chinese traditions, including Marxist theory, a topic which will be dealt with later on in the book (Chapter Eight). For now, it suffices to say that this particular view of Marxism as integrated with the rights-oriented discourse constitutes an attempt to argue for a change in the system from within. It could be said that Cheng and Wang represent the intelligentsia's fight for right in Rudolf von Jhering's sense. See Jhering, R (1915) [1872] *The Struggle for Law* Lalor, JJ (trans) Callaghan and Company.

[125] Incidentally, a vast anthropological literature has shown that ritual practices—even when they are structured according to seemingly rigid rules and roles—often involve a degree of personal re-elaboration of the meanings ascribed to the practice. See Tambiah, SJ (1985) *Culture, Thought, and Social Action* Harvard University Press; Goody, J (1977) *The Domestication of the Savage Mind* Cambridge University Press; Barth, F (1987) *Cosmologies in the Making: A Generative Approach to Cultural Variation in Inner New Guinea* Cambridge University Press; Csordas, TJ (1997) *The Sacred Self: A Cultural Phenomenology of Charismatic Healing* University of California Press. Anthropologists have also noted that often the need to follow ritual rules is more important than having a clear codification of what these rules might be. On this discussion see Humphrey, C and Laidlaw, J (1994) *The Archetypal Actions of Ritual: A Theory of Ritual Illustrated by the Jain Rite of Worship* Clarendon Press.

[126] These theories will be analysed in detail in Chapter Eight.

Confucianism: the thought of Mencius.[127] As noted by various scholars,[128] the Mencian account[129] is premised on the idea that humanity is not inherent in the person when she is born. Rather, a person, in Mencius' view, has to strive to become a full human being by entering a path of moral perfection and full realisation.[130]

Naturally, this account differs from the idea that individuals have innate value and dignity from birth, as found in the declarations of rights from the 18th century and in the 1948 Declaration of Human Rights. This might explain why current debates on human rights in China do not pivot on the idea of inalienable characteristics possessed

---

[127] Mencius, the Latinised name of Mengzi (孟子) (372–289 B.C.) is one of the most prominent Confucian philosophers. Confucian philosophy is mostly concerned with ethical and political theory. It was originally formulated by Confucius (551–476 B.C.) and was then carried on by his disciples Mencius and Xunzi (4th century B.C.). After a debate that lasted almost two hundred years, it was Mencius's version of Confucianism that became dominant. The challenges that Confucianism wrestled with in facing the moral arguments thrown at it by non-Confucian intellectuals were in part answered by Confucians and later by neo-Confucians and new-Confucians, and they are still being debated in contemporary China. On Mencius' philosophy see also Graham, AC (1967) 'The Background of the Mencian Theory of Human Nature' (6) *Tsing Hua Journal of Chinese Studies* 215; Graham, AC (1990) *Studies in Chinese philosophy and philosophical literature* State University of New York Press; Ivanhoe, PJ (2000) *Confucian Moral Self Cultivation* Hacket Publishing; Ivanhoe, PJ (2002) *Ethics in the Confucian Tradition: The Thought of Mengzi and Wang Yangming* Hacket Publishing; Lau, DC (1970) *Mencius* Penguin and Lau, DC (2003) *Mencius* (New Bilingual Edition) Chinese University Press.

[128] Ames, RT (1991) 'The Mencian Conception of Ren Xing: Does It mean "Human Nature"?' in Rosemont, HJ (ed) (2003) *Chinese Texts and Philosophical Contexts: Essays Dedicated to Angus C. Graham* Open Court 143 at 145. Graham, AC 'The Background' supra note 126; Graham, AC *Studies* supra note 126. Hall, DL and Ames, RT *Anticipating China* supra note 61 at 190-192; 272.

[129] The interpretation of the Mencian thought discussed here is the one given by Roger Ames and David Hall one of the most recent and authoritative.

[130] Ibid at 193-194. On the Confucian idea of human nature, see also Cua, AS (2005) *Human Nature, Ritual, and History: Studies in Xunzi and Chinese Philosophy* The Catholic University of America Press; and Foust, A (2017) *Confucianism and American Philosophy* SUNY Press at 84-95.

by every person from birth.[131] However, a closer analysis of the Confucian views reveals that, as suggested by Hall and Ames, the concept of the innate dignity of the human being is not, in itself, alien to the Chinese tradition. This concept, however, is expressed as an 'acquisition' rather than as an 'endowment from birth'.[132] Let us therefore unpack this idea of 'acquisition' of humanity.

First of all it is important to look at Confucian terminology with reference to human nature. In classical Confucian philosophy we find the notion of *xing*, 性, a term that is usually translated as 'nature'.[133] Different uses of this word can be found in Mencius, in the Analects and in Xunzi.[134] Interestingly, Ames and Hall note that Western scholars have translated the term as 'human nature', understood as what is naturally or genetically given. However, Mencius uses *xing* in a different way, as an achievement concept. This notion of personal development, according to Ames and Hall, possesses dynamic and creative aspects, which have been minimised by Western scholars due to a fundamental conceptual equivocation.

In the Confucian texts *xing* is understood as a potential that needs to be developed. On the one hand, *xing* is an Aristotelian potentiality: the potential of being human. On the other hand, *xing* differs from the Aristotelian notion of nature (φύσις) because it is a matter of nurture and culture, rather than of nature. *Xing* stands out as a distinctively cultural construction rather than a pre-cultural endowment. Humanity, in other words, is not given, but acquired through a constant, creative process of moral cultivation. In this perspective, human beings are not so much symbol users, or social animals, rather they are 'culturally refined beings' capable of ameliorating themselves. This point is particularly important to understand how human dignity is articulated within the Confucian framework.

Hall and Ames note that *xing* is rooted in the word *xin* (心) 'heart-and-mind'.[135] In the Confucian perspective, the sage is the person who actualises both *xing* and *xin* to the full.[136] The sage is

---

[131] Although it figures among the justification of rights in the reflection of some authoritative legal scholars (see Chapter Eight below).

[132] Hall, DL and Ames, RT *Anticipating China* supra note 61 at 272.

[133] Ibid at 188-189; 194.

[134] Foust, A *Confucianism* supra note 127 at 84-95.

[135] Hall, DL and Ames, RT *Anticipating China* supra note 61 at 193. Ames, RT 'The Mencian Conception' supra note 127 at 145.

[136] Hall, DL and Ames, RT *Anticipating China* supra note 61 at 193.

therefore the perfect human, with a perfect heart and a perfect mind. However, as Hall and Ames explain, being human does not necessarily entail being a sage.[137] *Xing* is a dynamic process, and the status of the sage constitutes the end-point of the process of cultivation. It follows, I would argue, that what characterises a human being is the potential to become a sage. Every human partakes in *xing* because each person involved in the constant process of maturation that one day will hopefully lead, through self-effort, to wisdom and full human actualisation. It is in this sense that Hall and Ames define the Confucian understanding of humanity as 'inspirational' (a model that inspires good conduct) rather than 'aspirational' (a standard that is predefined and needs to be replicated).[138]

To clarify this concept we can look at a fundamental difference between the Western and the Confucian understanding of the cosmos. The Confucian idea of the universe differs from the Greek philosophical notion of κόσμος, understood as an entity ordered by a defining principle or αρχή. In the κόσμος, the totality of things is ordered, regulated and generated by the αρχή from the beginning, or in principle.[139] In Confucianism, however, there is neither a creation nor a cosmogonic beginning of the universe. Therefore, as Hall and Ames note: 'the power of creativity and the responsibility for creative product reside more broadly in the phenomena themselves in their on-going interactive processes of becoming'.[140] Similarly, in the Mencian

---

[137] Ames, RT Ibid.

[138] Ibid at 159, 149, 165.

[139] Ibid at 148.

[140] Ibid. The absence of a 'given human nature' might also be related to the absence of a supreme God in Confucianism. Exploring this dynamic might be extremely revealing. However, such an endeavour goes beyond the scope of this book. Incidentally, according to Hall and Ames, this non-cosmogonic view leads to a specific understanding of the role of the thinker. In non-cosmogonic worldviews like Confucianism, the philosopher is not expected to unveil the origin of things, nor is he supposed to answer fundamental questions about the universe. Rather the philosopher is required to create a model of humanity that is persuasive, and that can be enacted and emulated (Hall, DL and Ames, RT (1995) *Anticipating China* supra note 61 at 11-12; 36; 92-115). It might be argued, perhaps simplistically but certainly suggestively, that in China this specific understanding of philosophy—not as interpretation of the world but as creation of a model of humanity—might have created a particularly fertile intellectual ground for the acceptance of Marxist

account, humanity is not a 'given' regulated by a defining principle, but a creative tendency that is grounded in humans themselves as the very possibility of becoming fully human. In Tu's words, 'the ultimate ground of one's becoming good is located within oneself'.[141]

This potential for amelioration, rooted within the individual, is the Confucian notion of human dignity. It is true that, if a human being fails to cultivate herself, she is considered a 'non-human', a 'failed human being' (*fei ren* 非人). However, even the non-human has, or has had at some point, the potential to become human. This is a fundamental clarification that allows us to understand that, though different from the Western views, Confucianism provides some ground for the attribution of rights, in the sense that it is important to secure the fundamental rights that allow a person to enter the path of full realisation, and develop his personality in creative ways.

It is also important to clarify that this process of self-realisation is not simply a matter of personal growth. The word *xing* does not have a strictly descriptive connotation, like the English word 'human'; instead, it indicates something which is defined and enacted in community.[142] Self-amelioration, therefore, is not achieved in isolation as with other traditions, like the Daoist doctrine. Rather it is reached by interacting with other individuals. The 'starting point' of a person, one might say, is therefore given by her relations, and 'This initial relationality is captured conceptually in the four categories of interpersonal bonds (*ren*), societal bonds of reference (*li*), meaning and value disclosing bonds (*yi*), and intellectual bonds (*zhi*), all of which are open to cultivation'.[143] Relationality included both the living and the dead, or the ancestors, because *xing* is mediated through the 'proper channelling of intense emotions and symbolic significance of honouring the dead'.[144]

In this perspective, self-cultivation undertaken in a relational manner is what characterises humanity, because 'the cultivated product of the four stirrings is human; mere consciousness and desires

---

theories. As Marx famously argued in the Eleven Theses on Feuerbach, 'The philosophers have only *interpreted* the world, in various ways. The point, however, is to *change* it.'

[141] Tu Weiming *Centrality and commonality* supra note 55 at 51.

[142] Ames, RT 'The Mencian Conception' supra note 127.

[143] Ibid at 155.

[144] The Confucian mourning ritual was public. The performance of correct ritual behaviour—and its effects on society—were therefore considered to be very important matters.

are animal'.[145] *Xing* is therefore 'an on-going poietic process'[146] which is 'conditioned by its particular context'.[147] It denotes an inherent human capacity for radical changeability and a vocation to refinement, but only as a result of interaction with the environment, understood as both social and natural reality. *Xing* has normative implications, but only in the sense that it is the best way to identify what is 'relationally good as "good at" or "good for" developing for oneself those bonds which tie one into family and community'.[148] Incidentally, this means that, as Hall and Ames conclude, 'what is "best" is only retrospectively understood. The norm comes into being *pari passu* with the process. That is, the norm itself is an emergent product that depends on the context'.[149]

Implicit in the analysis of Hall and Ames is the notion that Confucian thought has both an understanding of the role of the individual and a strong sense of the community. In fact, the two are not seen as diametrically opposed, but only as two sides of the same spectrum. Nonetheless, to a Western observer, these views might still be seen to indicate that Confucianism creates a theoretical obstacle: it difficult to use Confucian notions to ground the rights of the person. Let me elaborate on this.

The Confucian stress on the relational aspect of humanity, Hall and Ames argue, is related to a classical Chinese understanding of the dichotomy of abstract and concrete. In their words: 'to call a person "individual" in the atomistic sense that we associate with some liberal

---

[145] Ibid at 158.

[146] Ibid at 153.

[147] Ibid.

[148] Ibid at 156. Apparently, the idea of men as good is a neo-Confucian metaphysical interpretation of a concept that did not have metaphysical implications in Mencius, this view is shared by Graham and Ames (Ibid). See also Graham, AC 'The Background' supra note 126.

[149] Ames, RT 'The Mencian Conception' supra note 127 at 158. With reference to this point it is important to stress that in non-cosmogonic thought, difference comes before—and is conceptually prior to—similarity. The categories of *genus* and *species* are therefore dependent upon analogy among *sui generis* phenomena: a dynamic which would explain why, in Confucianism, the relationship between rule and exception seems inverted, as there is no universally applicable rule, but only solutions for a particular case. On this matter see Ibid. at 148.

48

democratic traditions would be *to abstract* him from the value-invested network of particular and familial and cultural conditions and the immediate cognitive and practical relationships that define him initially, and which make possible his continuing growth'.[150] This attitude is compatible with Marxist theorisations that reject abstract rights and affirm that the only kind of existing rights are concrete rights that reflect the social context. However, the notion of an individual who is inseparable from her relations stands in opposition to the liberal notion of the individual as an independent entity capable of free choice.

With reference to this point, it is important to clarify that, even though the Confucian notion of acquired and relational personhood clashes with liberal views, this does not mean to say that within Confucianism there is no room for choice. If the Western liberal paradigm understands choice as the faculty of a sovereign individual free from constraints, in Confucian thought choice is dependent on the context and implies responsibility towards one's relations. For instance, someone has a certain set of choices of behaviour when she interacts with her father, but this set of choices would be different when she interacts with a friend. The Confucian attitude, therefore, does value choice, but with an understanding of choice that differs from the Western one. This understanding is based on the essential relational component of the human being.

Choice is a fundamental aspect of the process of acquisition of humanity and amelioration: a point that, in order to be clarified, requires a brief analysis of the relationship between transcendence and immanence in Confucianism. According to some intellectuals,[151], the 'sky' or 'Heaven' (*tian* 天) is a fundamentally transcendental reality.

---

[150] Hall, DR and Ames, RT (1998) *Thinking From the Han: Self, Truth, and Transcendence in Chinese and Western Culture* State University of New York Press at 278. Emphasis added. This dynamic is also related to the fact that Chinese classical thought does not see 'inner' (*nei* 内) and 'outer' (*wai* 外) as a dichotomy of two opposites. According to Hall and Ames the absence of the dichotomy inner/outer, external/internal, is another element that contributes to a view of man as inseparable from the community (Ibid at 156). Significantly, Tu Weiming—who, as we have seen, has an individual-oriented interpretation of Confucianism—does not agree with this view. See Tu Weiming (1989) *Centrality and commonality* supra note 55.

[151] Liu Yuli (2004) *The Unity of Rule and Virtue: A Critique of a Supposed Parallel Between Confucian Ethics and Virtue Ethics* Eastern Universities Press.

The prevailing interpretation,[152] however, is that *tian* forms an inextricable continuum with earth and with man (*tian ren he yi* 天人 合一). Thus, following the same logic that regulates the relation between individual and community, transcendence and immanence are two sides of the same spectrum.

In progressing along the path of the acquisition of humanity, an individual transcends her being and passes through higher levels of wisdom, while always remaining the same individual, so that the process of amelioration is both transcendental and immanent. These two aspects are embodied by two aspects of the self: the transcendent self and the active self. In the process of amelioration the transcendent self is capable of reshaping the self by reflecting on the actions and attitudes of the active self. In this process the person makes free choices, and particularly the free, responsible choice of committing to the path of humanity by being faithful to his/her particular context and to his/her relationships. These considerations on personhood are key if one wants to reflect on current legal debates in China.

Indeed, as suggested by Hall and Ames, the notion of an acquired humanity underlies not only the classical Chinese tradition, but also contemporary Chinese society.[153] The foundation of human moral worth is therefore understood not as an endowment with innate prerogatives (liberty or freedom, property, and so on) but as the individual potential for amelioration, considering relationality as a fundamental trait of the person, and free choice as the choice to be faithful to one's context and relationships. In this sense, the Confucian understanding is far from the notions of individual autonomy and sovereignty espoused in the liberal tradition.

The traditional Confucian view of society as made up of different groups, and in which different responsibilities attach to different social roles, rests on a specific principle: the need to exercise rights in a way that takes into account the situation of the different individuals belonging to social groups with significant characteristics. Particularly when it comes to vulnerable groups like women, children,

---

[152] Mou, B (ed) (2009) *History of Chinese Philosophy* vol. 3 of *History of World Philosophies* Routledge.

[153] Ames, RT (1991) 'The Mencian Conception' supra note 127 at 164.

or the elderly, specific rights should be recognised in virtue of specific circumstances. On a deeper level, however, this focus on the needs of different social groups is based on a true situational anthropology of rights, which in turn is based on a contextual view of personhood that resonates with the previously described Chinese traditional philosophy.[154]

Bearing this in mind, later on in the book I will return to the ideas I have analysed in this section—human dignity as potential for amelioration, relationality as a fundamental trait of the individual, and free choice as the choice to be faithful to one's context and relationships—but with reference to human rights. As we will see, Chinese scholars do not explicitly refer to these notions, but they implicitly apply them and individuate grounds for human rights that are more applicable to China than liberal notions of the 'autonomy' and 'sovereignty' of the individual. Postponing a detailed discussion on these matters to Chapter Eight, I will now consider another concept from the Confucian tradition which is relevant for a discussion on human rights in China: mediation.

Chinese Mediation and the Global Discourse on Human Rights
Conflict resolution plays an important role in Chinese culture and its philosophical premises are to be found in the Confucian doctrine of harmony. Confucianism has as its paramount values the avoidance of conflicts, the safeguarding of social harmony and relationships, and the necessity to educate and enlighten the conflicting parties. In actualising these values of harmony and education, mediation takes into account the role a person occupies in a relationship. Though characterised by reciprocity, the five basic relationships identified in Confucianism (father and son, ruler and ministers, husband and wife, elder and younger brother, friend and friend) are mostly asymmetrical. Therefore, in mediation, the positions associated with the parties at the lower end of the relationship is typically one of 'obligation' or 'subjection', while the ones associated with the higher are 'privilege', 'immunity' and so on. Furthermore, mediation is supposed to be a process carried out by the wise and the elderly, who should act as mediators.

---

[154] Rosemont, HJ (2004) 'Whose Democracy? Which Rights? A Confucian Critique' in Kwong-loi Shun and David B. Wong (2004) *Confucian Ethics: A Comparative Study of Self, Autonomy, and Community* Cambridge University Press 49; De Bary, WT, and Tu Weiming (eds) (1998) *Confucianism and Human Rights* Columbia University Press.

The transition from the Empire to the Republic and the creation of the new PRC modified institutions and the organisation of the state, but the importance attached to mediation did not change. After the creation of the PRC, the law came to include among mediation's goals: 'the resolution of disputes, the reinforcement of people's patriotism, education on observance of the law, fostering unity among the people, the people's production, and the people's construction of China'. [155] The educational element and the safeguarding of social cohesion are therefore still at the core of mediation activities. While in Confucian China mediation was a social process, nowadays mediation is a legal institution aimed at guaranteeing the 'timely mediation of civil disputes, improving the unity of the people and safeguarding social stability, in order to facilitate the construction of socialist modernisation'.[156]

In today's China there are three forms of mediation: judicial, which is conducted by the court, semi-formal, and informal—or extra-judicial—mediation.[157] In the latter two models moral tenets usually play a stronger role than legal principles. For instance, a wholeheartedly felt apology from the party perceived to be at fault is considered to be part and parcel of the successful conclusion of the mediation process.[158] Judicial mediation, on the other hand, places more value on legal principles, but nevertheless makes use of compromises.[159] The role of compromise in the context of judicial mediation is greater 'in disputes where there is no clear-cut legal right and wrong, such as working out the details of divorce or tort settlements, or in disputes over roughly equal obligations, such as how

---

[155] People's Mediation Law of the PRC promulgated by the Standing Committee of the National People's Congress on 28/08/2010, in force 01/01/2011.

[156] Article 1, People's Mediation Law of the PRC.

[157] Palmer, M (1987) 'The Revival of Mediation in the PRC: (1) Extra-Judicial Mediation' in Butler, WE (ed) (1987) *Yearbook on Socialist Legal Systems* 143 at 145. See also Fu, H and Palmer, M (2017) *Mediation in Contemporary China* Wildy, Simmonds and Hill Publishing.

[158] The expectation of apologies in order to repair a damaged relationship, a moral tort or offence in addition to material damage, is less common in the cities than in villages. This is due to the fact that nowadays the community of citizens in urban areas is perceived to be a community of strangers.

[159] If court mediation fails, the dispute is the object of a formal adjudication.

to distribute among siblings the burden for maintaining the parents in their old age'.[160]

In examining the relationship between the current and the ancient understanding of mediation, Cheng and Wang note that there is a certain continuity in terms of aims (harmony, etc), but also some strong differences. Firstly, Cheng and Wang claim that there is a discrepancy between the type of settlement rules that are in force and the expectations of those involved in disputes, as the formal mediation system does not necessarily imply apologies and the education of those at fault.[161]

Secondly, in their view, there is a difference in the object of mediation. The object of contemporary mediation can be: 'disputes over property rights and interests, including land use rights and income rights disputes; homestead and property, the sale of housing, rental disputes; debt disputes and neighbours' rights disputes; disputes on assault, injury, damage, minor insult and slander, libel, interference in the freedom of marriage and other disputes.'[162] In this context, the principle of making concessions in order to maintain social harmony and cohesion conflicts with the idea and operational logic of legal rights.

Cheng and Wang highlight that mediation should not ignore or waive the rights of the person involved. The values of harmony, social order, and restoration of relationships between citizens in a dispute cannot prevail over the satisfaction, protection and guarantee of legal rights. Modern mediation, Cheng and Wang point out, is based on the principle of legality and respect for the parties' rights is part of the mediation process, which in fact provides specific restrictions limiting the action of the mediators.[163] Cheng and Wang thus emphasise that Chinese contemporary mediation should adjust its own goals and include among them the guarantee of people's rights. In his words: 'it is necessary to move beyond the traditional mediation that was only focusing on the reconstruction of order and ignoring the value of the right's guarantee'.[164]

---

[160] Huang, PC (2015) 'Morality and Law in China Past and Present' (41, 1) *Modern China* 39.

[161] Cheng Liaoyuan and Wang Renbo *Quan li lun* supra note 2.

[162] Ibid.

[163] Articles 13-16 of the People's Mediation Law of the People's Republic of China.

[164] Anthropological research persuasively demonstrates that the people coming in front of the wise or elderly people in the village in order to mediate a dispute do not perceive the mediation process as being governed by impartiality. On this matter see

In putting forward these arguments Cheng and Wang clarify that in some areas of law the traditional logic of mediation can play a stronger role. He refers particularly to areas where there are not clear rights and corresponding obligations, and where the line between legally provided rights and duties is blurred, such as with the regulations on marriage and divorce. In these areas, Cheng and Wang argue, the Chinese legal tradition could bring a valuable contribution to the global human rights discourse. With reference to other, more clear-cut areas of law, however, Cheng and Wang see a complete incompatibility with the protection and guarantee of legal rights.[165] Interestingly, however, other contemporary Chinese scholars have a less negative view of traditional mediation processes.

Renowned scholar Huang, for instance, argues that: 'the settlement of disputes by mediation can be seen as a major example of the Chinese legal system's practising of moral principles'.[166] In Huang's view the very concept of mediation is based on the issue of what morally ought to be, instead of the issue of what is legal and what is not. Mediation, according to Huang, 'is about virtue, even more than justice. It is about harmony, not rights and their violations, and about resolution of disputes through compromise, not adjudication of legal right and wrong. It is about drawing on the compromising and forgiving side of humans to build a moral society, not just about the forbidding and punishment of illegal behaviour'.[167] This logic is based on relationality and empathy, the human capacity to understand

---

Hoque, A (2015) 'Does the Law Work in a Village Like Gulapbari? An Anthropological Insight' (1) *University of Asia Pacific Journal of Law and Policy* 33 at 41-45.

[165] Cheng argues that in ancient China mediation processes contributed to maintain the hierarchical structure of society. In Cheng's view, the logic of mediation thus differs from legal logic, as he puts it: 'In order to protect the ethical order and restore interpersonal harmony, mediation could put aside the legal texts or provisions and follow the feudal etiquette instead' (Cheng Liaoyuan and Wang Renbo *Quan li lun* supra note 2 at 576). Cheng is certainly a scholar with liberal tendencies, but his position on this particular point resembles the classic Marxist critique of ideology understood as principles that are presented as natural in order to justify inequality and exploitation.

[166] Huang, PC 'Morality' supra note 159 at 7.
[167] Ibid.

someone else's context,[168] and it is thus 'very different from a legal system based on the premise of individual rights and then elaborated logically with regard to what violates individual rights'.[169]

The views held by Huang, Cheng and Wang on mediation stand out as yet another example of critical engagement with tradition. I should also add that Huang's view is valuable in arguing that a synthesis between the goals and values associated with Chinese traditional mediation and rights provided by law may begin a new trend in legal development, capitalising on the capacity of the Chinese legal system to represent a unique 'continuum of shadings from mediation to adjudication and of the two working in tandem'.[170] The joining together of law and morality in the mediation system reflects a major characteristic of the Chinese conception of law and legal practice. I will therefore refer to it in other sections of the book, including the one that follows. As Huang affirms, it is by focusing on this aspect that 'a new, modern, and distinctively Chinese legal system can and will be constituted'.[171]

Conclusion

In this chapter I have introduced some key concepts from Chinese classical legal thought that will be relevant for our discussion on human rights in China. As we have seen, far from being static and clear-cut, these notions give rise to a plethora of different interpretations within Chinese legal discussions. Contemporary

---

[168] Ibid.

[169] Ibid. Some Western theorisations see the possibility to activate judicial enforcement against the violation of the right as an essential aspect of human rights. For a critical and complete account of the role played by institutionalisation, legislation and judicial protection of rights, see Trujillo, I and Viola, F (2016) *What Human Rights Are Not (or Not Only): A Negative Path to Human Rights Practice* Nova Science Publishers at 37-40. More broadly, the interpretation in discussion implies, though with different outcomes, Weber's famous distinction between formal and informal law. According to Max Weber, the formal, rational ideal-type of law is the one that guarantees predictability and certainty, derived from practice rather than from other systems such as religion or morality (Weber, M (2013) [1922] *Economy and Society* University of California Press. Chinese traditional mediation, on the contrary, follows a moral logic. In Huang's words, 'if one were to employ Weberian categories, it is in the end about substantivism, and about substantive irrationality and rationality not formal rationality'. Huang, PC 'Morality' supra note 159 at 7.

[170] Huang, PC 'Morality' supra note 159 at 9.

[171] Ibid at 7.

scholars thus critically engage with their tradition, accepting or rejecting its notions and ideas, in whole or in part. In a sense, one might argue that scholars reject tradition and feel the necessity to explore legal systems or traditions other than China's when they feel that the answers it provides are not adequate to deal with new, contemporary challenges.

Bearing this in mind, the following chapter will explore the relation between Chinese legal scholars and Western legal thought. In particular, it will be shown how scholars critically engage not only with their own tradition, but also with Western frameworks. This discussion will also provide the chance to contextualise the theoretical positions of Chinese scholars within some major changes that have taken place in China, particularly the shift to the social market economy.

CHAPTER THREE

Engaging With The Concept of Rule of Law

Introduction

The previous analysis has shown how contemporary Chinese scholars engage with their own classical legal tradition in theorising human rights. This new and more mature attitude, liberated from the prejudices of the past, reflects a renewed interest in Chinese intellectual heritage. However, the result of this new attitude is not the wholesale, blind recovery of ancient theorisations, but the rejection or recovery of some of its components, in a process of critical engagement. As shown in the preceding pages, the legal scholars argue for or against the use of elements retrieved from the classics, including Confucian ones, striving to articulate theories that may better respond to present predicaments, in line with what they perceive as the Chinese identity.

In the same fashion and with the same purpose, Chinese legal scholars have been engaging with Western ideas, concepts and legal institutions. To understand the dynamics of critical engagement, the following pages will explore how the Chinese scholars discuss a specific notion, linked[172] with the affirmation and protection of human rights: the idea of 'the rule of law'.

The concept of the rule of law[173] expresses the autonomy of law from politics. In this specific sense there is a relationship between

---

[172] There is a philosophical disagreement on the nature and strength of this connection or mutual implication between respect for the rule of law and protection of rights. Ronal Dworkin and Lord Bingham defended the right thesis (Dworkin, R (1985) *A Matter of Principle* Oxford University Press; Bingham, T (2010) *The Rule of Law* Allen Lane), while Joseph Raz held the opposite view called no-right thesis (Raz, J (1979) 'The Rule of Law and Its Virtue' in *The Authority of Law. Essays on Law and Morality* Clarendon Press 211).

[173] The rule of law is an 'essentially contested notion' and is at the centre of debates in the philosophy of law and politics. In a 'thinner' sense, the rule of law consists of the mere subjection of authorities to pre-existing legal norms that have certain formal characteristics and whose application can be predicted with sufficient certainty, whatever the substance of the norms. The formal and procedural accounts of the rule of law advocate for this thesis. According to Fuller, a legal system is a rule of law system in which the law generally possesses specific formal and

the rule of law and the protection of rights. A basic condition for the respect of rights provided by law is that the exercise of power and the use of coercive means, necessary to govern any society, must be carried out according to the law; the enactment and the application of laws should respect previously stated procedures in order to be legitimate and obligatory for its subjects. According to the principle of legality, all powers must be exercised under the law, and the law must be applied to all in compliance with the principle of formal equality (equality before the law). This account of the rule of law is called 'thin', because it does not provide any indication about the content that legal dispositions should have.

However, some believe that respect for existing norms and procedures is a necessary but not sufficient condition for the protection of basic rights: legality ensures the protection of rights only where enacted legal rules recognise and protect such rights. The 'thick', substantive accounts of the rule of law accept a tighter link between the rule of law and rights, a link that for some authors is conceptual in nature. According to 'thick' theories, the rule of law necessarily involves the protection of certain rights (property,[174]

---

procedural characteristics, including clarity, publicity, non-retroactivity, non-contradiction, stability, possibility, and promulgation; also, the application of the law should be consistent with the letter of the law (Fuller, LL (1969) *The Morality of Law: Revised Edition* Yale University Press; Fuller, LL (1976) *Anatomy of the Law* Greenwood Press) Understood in this way, the rule of law does not give any indication of the contents of the law, but a system that possesses the desiderata indicated by Fuller to a sufficient degree can still be instrumental to the protection of rights, since the protection of individual rights presupposes that authorities are subject to legal norms, and the fairness of the system resulting from respect for the formal and procedural requirements is necessary for treating the individuals subject to the system with respect. See Celano, B (2011) 'Liberal Multiculturalism, neutrality and the Rule of Law' in (11) *Diritto e Questioni Pubbliche* 559; and Celano, B (2013) 'Publicity and the Rule of Law' in Green, BLL (ed) *Oxford Studies in Philosophy of Law: Volume 2* Oxford University Press 122. Celano highlights the value of neutrality in law, which consists of the law's fairness, public character, coherence, consistency and practicability, and the equivalence of positions of power.
[174] Montesquieu, C (1989) [1748] *The Spirit of the Laws* Penguin; Cohler, A; Miller, C and Stone, H (eds) Cambridge University Press; Cass, R (2004) 'Property Rights Systems and the Rule of Law' in Colombatto, E (ed) (2004) *The Elgar Companion*

freedom) or specific political preferences, as for instance the separation of governmental powers within a system of checks and balances, or democratic elections with multiple political parties.

An intermediate position between the formal and the substantive approaches described above holds that a legal system is regulated by the rule of law if there is a tension between the exercise of political power and specific legal principles enabling and constraining this exercise.[175] However, according to this theory, the rule of law does not require that the principles constraining political power have a specific content, their content being a matter for positive law.[176] A different debate is whether the rule of law represents a political ideal, external to the concept of law, or if, on the contrary, it is part of the very concept of law,[177] but this debate cannot be discussed here.

Chinese scholars have debated the model of the rule of law in relation to the two theories of the exercise of power that have been alternately dominant throughout Chinese history: the rule of man (*renzhi* 人治)[178] and the rule by law (*fazhi* 法治).[179] Although this chapter focuses on the contemporary conceptions rather than the traditional ones (on which the previous chapter was focused), there will be space to discuss the traditional opposition of rule of man and rule by law, as reinterpreted through contemporary lenses. Neglecting this portion of the debate would be simplistic, not only because advocates of the rule of man still exist, but also because even supporters of more liberal accounts of the rule of law do explore the arguments of classical Chinese philosophies on the rule of man. In addition, some underlying premises of the contemporary discussion

---

to the Economics of Property Right Edward Elgar Publications 131; Bingham, T *The Rule* supra note 171.

[175] Palombella, G (2009) 'Rule of Law. Argomenti di una teoria giuridica istituzionale' (1) *Sociologia del diritto* 27.

[176] Ibid.

[177] Jeremy Waldron argues for a conceptual, necessary relationship between the concept of law and the rule of law (Waldron, J (2008) 'The Concept and the Rule of Law' (43) *Georgia Law Review*, 59). In contrast, Joseph Raz defines the rule of law as the 'virtue' of legal systems, and understands the rule of law as a political ideal (Raz, J *The Authority of Law* supra note 171).

[178] The rule of man, once advocated by Confucian scholars, values benevolent government by wise persons.

[179] The rule by law, normally ascribed to the Legalist school, in opposition to the Confucian school, advocated enacted law as an instrument serving political objectives.

can be made clear by identifying the core ideas professed by the Confucian and the Legalist schools between the 3rd and 5th century BC, the first advocating for the rule of man, the latter purporting a system of rule by law.[180] The majority of contemporary advocates of the rule of law argue for the variant called socialist rule of law, a view which is in line with Chinese socialism, but could be interpreted as a modern, unspoken but rather sophisticated re-articulation of earlier Confucian and Legalist ideas.

It will be contended that the scholars who advocate positions similar to Western liberal conceptions of the rule of law are not motivated by a mixture of awe and a sense of technical or moral inferiority towards Western legal values. On the contrary, the reasoning behind the specific model they advocate is animated by the strong belief that it will provide the best response to the challenges[181] that China is experiencing, and by a new understanding of the value of law within the same Chinese tradition.

It will be argued that the most relevant and recent change that has affected the debate on the rule of law is the shift to the socialist market economy. The attribution of rights to individuals who are active agents in the market, and have interests to protect (economic interests, for instance), catalysed the appreciation of law per se and not as a mere tool to reach political goals. In particular, Chinese intellectuals revolving now around the idea that a legal system possessing autonomy and authority is necessary for the protection of individual rights, show a different understanding of the role and functions of law. The debate on the rule of law lacks coherence and

---

[180] For an account of the difference between 'rule of law' and 'rule by law' see Palombella, G 'Rule of Law' supra note 174 and Morlino, L and Palombella, G 2010 *Rule of Law and Democracy: Inquiries into Internal and External Issues* Brill. In the Chinese debate see Cheng Liaoyuan (1999) *Cong fazhi dao fazhi* [From Legal System to Rule of Law] Falu chubanshe; and Cheng Liaoyuan and Wang Renbo *Quan li lun* supra note 2.

[181] Some of these challenges are due to long-standing problems such as the urban-rural divide, local protectionism, and corruption. Others have been brought about more recently by the shift to the socialist market economy, such as the widening of the gap between the rich and the poor, or generated by economic development, such as the environmental issues.

consistency, and the trajectory of its development is not clear.[182] However, it is still significant because it represents the attempt of the Chinese intelligentsia to finding its own definition of the role and importance of the law in protecting rights. This debate is heavily controlled at present, due to the strong censorship imposed by the political agenda of the current elite in power.[183] In the light of the changes brought about by the market, the following pages will discuss the function attached to law, the value of the autonomy of law, the ideal of faith in law, and the relationship between law, justice and rights.

The Debate about the Rule of Law after the Cultural Revolution
Having experienced the effects of an unrestrained and arbitrary power, after the Cultural Revolution the same elite of the CCP called for a system of governance where the law would play a more important role.[184] Thus, the contemporary debate about the rule of law was promoted from above.[185] Since then, a number of Chinese scholars and intellectuals started a reflection, which is still ongoing today, on the significance of the model of the rule of law, and on its advantages with respect to the models of rule by law and rule of man.[186] The scholarly discussion had different phases of evolution. While during the 1980s the debate was focused upon the opposition between the

---

[182] Seppänen, S (2016) *Ideological Conflict and the Rule of Law in Contemporary China: Useful Paradoxes* Cambridge University Press.

[183] See Chapters Four and Five.

[184] The debate was initiated due to a 'visceral and personal reaction to the arbitrariness of the Cultural Revolution by many senior Party leaders' (Peerenboom, RP (2006) 'A Government of Laws. Democracy, Rule of Law, and Administrative Law Reform in China' in Zhao, S (ed) *Debating Political Reform in China. Rule of Law vs. Democratisation* Routledge 58 at 59). See also Keith, RC (1994) *China's Struggle for the Rule of Law* St. Martin's Press.

[185] Keith, RC Ibid; Peerenboom, RP (2001) 'Globalization, Path Dependency and the Limits of Law: Administrative Law Reform and the Rule of Law in the PRC' (19) *Berkeley Journal of International Law* 161 at 164; He Weifang (2012) *In the Name of Justice* supra note 1.

[186] For a comprehensive exposition of the scholarly debate on the rule of law from 1996 to 2000 see Chen, AHY (2000) 'Toward A Legal Enlightenment: Discussion in Contemporary China on the Rule of Law' in The Mansfield Center For Pacific Affairs (2010) *The Rule of Law: Perspectives from the Pacific Rim* The Mansfield Center For Pacific Affairs 13 at 13-54; Seppänen, S *Ideological Conflict* supra note 181.

rule by law and the rule of man,[187] subsequently the debate focused instead on the opposition between rule of law and rule by law.[188]

Most recently, Albert Chen, Randall Peerenboom and Samuli Seppänen have analysed the Chinese debates on the rule of law. Albert Chen compiled an overview of Chinese theories of the rule of law elaborated at the end of the 20th century and the beginning of the 21st century, distinguishing between mainstream and minority views. Chen argues that in that particular period of time, among the most prominent scholars there seemed to be an agreement on a core point:

---

[187] Liang Zhiping (1999) *Cong lizhi dao fazhi* [From rule of *li* to rule of law] (126) *Kaifang shidai* 78.

[188] See Ibid. The characteristics of a 'Chinese' rule of law have been highlighted by Castellucci, Ignazio (2007) 'Rule of Law with Chinese Characteristics' (13) Annual Survey of International and Comparative Law 35. See also Wang, J (2004) 'The Rule of Law in China: a Realistic View of the Jurisprudence, the Impact of the WTO and the Prospects for Future Development' *Singapore Journal of Legal Studies* 347; Catá Backer, L (2006-2007) 'The Rule of Law, The Chinese Communist Party, and Ideological Campaigns: *Sange Daibiao* (The Three Represents) Socialist Rule of Law and Modern Chinese Constitutionalism' (16) *Transnational Law and Contemporary Problems* 29; Chen, J (2004) 'To have a Cake and Eat it Too?: China and the Rule of Law' in Doeker-Mach, G and Ziegert, KA (eds) (2004) *Law, Legal Culture and Politics in the Twenty First Century* Franz Steiner Verlag 250; Chen, AHY 'Toward A Legal Enlightenment' supra note 185; Crespi RG (1999) 'Verso il mercato e lo Stato di diritto: recenti riforme costituzionali in Cina' (2) *Diritto pubblico comparato ed europeo* 485; Delmas-Matry, M (2003) 'Present Day China and the Rule of Law: Progress and Resistance' (2) *Chinese J. Int'l L.* 11; Keith, RC (1991) 'Chinese Politics and the New Theory of "Rule of Law"' (125) *The China Quarterly* 109; Keith, RC *China's Struggle* supra note 184; Li, Z (2004) 'NPC: The Rule of Law' (47) *Beijing Review* 10; Lidija, R and Basta, F (eds) (2000) *Rule of Law and Organisation of the State in Asia: the Multicultural Challenge* Helbing et Lichtenhahn; Liu, H (2009) 'Protection of Human Rights and the Establishment of Rule of Law in China' in Li, L (ed) (2009) *The China Legal Development Yearbook II* Brill, 279; Liu, H (2008) 'International Human Rights Law and the Establishment of Rule of Law in China' in Li, HW; Feng, J; Wang, M; Wu, Y; Zhang, G and Zou, H (eds) (2008) *The China Legal development Yearbook I* Brill 209; Peerenboom, RP 'Globalization' supra note 184; Peerenboom, RP (2002) *China's Long March toward Rule of Law* Cambridge University Press; Peerenboom, RP (ed) (2004) *Asian Discourses of Rule of Law: Theories and Implementation of Rule of Law in Twelve Asian Countries, France and the U.S.* Routledge Curzon; Chen AHY (2016) 'China's Long March Towards the Rule of Law or Chinese Turn Against Law?' (4) *The Chinese Journal of Comparative Law* 1.

'that the Rule of Law connotes the binding authority of democratically generated law on both subjects (citizens) and rulers (government), and submission to such law on the part of all members of the community, including the most senior government officials'.[189] In his work Chen proves that, rather than looking at the 'intellectual resources' consisting of 'the heritage of intellectual history, particularly concepts and theories developed by great thinkers in the past', Chinese legal scholars took inspiration from 'the Western tradition in order to find the intellectual resources for their theory of the rule of law'.[190] However, from Chen's overview it emerges that this engagement with Western culture is critical and mature. In fact, as Chen notes, in discussing Western legal thought on the rule of law, Chinese scholars not only acknowledged the origin and rationale of the rule of law in the works of philosophers from ancient, modern and contemporary legal thought such as Aristotle,[191] the thinkers of the Enlightenment, and the liberal tradition, but also acknowledged the historical development of this concept in the context of the evolution of the Western states. Significantly, the scholars analysed the concept of the rule of law taking into account the contextual specificities of the periods of ancient Greece, modern French and American revolutions, and also the different stages of capitalism followed by the later developments of the welfare state. In addition to that, even if they have considered the rule of law as an idea that could be beneficial to China, the Chinese legal thinkers have always been conscious that the political and institutional path of evolution of the Chinese state will differ from that of Western constitutional democracies. Rightly, they affirm that the evolution of this concept in China will follow a different and specific path. Consequently, they are cautious about transposing the Western idea of the rule of law to China in a rigid fashion.

Alternative theories argue for a model of the rule of law which differs from those inspired by Western theories. They criticise the Western model because it fails to consider the actual circumstances of Chinese social reality, including the importance and effectiveness of informal customary institutions, such as mediation, communal networks and informal patterns of behaviour. These elements should be considered and incorporated in the discourse on the rule of law in

---

[189] Chen, AHY 'Toward A Legal Enlightenment' supra note 185 at 21.
[190] Ibid at 18.
[191] Wang, J; Hainian, L and Li Buyun (1989) 'Lun Fazhi Gaige' [On the Reform of the Legal System] (8) *Faxue Yanjiu* [Studies in Law] 1.

China because they constitute the Chinese 'local resources'. For the alternative theorists of the rule of law, the Western model of the rule of law is not suited to meet Chinese needs within a system in rapid economic and social evolution. In fact, upholding the supremacy of the law would reduce the speed of social progress and economic development or prevent it altogether. Moreover, the predicament of such a system is in their view the increase of public discontent due to the lack of respect and even application of the law. Later on, the analysis will elaborate more on the views of one of the most prominent advocates of the 'rule of law with Chinese characteristics', professor Zhu Suli of Peking University.

Peerenboom provides a systematic account of the rule of law theories in China. In particular, in order to 'theorise the rule of law in ways that do not assume a liberal democratic framework, and explore alternative conceptions of rule of law that are consistent with China's own circumstances', [192] Peerenboom distinguishes four different political ideal types, analogous to different political strategies: Statist Socialist, Neo-Authoritarian, Communitarian, and Liberal Democratic. Peerenboom clarifies how each of these four groups interprets differently both the notion of rights and the relationship between rights and the rule of law.

Neo-Authoritarians aim at protecting individual rights but set limits to their guarantee and do not consider the protection of rights as a priority. Neo-Authoritarians hold an 'Asian values or communitarian' conception of rights. They emphasise the indivisibility of rights, and prioritise collective rights, privilege economic growth at the expense of rights (liberty trade-off), hold a utilitarian or pragmatic conception of rights, and privilege stability and order over freedom and social solidarity and harmony over autonomy. For them, freedom of thought and the right to think are to be limited by a need to preserve a common ground and consensus on important social issues. They justify limitations on the right to criticise the government, and pay attention to character building, virtues and duties.

---

[192] Peerenboom, RP *China's Long March* supra note 187 at 475.

Statist Socialists accept that the rule of law includes the protection of individual rights, but do not view this as a priority. Moreover, for them rights have a limited scope. Statist Socialists emphasise social rights at the expense of civil and political rights (liberty trade-off). They support state sovereignty and uphold a utilitarian or pragmatic conception of rights, which they consider as being granted by the state. They favour stability and order over freedom, social solidarity and harmony over autonomy. They prefer unity of thought to freedom of thought, the right thinking to the right to think. They have a tendency to exercise strict thought control if possible. At a minimum, they set strict limits on attacks against the ruling party. They emphasise the need to ensure common ground and consensus on important social issues and pay attention to character building, virtues and duties.

Both Liberal Democrats and Communitarians view the protection of individual rights as a key aspect of the rule of law. The Liberal Democrats hold a liberal view on rights, with an emphasis on civil and political rights; they defend a deontological view of rights as anti-majoritarian trumps on the social good. They privilege freedom over order, autonomy over social solidarity and harmony, freedom of thought over restrictions based on the need to preserve a common ground, and right thinking on important social issues. They pay more attention to rights than character building, virtues and duties. The Chinese Communitarians have a communitarian approach to human rights, with an emphasis on the indivisibility of rights and collective rights. They accept economic growth at the expense of rights (liberty trade-off), adopt a utilitarian or pragmatic conception of rights, privilege stability and order over freedom, and consider social solidarity and harmony to be as important as autonomy and freedom of thought, if not more so. The right to freedom of opinion is limited by a need for common ground and consensus on important social issues. They pay attention to character building, virtues and duties as well as to rights.

Lastly, Samuli Seppänen has critically explored the Chinese theories of the rule of law, exposing the apparent paradoxes and the ideological conflicts, which are internal to the theories themselves.[193]

Moving on from the categorisations summarised above and following Albert Chen's example, the following pages will present an overview of some representative theories of contemporary Chinese

---

[193] Seppänen, S *Ideological Conflict* supra note 181.

scholars on the rule of man and the rule by law, situating the current debate within its legal philosophical and historical context.

Rule of Man (*renzhi* 人治) and Rule by Law (*fazhi* 法治)

The model of the rule of man is an ancient idea, but nonetheless it has contemporary supporters. More specifically, the rule of man (*renzhi* 人治) lies at the core of the Confucian doctrine of good governance. It is based on the notion that wise men should adjudicate disputes, administer the state, rule the country and govern through moral authority. Confucians regarded law as a rudimental means to rule, in comparison to the moral way learned through rites and self-cultivation. The normative dimension of the reciprocal relationships between the rulers and the ruled, the rulers and the ministers, along with the other basic relationships, constituted the structure of the 'fiduciary community'.[194] In this framework, the wise man, in a position of authority, creates and applies the rules exercising *ren* 仁 (usually translated as benevolence or compassion, or humanity), a moral virtue possessing epistemic value and paramount importance.[195] According to this model, in determining the rule for a specific case, the sage should take into account not only human reason, but also the commonly shared human feelings and the diffuse social reactions.[196] The prominent role of moral principles, rules and virtues emerges

---

[194] Tu Weiming *Centrality and commonality* supra note 55.

[195] Munro, DJ (2008) *Ethics in Action. Workable Guidelines for Public and Private Choices* The Chinese University Press.

[196] Chang, W (2012) 'Classical Chinese Jurisprudence and the Development of the Chinese Legal System' (2) *Tsinghua China Law Review* 207. Interestingly, as it will be discussed below in the section on empathy in law making and the interpretation of law, general human reactions, feelings and beliefs commonly shared by the people are taken into account by contemporary Chinese scholars in their theories of law making and interpretation. According to these theorists, the principle of empathy must play a role in contemporary legal practice. Judges must adjudicate and legislators must enact law by 'putting themselves in the other's shoes', and follow the *san chang* with the purpose of respecting the people's sense of justice. The theory of law elaborated by Chen Zhonglin explicitly mentions common human feelings as a criterion to individuate the legal discipline in 'hard' cases, as for instance cases lacking explicit legal discipline Chen Zhonglin (2009) 'Guanyu renquan gainian de ji ge jiben wenti' [Several Basic Issues on the Concept of Human Right] unpublished article on file with the author, trans. by Ma Xiao-wei.

from the hierarchy of norms. Chang represents the normative hierarchy according to the Confucian school as a pyramid in reverse, composed of the moral norms and principles called *de*, 德, at its apex; in the second position the *li*, 禮, or rites; in the third position, *zheng*, 政, or government decrees, and finally *xing*, 刑, the criminal laws. The rank of a norm was determined by two standards: acceptability, indicating how close a norm was to reason and human feelings, and effectiveness, indicating 'how great a good for humanity it helped achieve'.[197] At the top of the normative hierarchy, therefore, there were the moral rules, while law was at the bottom, only to be used when moral persuasion and education had failed.

This model of the rule of man illuminates some unarticulated broad premises of the contemporary legal philosophical debate. In particular, it shows how tight is the connection between law and morality,[198] and how the political realm is juxtaposed to the moral realm, constituting an inextricable whole.[199] As a matter of fact, the tight connection between law and morality was maintained throughout the imperial period[200] and it is still remarkably visible in the theorisations on socialist law. Law, according to this conception, does not possess an autonomous position in respect to morality. It is important to stress that, in this context, morality is defined by an illuminated, and virtuous elite, that is not acting as people's representative in the exercise of powers conferred by the people's vote, but because of its merits. The other constant characteristic of Chinese political and legal thinking is related to the notion of 'politics'.[201] The meaning usually associated with the term *zheng*, 政, 'politics', is the art of good government. More precisely, however, in

---

[197] Chang, W Ibid at 207.

[198] On the relationship between law and morality in Chinese philosophy and law, see: Peerenboom, RP (1993) *Law and Morality in Ancient China: The Silk Manuscripts of Huang-Lao* State University of New York Press; Consiglio, E (2015) 'Early Confucian Legal Thought: A Theory of Natural Law?' (4) *Rivista di Filosofia del Diritto* 359; Kim, HI (1981) *Fundamental Legal Concepts of China and the West: A Comparative Study* Kennikat Press.

[199] Schwartz, BI (1965) 'Modernization and the Maoist Vision – Some Reflections on Chinese Communist Goal' (21) *China Quarterly* 51.

[200] MacCormack, G (1996) *The Spirit of Traditional Chinese Law* University of Georgia Press.

[201] Tu Weiming *Centrality and commonality* supra note 55 at 48. See also Anonymous (2003) 'Chung-yung' [The Doctrine of the Mean] in Plaks, A (trans) (2003) *Ta Hsüeh and Chung Yung: The Highest Order of Cultivation and On the Practice of the Mean* Penguin 21.

Confucian writings especially, *zheng* means 'rectification'. The act of rectification is considered to start from the ruler and potentially to reach all the domains under his guidance, influencing even those territories that are not under his guidance. All the people below the ruler, beginning from his ministers, are involved in the process of rectification. The ideal accomplishment of this process is the creation of a harmonious community.[202] Zheng is 'concerned with the organisation, direction and administration of all governmental units involved in the regulation and control of people in a given society'.[203] Therefore, the art of government is an extension of moral education: 'To govern is to be straight. If you steer straight, who would dare not to go straight?'[204] In particular, as argued by Shwartz,[205] in China the political dimension seems to be characterised as an ethical totality, and this characteristic is continuous throughout the history of China. While priority is attributed to the politico-ethical sphere, the legal domain is considered less important.

The alternative model of the rule by law (*fazhi* 法治), namely, the conception that attributes paramount importance to the law as a means to control the population and realise the political goals of the rulers, formulated for the first time by the Legalist school in China,

---

[202] The notion of harmonious community is apparently elusive, a notion whose meaning is vague. It will not be defined in the present work. However, on this concept see Wei Y (2006) 'Zhongguo gu dai de he xie zhi lu' ['The Ways of Harmony in Ancient China'] in Xian, Y (ed) (2006) *Falü wenhua yanjiu* [Research in Legal Culture] Zhongguo renmin chubanshe; Xu Xianming (2006) 'The Right to Harmony: Human Rights of the Fourth Generation' (3) *Human Rights* 20; Cheng, CY (2006) 'Toward Constructing a Dialectics of Harmonization: Harmony and Conflict in Chinese Philosophy' (33) *Journal of Chinese Philosophy* 25; Fox, A (1995) 'The Aesthetics of Justice: Harmony and Order in Chinese Thought' (14) *Legal Studies Forum* 43; Hermann, M (2007) 'A Critical Evaluation of Fang Dongmei's Philosophy of Comprehensive Harmony' *Journal of Chinese Philosophy* 59.

[203] Tu Weiming *Centrality and commonality* supra note 44 at 49. Tu Weiming's interpretation adds the ethico-religious dimension. His interpretation of Confucianism sees it as religious thought. This is one of the interpretations which can be given of Confucianism, but it is not possible to discuss the religious character of Confucianism in this study.

[204] Confucius (1979) *The Analects*, Penguin at 17.

[205] Schwartz, BI 'Modernization' supra note 198 at 51.

was paradigmatically opposed to the rule of man. Also called 'ruling the country through law' (*fazhiguo* 法治國), the rule by law attributes to law an instrumental value. During imperial times, the dichotomy between rule of man and rule by law was a constant feature of the legal debates between opposing schools, which alternately became the imperial orthodoxy. Over time, the dynasties managed to mould the relevant aspects of both into a powerful synthesis, still perceived as a major characteristic of the Chinese state, as suggested by the figurative expression invented by Chinese jurisprudence to describe the essence of the Chinese state: 'outwardly Confucian, internally Legalist' (*wai ru nei fa* 外儒內法). This expression refers to the image that the state wants to offer to the population: the state's 'face' is that of a benevolent government which cares for the wellbeing of its people, seemingly following the Confucian doctrine. But the true structure, nature and purposes of the state is Legalist, and the law is used as an instrument to realise the political ends of the ruling elite.

The question is whether the models of the rule of man and the rule by law can adequately protect the citizens from the risk of abuses of power. The crucial point is that according to the model of the rule of man, but also according to the model of the rule by law, the law is not theorised as a limitation on the arbitrary exercise of power. In the rule by law model, the law is a tool in the hands of the power holders to achieve their political objectives. In the opposite model of the rule of man, the law is also viewed as a tool, to be used as a last resort when the rule of morals has failed. The exercise of authority is entrusted to the wise persons, the *junzi* (君子), who should exercise power benevolently, according to the rule of morals. In principle, the rule of morals could also be a viable way to limit arbitrary power, provided that it is perceived as binding by the members of the community, including, above all, the rulers of that community. However, the mechanisms to control the power holders developed by the supporters of the rule of man model are perceived by its critics as less reliable than those developed by the supporters of the rule of law.

Notwithstanding this limitation, the Confucian model of the rule of man has been proposed as a valid model for Chinese institutional evolution.[206] The scholar Jiang Qing, in particular, relies on this concept as part of a general attempt to theorise a constitutional

---

[206] On the cultural level, a group of scholars called New-Confucians are engaged in reinterpreting Confucian doctrines in response to the cultural predicaments of the present day, such as the spread of an exaggerated individualism.

order based on the Confucian institutional framework.[207] Jiang Qing strongly rejects the possibility of integrating Chinese and Western ideas and regards the focus of Chinese political orthodoxy on Marxism as a mistake, because Marxism has been 'imported' from the West. As Qing argues in his works *Political Confucianism* and *A Confucian Constitutional Order*, China has its own intellectual resources to draw upon, and should cultivate the 'ability to think independently about political questions'[208] without resorting to Western ideas. It is in this perspective that Qing advocates for the use of Confucian notions like that of the rule of man.

From a political perspective, Jiang Qing denies that Western-style democracy with multi-party electoral contests could be the way ahead for China. On the contrary, to address the present predicaments generated by the shift to a socialist market economy, above all the increasing inequality between rich and poor, Jiang Qing advocates the Way of the Humane Authority,[209] a Confucian-inspired democracy and the institutionalisation project of political Confucianism. In his opinion: 'the biggest problem facing China as regards a constitution is the failure to produce a plan for a constitution that reflects China's own political civilisation and that gives room for basic Confucian ideas at the level of legitimisation'.[210] His criticism targets Westernisation and the imitation of Western politics, regarded as symptoms of the failure of Chinese intellectuals to provide a viable alternative.

For Jiang Qing, re-establishing Confucian constitutionalism is a way to demonstrate 'to the world that contemporary Chinese intellectuals [...] have the courage, wisdom and ability to create a bright political system for humanity' and 'to prove to the world that the Confucian civilisation is able to create a political structure that has rich resources, great vitality, and creativity.' He views this as 'the common historical mission, cultural responsibility, and sacred task of

---

[207] Jiang Qing; Bell, DA and Ruiping, F (eds) (2013) *A Confucian Constitutional Order, How China's Ancient Past Can Shape Its Political Future* Princeton University Press.
[208] Ibid at 27.
[209] Ibid.
[210] Ibid at 69.

contemporary intellectuals in China', [211] which should lead to the collective creation of the Way of the Humane Authority. It is precisely because his account explicitly and directly draws from the Confucian doctrine that Jiang Qing's theory is peculiar and unique. However, it is significant that Jiang Qing's theory was more successful overseas than in Mainland China. As a matter of fact, in general, Mainland Chinese scholars do not draw directly from traditional Chinese schools of thought in elaborating their theories, including theories of rights (as will be demonstrated in Chapters Seven and Eight).

Contrary to Jiang Qing, He Weifang [212] appreciates the introduction of Western legal thought into China since the beginning of modern times, because it offered an opportunity to overcome the tradition of autocracy, delayed due to a long history of government by absolute power. In He Weifang's view, the ancient Chinese theories are not much use for designing the way ahead for China. However, the reasoning behind He Weifang's appraisal of Western theory does not ignore the contents of tradition, and represents a fine example of critical engagement.

In particular, He Weifang sifts through the works by the classical Confucian author known as Mencius to assess the arguments that can be compared to the rule of law. He Weifang analyses Mencius' theory of 'people as the basis', which defines the duties and limitations of the imperial power. Notably, by attributing more importance to the people than the ruler, the theory of 'people as the basis' indicates that the purpose of the government is to nurture the people, and defines the relationship between the ruler and the ministers as one of reciprocity, trust, power and responsibility. He Weifang interprets Mencius' account of the relationship between ruler and subjects as 'revolutionary' because it led to the basis for a justification of rebellion against a tyrant. Truly, in Mencius' view, the emperor who failed to care effectively for the welfare of his subjects was no longer to be treated as an emperor, but rather as a 'robber and enemy'. Even murdering the ruler was legitimate in the case of a major failure to comply with the responsibilities towards the subjects.

However, He Weifang does not consider Mencius' theory helpful for solving the institutional predicaments that China is experiencing at present. In He Weifang's view, Mencius' theorisations ultimately failed to answer three core questions. First, is it possible to

---

[211] Ibid.

[212] He Weifang *In the Name of Justice* supra note 1.

control and restrain the power of the political authority or not? Second, what are the mechanisms and procedures that should be put in place to this end, suitable for rectifying mistakes on the part of the ruler promptly after their occurrence? And third, what are the criteria to determine that the exercise of the power has deteriorated into a tyranny? In He Weifang's view, Mencius did not offer a solution to any of these questions. In particular, it is not clear what remedy should be adopted if the ministers followed the normal procedure but this failed to restrain the ruler's ruthlessness.[213]

In addition, Mencius did not in any case discuss the approach that commoners should take when they are dissatisfied with their ruler. In He Weifang's view, at present, the same government that committed the abuse is entrusted with the power to control the propriety of its own acts. In particular, He Weifang considers that the control mechanisms provided by the Chinese Constitution are ineffective. Article 71 of the PRC's Constitution provides for a procedure to control the exercise of political power, promptly correct mistakes and reverse their negative effects. However, this mechanism has never been activated since the enactment of the Constitution in 1982. For this reason, He Weifang refers to it as a 'sleeping beauty'. The bitter reality, in his opinion, is that turning to classical theories would not be helpful to solve this problem.

As a result, He Weifang believes that 'Confucians face a legal predicament which stems both from its intrinsic theoretical framework and from the unique traditional social structure in China'.[214] The rigid ideology, the coincidence of moral and political authority, the supremacy of morality and politics over law, and the circumstance that a class of professionally trained judges administered the law according to a fixed set of standards are the traits of Chinese political and legal history that hindered the development of a mechanism of constraint upon the action of the holder of political power. For all these reasons, He Weifang does not consider Chinese traditional legal thinking helpful for defining the way ahead for China and turns to the West to look for viable solutions to the institutional, political and legal

---

[213] He Weifang *In the Name of Justice* supra note 1 at 48.
[214] Ibid.

predicament that his country is facing at present with regards to the particular method of law to govern the country.

Other Accounts of the Rule of Law: the Law as a *per se* value.
In contrast to the ideas described so far, He Weifang, Cheng Liaoyuan and Wang Renbo uphold a different theory of the rule of law. Their views are based on the firm belief that the rule of law is the way forward for China. Rather than defending the rule of law in opposition to tradition and in awe of Western culture, Cheng, Wang, and He defend a liberal conception of the rule of law because they consider that a socialist market economy should be regulated by a rule of law system. Cheng Liaoyuan and Wang Renbo argue for a substantive version of the rule of law, while He Weifang argues for a formal account. Both accounts strongly advocate for the autonomy of law from politics. I will summarise their views below, starting with the view of Cheng and Wang.

The starting point of the two author's reflection is the conceptual difference between the rule of law and the rule of man. Understanding of the respective characteristics, goals and methods of the two models is regarded as the fundamental argument for choosing one model over the other. Cheng and Wang individuate three main hindrances for the development of the rule of law in China. The first is the traditional legal culture, which neither constrains nor fosters the development of the idea of the rule of law, but rather purports ideas that conflict with this model. The second is traditional ethics: the idea of the family as a fiduciary community, the importance of personal ties and familial particularism, in their view, are at odds with the law as an abstract and impersonal method. Cheng and Wang mention for example the frequent choice of the practice of *guanxi*[215] instead of that of the law to solve controversies and problems between individuals and groups. The third obstacle to the establishment of the rule of law is, according to Cheng and Wang, the public expectations that the adoption of the method of law generates: the emphasis upon formal respect for the law would in fact imply the impartial application of the law by the judges. However, the judges are not perceived as impartial

---

[215] *Guanxi* means 'personal connection'. For a definition of the term and an assessment of the role that *guanxi* might have played in the market reform, see above in this Chapter.

and therefore the application of the law is largely felt as a form of injustice.[216]

Cheng and Wang consider it nonsensical to equate the existence of a system of law with the rule of law, because, they affirm, the 'rule of law does not only mean that law is supreme, but also that law has an intrinsic value. Law is constant; it possesses its own procedures. Thus, the measure of the rule of law consists of the value of law and the method (or procedure) of law'.[217]

In his book *In the Name of Justice. Striving for the Rule of Law in China*, He Weifang advocates the liberal account of the rule of law as a way to limit and control the exercise of political power by the elites. He demands clearly established legal procedures to supervise the action of the top leaders. He admits that everyone, including the CCP, affirms that the party should exercise its power under 'supervision'. However, the problem is that in the current institutional framework there is no mechanism that can be effectively used to supervise the exercise of power by the party.

He Weifang argues for a Western-inspired model of the rule of law. In the Prologue of his book *An Open Letter to Legal Professionals in Chongqing,* He advocates the rule of law as a stronghold against the widespread corruption in contemporary China. The letter uses very passionate words to recall the mission of the legal scholars to provide and reinforce support for the principle of legality, the cornerstone of every healthy institutional system. He calls upon the legal scholars to issue clear, firm criticism and opposition to the intrusion on judicial independence, the violation of legal procedures, and any conduct that infringes upon the civil rights of citizens. In addition, He urges the police to balance order and freedom without emphasising order too much because otherwise freedom would suffer. Lastly, he urges the leaders and the legal scholars to deal 'with the problem at its roots' by building relevant systems to ensure that

---

[216] Cheng Liaoyuan and Wang Renbo (1989) *Fa zhi lun* [Rule of Law] Shandong People's Publishing House. He Weifang shares the same idea. See He Weifang (1999) *Juti Fazhi* [The Specific Rule of Law] Falü Chubanshe; He Weifang (2005-2006) 'China's Legal Profession: The Nascence and Growing Pains of a Professionalized Legal Class' (19) *Columbia Journal of Asian Law* 138.

[217] Cheng Liaoyuan and Wang Renbo Ibid.

government administration is in accordance with the law and that the courts are just. Finally, He condemns the government's use of illegal means to combat illegal activities, as the consequences of this action are that citizens' idea of the law will be distorted: 'people may get the unfortunate idea that might is right, that black means can be used to deal with black phenomena', and concludes with a warning: 'without judicial independence no one is safe'.[218]

In conclusion, Cheng and He do not argue for the rule of law because it is considered as superior to traditional Chinese concepts, but because they consider it more apt to solve Chinese problems and more valid from a philosophical point of view. Their view is not isolated. Indeed, other scholars in a similar fashion[219] advocate the value of law as an end in itself, in opposition to the view of the law as an instrument to realise political ends. As Albert Chen noted, there is a trend in scholarly discussion which affirms that the law expresses the values, needs and aspirations of the community, and reflects the ideals of reason, liberty and equality.[220] This is completely at odds with the political understanding of 'the rule of law with Chinese characteristics', which means government by law and party rule.

Authority of the Law and Faith in the Law

The Chinese scholarly discussion on 'faith in the law' (*falu xinyang* 法律信仰) is particularly interesting as it is entangled with the idea of the autonomy and supremacy of law. Indeed, a core feature of legal systems based on the rule of law is the widespread acceptance of the 'authority of the law'[221] by every person subject to a given system of

---

[218] He Weifang *In the Name of Justice* supra note 1 at 5.

[219] Shen Zhonglin (1996) 'Ruling the Country According to the Law, Constructing a Socialist Legal System State' (6) *Beijingdaxue Xuebao Zhesheban* 4; Xie Hui (1994) 'On Legal Instrumentalism' (1) *Zhongguo Faxue* 50.

[220] Chen, AHY 'Toward A Legal Enlightenment' supra note 185 at 21.

[221] For the rule of law to be effective it is necessary that legal rules be considered as prevailing over other kinds of rules: 'exclusionary reason' (Raz, J *The Authority of Law* supra note 171 at 16-19; Raz, J (1985) 'Authority and Justification' (14) *Philosophy and Public Affairs* 3 at 10-18; Raz J (1975) *Practical Reason and Norms* Hutchinson at 35-46; Raz, J (1975) 'Reasons for Action, Decisions and Norms' (84) *Mind* 481). In other words, the fact that the law requires certain behaviour must not only be viewed as a reason to behave accordingly. It must also be viewed as a reason that outweighs or even excludes any reasons—pertaining to private interests or to political objectives—to depart from what is legally required. It has also been argued that the law really deserves such authority, ie its authority is legitimate, if complying with the law really contributes to make citizens behave as they should, according to the (moral) reasons that apply to them. Chen notes how the debate among Chinese

law: state functionaries, officers, and citizens alike. Harold Berman[222] linked the idea of the authority of the law to the idea of 'faith in the law', namely the view that the law, at least in the Western tradition, not only was historically influenced by religious ideas, but also was the object of quasi-religious faith in its capacity to deliver peace, progress and emancipation. Berman's thesis has affected the Chinese discussion.[223] The contemporary Chinese academic debate over the authority of the law and faith in the law concerns the reasons that should anchor the respect, trust and use of law by citizens. Chinese scholars dispute whether it is appropriate to ground the authority of the law on the 'faith in the law', as Harold Berman describes it.[224] Some scholars criticise the idea of the autonomy of the law, its supremacy over political imperatives, and the idea that officers and citizens should have 'faith in the law', while others strongly support it.

Xu Xianming and Qi Yanping criticise Chinese jurisprudence's tendency to idealise law as a means to solve social problems. They argue that, in the process of Westernisation, part of Chinese jurisprudence supported the idea of 'faith in the law' in order to foster people's compliance with newly enacted laws, wrongly assuming the lack of legal faith as the fundamental cause of the inertia preventing compliance with newly enacted laws by the Chinese population. For Xu and Qi, on the contrary, reliance on a quasi-religious 'legal faith' is misleading. The two authors critically examine the way in which other scholars have reinterpreted the works by Harold Berman and in particular his idea that faith in the law is the element that distinguishes the law from mere dogma. They claim that

---

scholars pivoted on the works by Roberto Unger, which highlight substantive, institutional, methodological and occupational autonomy. Chen, AHY 'Toward A Legal Enlightenment' supra note 185 at 28; Zheng Chenglian (1996) 'The Essence of the Jurisprudence of Ruling the Country According to Law' in Liu, H et al (eds) (1996) *Yifa Zhiguo jianshe zhuyi fazhi guojia* [Ruling the Country According to Law, Constructing a Socialist Rule-of-Law State] Zhongguo fa zhi chu ban she 126 at 126-127.

[222] Berman, HJ (1993) *Faith and Order. The Reconciliation of Law and Religion* Wm. B. Eerdman Publishing.

[223] Xu Xianming and Qi Yongpin (2007) 'Practicality, Questions, and Characteristics of Chinese Jurisprudence' (1) *Chinese Jurisprudence* 111.

[224] Berman, HJ *Faith and Order* supra note 221.

the notion of legal faith should be understood as meaning merely 'legal authority', without a religious or quasi-religious dimension. Therefore, they criticise 'the Chinese researchers who adhere to a quasi-religious notion of legal faith', arguing that such researchers 'wanted to design a semi-religious system by combining law and religion in some way', but failed. The mistake in their view is based on a misperception of the characteristics of Chinese culture, since 'religious belief is not widespread in China'.[225] Anchoring respect for the law on legal faith is described as 'something that puts Mr John's hat on Mr Lee's head'.[226] Those scholars quoting Berman's 'belief in the law' in relation to China went wrong because they lost 'the original context' of Berman's thesis. According to Xu and Qi: 'The law is not faith; it cannot be the object of belief'.[227] They affirm that after the process of rationalisation of law, it becomes 'something that people like to maintain and use to seek justice': 'people believe in the law', but not as though it were a religion.

Guo Zhong and Zhang Yong advance a more radical critique, arguing that in China the practice of the law cannot be revived by attributing value to its autonomy, but rather by linking the law to traditional values. Using an argument that resonates deeply with the socialist idea of law, Guo Zhong affirms that the law and the legal system must be anchored in the traditional social spirit and on those social values that are still alive and practised by the people; otherwise it will be detached from the basis and not complied with. Guo believes that:

> In modern times China has established a complete legal system by transplanting the Western legal system on a large scale. But we gave up China's traditional humanity, which led to the lack of a socially unifying spirit, therefore our legal system has no root. The legal system has to be set up on the basis of the traditional social spirit and then it will have social life. Only if China forms such a kind of unifying spirit can the crises of the Chinese spirit be solved.[228]

In the same vein, Zhang Yong[229] holds that 'there is a fundamental difference between Chinese and Western legal systems. Promoting 'faith in the law' would be a misunderstanding of the

---

[225] Xu Xianming and Qi Yongpin 'Practicality' supra note 222.
[226] Ibid.
[227] Ibid.
[228] Ibid.
[229] Ibid.

Chinese legal system because it looks at the wrong side of the crisis in social values and confuses 'legal authority' with 'legal faith'. The solution for the crisis in social values should come instead from the recovery of societal values (filial piety, humaneness, loyalty) and their recognition in law.

However, some other scholars have adopted and developed the notion of 'faith in the law' as possessing manifold significance. In Cheng's view: 'Such faith means that people not only understand the law, but respect it, trust it and rely on it for the purpose of defending their interests. It is also an attitude of fidelity to law, a commitment to uphold its values and principles, which manifests itself when people feel strongly about and fight against violations of the law and its values and principles.' Hence it is pointed out that faith in the law is not only a matter of knowledge; it is also a matter of emotion and will. It is a sublimation of law, reason and passion, or what Cheng describes as 'passionate reason' or 'rationalised passion'.[230] On this complex attitude towards law it is possible to ground the 'authority of the law', much needed for the affirmation of the rule of law that Cheng advocates.

The debate on faith in the law stands against the background of the construction and reform of the legal system, that, since the 1978 was used to support and develop the emerging socialist market economy.[231] As explained above, adherence to a formal rule of law may work as a guarantee for the protection of human rights. In particular, the rule of law represents a protection against the arbitrary exercise of political discretion, a stronghold for respect and effective enjoyment of the rights abstractly provided by law. The following pages will not describe the reforms extensively, but will focus on

---

[230] Cheng, Liaoyuan (1999) *Cong fazhi dao fazhi* supra note 179 at 29. See also Chen, J (1999) *Chinese Law: Towards an Understanding of Chinese Law, its Nature and Development* Kluwer Law International.

[231] Chen, AHY (1996) 'The Developing Theory of Law and Market Economy in Contemporary China' in Wang, G and Wei, Z (eds) (1996) *Legal Developments in China. Market Economy and Law* Sweet and Maxwell in collaboration with [the] Centre for Chinese and Comparative Law, City University of Hong Kong 3; Dowdle, MW (2002-2003) 'Of Parliaments, Pragmatism and the Dynamics of Constitutional Development: The Curious Case of China' (35) *New York University Journal of International Law and Politics* 1.

some of the effects generated by the socialist market economy on the conception of law and rights. Even recognising the autonomous value of the law, Chinese legal scholars maintain a tight connection between law, morality, and people's feelings and beliefs. A feature of the debate that will be now discussed.

Empathy in Law Making and the Interpretation of Law

When contextualised within the discussion on human nature that I have previously presented, the instrument of mediation—particularly in the interpretation articulated by Huang—offer a valuable contribution to the global legal debate. I refer in particular to the role that empathy should play, both in mediation and, more broadly, in law making, legal interpretation and adjudication. By looking at the importance of empathy within Chinese legal debates, one realises that Chinese traditional principles have the potential to counter-balance some of the limitations that characterise Western liberal discourses on law. With reference to this point, I believe that the global discussion on law should attempt to elucidate, rationalise, adjust and codify the principle of empathy in order for it to be used as a legal principle, together with the notions of equality and freedom.

The importance of empathy is expressed with particular emphasis in the writings of Chen Zhonglin, a contemporary Chinese legal scholar and member of the National People's Congress, the organ of the state endowed with legislative power and the power to interpret the law. Chen advocates empathy as the guiding criterion of both legislation and interpretation of law, and argues that 'the process of sentencing a crime should be a process where the general public, including the accused, "put themselves in other people's shoes".'[232] Chen holds that law does not take into account only legal dispositions, but also 'humanity' (*ren xin* 人性), and 'consciousness' (*liang xin* 良心). These two traits, according to Chen, are 'the prototype of human nature, the minimum requirements of society, and also constitute the common sense which is used to determine the best interest of the people'.[233]

The idea of a neutral law devoid of empathy and common sense is, in Chen's view, faulty. The place where each person's judgments about right and wrong are formed is the individual

---

[232] Chen, Zhonglin (2007) *Xingfa zong lun* [General theories of criminal law] Gaodeng jiaoyu chuban she at 16.
[233] Ibid at 17.

consciousness. However, as Chen argues with a certain psychoanalytical acumen, the basis of conscience is formed in a subconscious way, and consciousness is always influenced by social norms that are unconsciously accepted and taken as natural by the individual. In addressing these points, Chen elaborates a normative theory based on the notion of the 'three commons' (*san chang* 三常), namely 'common knowledge, common opinion and common feelings which are widely accepted by the general public'.[234] The *san chang* thus embody the values and ethical standards shared by the public in their inner conscience, and include principles such as 'everybody knows that you cannot harm other people's interests for no reason'.[235]

According to Chen, lawmakers need to take these standards into account when it comes to legislation.[236] If they do, then people will feel naturally inclined to conform to legal provisions. Chen argues that those who apply the law should also bear these standards in mind. A judicial official (*sifa renyuan* 司法人员), should adjudicate matters according to the law, but she or he should also follow common sense as well as her/his own interpretation of the law and her/his conscience.[237] In Chen's view this attitude constitutes a core element of judicial independence.[238] Chen thus supports the integration between law and morality, and a synergy between the rule of law and the rule of morals that can only be achieved using the 'three commons' as guidance for interpretation.

Naturally, this position clashes with the notion of rule by law, that is with the instrumental use of law that seems the view upheld by the elite in power:[239] 'The law', Chen argues, 'should not become a

---

[234] Ibid.

[235] Ibid.

[236] Ibid.

[237] Chen's theory of law can be defined as 'hermeneutic' because it holds that the activity of interpretation coincides with the application of law.

[238] Chen's theory is in line with the socialist idea of law.

[239] Other contemporary Chinese scholars agree with Chen on the importance of the principle of legality and the supremacy of law. Among others, Xu and Qi affirm that: 'The basic feature of legal reasoning is the reasoning that is based on the supremacy of the law. It is the judicial system which puts rights at its centre, the rule as the basis and the defence as the guarantee' (Xu Xianming and Qi Yongpin (2008) 'Practicality' supra note 222). Nonetheless, recent Chinese jurisprudence has

mechanical tool to go against the interest of the people. The process of maintaining the law for the benefit of the people should not be treated as a mechanical tool to go against the people's interest without considering people's voices and the possibility to go against the common sense widely accepted by the people'.[240] On the contrary, 'understanding people's situations, following people's desires, reflecting people's needs'[241] is the fundamental starting point in law making. Interestingly, Chen's position also offers a criticism of some Marxist interpretations of the role of the vanguard as sources of guidance.

For instance, Chen strongly advocates against the instrumental use of the law to impose 'the advanced ideas of the vanguard élite on the general public when the advanced ideas are not universally accepted'.[242] To guarantee consistency between the experience of the general public and the law enacted by the vanguard elite (be it intellectuals, teachers or educators), Chen advocates full protection of the freedom of speech by the law.[243] In his words: 'the task for us is to convert commonly accepted advanced ideas and values into laws and interpret and apply laws based on the common sense of the general public. It is the thinker's and the educator's task to convert advanced ideas, values and views into the general knowledge, reasoning and feelings accepted by the public'.[244] In this sense, knowledge and systematic understanding of the law is not enough: social experience too is required in order to create and enforce law.[245]

---

acknowledged the importance of legal principles in the interpretation of legal dispositions and their prominent position with respect to rules. Xu and Qi write that when the content of principles and rules is consistent, principles are the guidance for the interpretation of the rules. In the absence of rules, the principles should be interpreted in order to find a rule to fill the normative gap. In case of conflict between principles and rules, the principles shall prevail. If, instead, the conflict is between two principles, the legal interest should prevail (Ibid at 8).

[240] Chen, Zhonglin *Xingfa* supra note 61 at 17.

[241] Ibid.

[242] Chen Zhonglin (2009) '"E fa" fei fa. Dui chuantong faxue lilun defansi' [The "Evil Law" is Illegal. Theoretical Reflection from Traditional Jurisprudence] (142) *Social Scientist* 9.

[243] Chen, Zhonglin *Xingfa* supra note 61 at 17.

[244] Chen Zhonglin '"E fa" fei fa' Supra note 241 at 10.

[245] The issue of the role of the vanguard in the Marxist framework is a complex one. Marx and Engels discuss it in their writings, but different Marxist thinkers have different interpretations on this matter. Gramsci, for instance, is suspicious of vanguard oligarchism and advocates the creation of a broad-based party that is linked with popular structures. Gramsci's ideas might seem similar to Chen's, but

Chen also anticipates the critique that it would impossible to reach a common understanding of the 'three commons' because different individuals might disagree on what constitutes common knowledge, common feelings and common opinion. In response to this criticism Chen argues that understanding what is common is a question of legal practice. The *san chang* must therefore be identified within and through legal practice, because 'from the point of view of legal practice the three terms are the most basic tools to communicate with nature and human beings'.[246] Incidentally, this understanding of law making and interpretation resonates with the way in which many Chinese legal practitioners currently approach law making and adjudication in China.

For instance, Huang observes that one of the general principles that currently guide judges is the notion that their decisions must reflect the common feeling of the people. Huang affirms that:

> Chinese judges acknowledge in interviews that they routinely strive to achieve decisions that will be perceived as fair and that will minimise popular unhappiness with courts even in the face of laws and regulations that dictate other outcomes. Courts in China may be expected to adjust their interpretations of the law to achieve popular outcomes or outcomes that minimise social unrest. But they are not expected to do so in such an explicit manner.[247]

Huang also notes that the pattern of legislation that has become standard in contemporary Chinese law is that of 'no formal adoption and codification until an extended period of trial and error has shown a legal principle to be acceptable to the people and workable',[248] and

---

the two have a diametrically opposed view on common sense: for Chen it is the foundation of the law, for Gramsci it is the most rooted expression of ideology. Famously, the role of the vanguard was a source of deep disagreement between Lenin and Trotsky. See: Marx, K and Engels, F (1996) *Collected Works Vol. 35* International Publishers. Gramsci, A (1974) [1921-1922] *Socialismo e Fascismo: L'Ordine Nuovo 1921-22* Einaudi; Lenin, VI (2013) [1902] *What is to be done?* Martino Fine Books. Trotsky, L (1979) [1904] *Our Political Tasks* New Park Publications.

[246] Chen Zhonglin '"E fa" fei fa' supra note 241.

[247] Huang, PC 'Morality' supra note 159 at 20.

[248] Ibid.

that lawmakers are currently supposed to produce legislation that is 'both in accord with social reality and yet still provides a prospective moral ideal to guide societal development'.[249]

These practices embody Chen's view of the lawmaker and the judge as figures that need to be in tune with human nature and with social feelings because 'having the knowledge to deal with nature is the pre-requisite of a person who knows better'.[250] Bearing this in mind, it is important to stress that Chen's views directly evoke the Confucian model of the sage capable of adjudicating between right and wrong because he is in harmony with his relational context and with the values of society. In this perspective, the similarity between Confucianism and Chen's theory of the 'three commons' is striking. In the Confucian tradition, the paramount criterion for ranking norms in the hierarchy of rules was the degree to which a norm was in accordance with feelings, reason and relationships. The cultivation of empathy thus lies at the very core of both Chen's theories and Confucian legal thinking.[251]

Given Chen's link with traditional sensibility it is not surprising that, as Liebman observed, in the case of a legal vacuum, Chinese judges often draw from the Confucian tradition to elucidate the grounds for the decision.[252] Nonetheless, it is important to clarify that Chen's theory also presents some differences from Confucian thought. In Confucianism the person who adjudicates is the, the 'righteous man' (*jun zi* 君子) while in contemporary China the person who is empowered to issue legal interpretation is the professional magistrate, trained in law and qualified through a national judicial examination.[253] Another major difference between Confucianism and the approach advocated by Chen lies in the fact that contemporary legal practice in China is based, at least theoretically, on the idea of the supremacy of law in adjudication, which is based in turn on the attribution of individual rights to the parties.

---

[249] Ibid.

[250] Chen Zhonglin '"E fa" fei fa' supra note 241. The opposite of the 'person who knows better' is either 'a person whose intelligence is underdeveloped or a person who has lost the core functions of his nervous system, has lost the ability to discriminate and control his behaviour, and has lost the basic knowledge and reasoning required to discriminate and control one's behaviour' Ibid.

[251] Ibid at 9.

[252] Liebman, BL (2008) 'China's courts: Restricted reform' (21) *Columbia Journal of Asian Law* 2.

[253] The National Judicial Examination was introduced in 2001 for the whole China.

These two differences illuminate an important fact: in the end, China remains a context where the rule of man takes the normative precedence. Nonetheless, Chen's theorisations show that morality and empathy are not wholly incompatible with contemporary approaches to legal theory. Interestingly, this position is also shared by some Western legal scholars who have sought to refute the idea of a purely mechanical jurisprudence. One example is Corso, who recently argued that a degree of empathy would be beneficial to adjudication.[254] The methods used in Western jurisprudence, such as the appeal to principles, can be usefully integrated with the notion of empathy, favouring a deeper development of law through judicial adjudication and administrative activity.

---

[254] Corso, L (2014) 'Should Empathy Play Any Role in the Interpretation of Constitutional Rights?' (27-1) *Ratio Juris* 94.

CHAPTER FOUR

Socialist Market Economy, Social Stability, and Legal Instrumentalism

Debating Socialist Rule of Law's Relation to Justice

Contemporary socialist theorists have refuted the view that the rule of law is a bourgeois concept. However, socialist scholars claim that the socialist rule of law is different from the rule of law in a capitalist system,[255] in particular because it allows for a political actor (the party) to influence the application of the law. They claim that the socialist conception of the rule of law alone can provide the full realisation of freedom, equality, and the protection of individual rights.

Scholars within China disagree on whether societies should aim at 'thinner' or 'thicker' theories of the rule of law. Some argue that theories of the rule of law lacking the robust normative backing provided by a 'thick' theory do not break out of the confines of mere 'rule by law'.[256] Based on this premise, Liu describes the Chinese legal system as a 'thin rule of law system', comparable to rule by law, and ultimately failing to provide adequate protection to human rights. On the other side, the rule by law defenders emphasise that the protection of rights should be subordinated to the higher goals of subsistence and economic growth. Some commit to the socialist conception of rights as bourgeois and keep their emphasis on duties, rather than rights, and in particular on duties to the state.

In the first decade of the 21st century, Chinese jurisprudence critically addressed the socialist concept of the rule of law, debating the core connotations of the socialist concept of legality. One of the major issues in dispute is the importance of fairness and justice and the degree to which they must be pursued according to a socialist concept of the rule of law. Recent systematic and in-depth jurisprudential analysis on the concept of socialist law has explicitly addressed the connection between law and justice. The most recent Chinese jurisprudence is converging on the idea that the socialist rule

---

[255] Chen, AH 'The Developing Theory' supra note 230. This conception is consistent both with the public ownership of the means of production and with the leadership of the CCP.

[256] Liu Yongping *Origins* supra note 35; Cheng Liaoyuan and Wang Renbo *Fa zhi lun* supra note 215.

of law pursues the values of fairness and justice. In the broad debate about the rule of law and justice there are two main views: some view justice and the rule of law as separate criteria for the evaluation of a legal and political system, while others consider that the two concepts are interrelated, having elements in common.

For instance, Xu Xianming[257] advances a substantive approach to the rule of law, claiming that socialist rule of law pursues the values of fairness and justice, to build a steady process towards 'people-oriented', 'scientific' development. In his view, the construction of the 'harmonious society', fairness and justice are primary objectives and must be set as the social standard to evaluate good and evil. Similarly, Zhang Hengshan[258] indicates justice, and namely judicial justice, as the core element of the concept of socialist rule of law. Zhang Zhiming[259] believes that the concept of social justice and the rule of law must be a practical concern and, in particular, that they should guide China's judicial reform. Wu Yuzhang[260] considers rights as a crucial element for the development of public law because rights provide protection from administrative power. In his view 'the practice of private law, the change in ideology, the enhancement of the legal system and the principle of the rule of law' are the instruments to support the reform in public law.[261]

Zhu Jingwen[262] holds that the idea of rule of law as a stronghold of justice is consistent and not in contradiction with traditional Chinese legal culture. On the contrary, Liang Zhiping,[263] stresses that the notion of law as it was understood and elaborated in traditional China does not possess the dimension that is entailed by the term 'ius', which is the same one contained in the root of the term

---

[257] Xu Xianming (1996) 'The Main Constitutive Elements of the Rule of Law-And Some Rule of Law Principles and Concepts' (5) *Chinese Journal of Chinese Law*.
[258] Xu Xianming, Qi Yongping (2007) 'Practicality, Questions and China Characteristics of Jurisprudence' (1) *Chinese Legal Science* 111 at 114
[259] Ibid.
[260] Ibid.
[261] Ibid. at 115.
[262] Zhu Jingwen (2004) 'Contradictions in the rule of Law' in Xia Yong (ed) *The Rule of Law and the 21st Century* Social Science Documentation Publishing House.
[263] Liang, Z (1989) 'Explicating Law: A Comparative Perspective of Chinese and Western Legal Culture' (3) *Journal of Chinese Law* J. 55.

'*iustitia*'. This dimension was instead already present in Western law from its very origins. Liang Zhiping affirms that it is this particular dimension that makes the law a protection to be invoked by individuals who are less fortunate, rich, and powerful, the socially weaker, and the vigilant who abide by the law (those who remembered to keep copies of documents, who were punctual in fulfilling their obligations, who paid taxes, and so on). These categories of people, according to Liang Zhiping, should enjoy the protection of the law against the power holders, always inclined to expand their prerogatives and licences at the expense of others.

However, the recent evolution of the legal system has brought about a new procedural dimension possessing paramount importance for the guarantee of both justice and fairness. It is remarkable how procedural approaches to justice have acquired an increasing importance in recent years, in contrast, at least on the theoretical level, to the priority that was historically attributed to substantive justice in China's legal history.[264] In the past, most works by Chinese scholars adopted a negative view of legal formalisms (*xing shi zhu yi* 形式主义). The term translated was understood as having a derogatory meaning, ie as referring to a 'burocratized concern with form rather than substance', or to a 'strictly literal application of the law'.[265] In recent debates, the formal rationality of law has re-gained value, being understood as expressing the commitment to the faithful application of enacted law, according to established procedures.[266]

A poignant view regarding the relationship between formal and substantive legal rationality in the application of law is proposed by Zheng Chengliang.[267] Zheng affirms that, as a rule, formal legal rationality should prevail in judicial process. When formal and substantial rationality are compatible and can both be realised to the same degree, these two values should be harmonised. The problematic cases are those in which the two values of formal and substantive legal rationality are in contrast. Zheng suggests that in those cases the principle of formal legal rationality should be realised first and

---

[264] Keith, RC and Lin, Z (2001) *Law and Justice in China's New Marketplace* Palgrave at 181-188.

[265] Huang, PC 'Morality' supra note 159 at 5.

[266] See Keith, R and Lin, Z *Law and Justice* supra note 263, Chapter Five on the importance of procedure in the theorisation of Criminal Law and Criminal Procedure Law.

[267] Zheng Chengliang (2000) 'On Legal Consciousness and Law-Based Mentality' (4) *Jilin University Journal Social Science Edition*.

foremost. Only in exceptional cases and under exceptional circumstances may substantive rationality prevail over formal rationality, because 'the basic feature of legal reasoning is the reasoning that is based on the supremacy of the law'.[268] In Zheng's account, the form of law acquired an independent and autonomous value with respect to the substance of law, a very important turn in Chinese legal speculation.

The debate on justice and the rule of law is related to the discussion on judicial independence because the consistent application of law helps in achieving formal equality, a core element of justice. The following section will discuss the socialist notion of judicial independence and the doctrinal interpretations of this notion in a system of socialist rule of law, offering a brief account of the ways in which social practices and institutional arrangements constitute an encroachment on the activities of the courts.

Debating Judicial Independence in a Socialist Legal System

Let us start by describing relevant institutional and social factors that operate as a limitation on judicial independence in China,[269] beginning with the wording of the 1982 PRC Constitution. Article 126 states that the people's courts have the 'duty to independently exercise the right to adjudicate according to the law' and 'must not be subject to the interference of administrative organs, social organisations and individuals'. The dominant interpretation of this disposition is that courts, as collective entities, must be independent. Therefore, 'judicial independence' does not refer to individual judges but to the collegial panel of judges as a whole.

Widespread social practices constitute another element limiting the independence of courts and judges.[270] The most

---

[268] Xu Xianming and Qi Yaiping 'Practicality' supra note 257 at 116.

[269] On this matter, see also Fu Hualing (2011) 'The Varieties of Law in China' *Human Rights in China* available at https://www.hrichina.org/en/crf/article/5422, last accessed on 15 May 2017.

[270] *Guanxi* could be considered as an illegal practice, implying illegal interference in judicial work. See Lei, D (2005) '*Guanxi* and its Influence on Chinese Business Practices' (5-2) *Harvard China Review* 81; Guo Xuezhi (2001) 'Dimensions of *Guanxi* in Chinese Elite Politics' (46) *The China Journal* 69. However, it is socially widespread, therefore some authors do not regard *guanxi* as an illegal practice. See,

significant one is 关系 *guanxi*, an expression carrying a dense meaning, which could be translated as 'personal connection'. The practice of *guanxi* consists of using one's personal connections to request an influential person to act in favour of someone in order to obtain for the requesting person special services that are generally unavailable or not easily obtainable. Chinese people commonly use *guanxi* in everyday life, even when it bends legal rules. Recent research[271] has demonstrated that lawyers do use *guanxi* in order to win a case in court because *guanxi* actually weighs more than the content of black letter law and the circumstances of a case.[272] In this sense, the practice of *guanxi* significantly limits the independence of the courts.

Among the institutional arrangements limiting judicial independence are the judicial committees instituted by the Organic Law of the People's Court, in force since 1 January 1980, to 'support' and 'monitor' the activities of any court. Judicial committees are organs constituted by retired judges or non-judges who are party members. The law endows judicial committees with consultative functions only, including suggesting how to decide hard cases, deciding important questions in sensitive cases, and suggesting the

---

among others, Guthrie, D (1998) 'The Declining significance of *Guanxi* in China's Economic Transition' (154) *China Quarterly* 254.

[271] McConville, M and Pils, E (2013) *Comparative Perspectives on Criminal Justice in China* Edward Elgar Publishing at 450.

[272] This is especially true at the lower administrative levels. The Chinese central government is overtly fighting against corruption, or at least, this is the official line of the elite in power. However, the recent attempts by the central government to fight this kind of corruption have produced few results. The practice of *guanxi* is governed by its own rules. If *guanxi* is not used properly, it can result in punishment for the person using it. If a more powerful person does not approve of the conduct engaged in because of *guanxi*, it is possible to sanction the use of *guanxi*. In the vast majority of cases, sanctioning *guanxi* is an extra-legal practice too. In other words, people are not brought to court because they used *guanxi*. This practice is part of Chinese culture, a deeply rooted social practice. *Guanxi* allows the informal exchange of favours between people, for example money in exchange for a favourable judgment, or a meal in exchange for professional advice or other information. It would certainly be repressed according to the law; however, it is largely tolerated as social behaviour. However, it is difficult to frame the nature of *guanxi* as a kind of reciprocal obligation; it remains to be investigated if it can be better defined as an ethical obligation or a social obligation. This practice originated in the family-centred mentality ('family' interpreted as a broad concept, which extends far beyond the nuclear family members), coupled with a general rule of an ethico-social nature which states that one must help a person in one's family who is in need.

solution in cases which are extremely important due to their potential social and economic consequences. However, judicial committees exercise de facto adjudicatory functions in 'hard cases' (for instance, cases in which other state organs, important personalities or their interests are involved) and 'uncertain cases' (for instance, cases in which the facts are not clear). In practice, the judge in charge remits hard and controversial cases to the judicial committee, and decides later according to the indication of the committee.

In this respect, the activity of the judicial committees contradicts the principles of unity and concentration of the process, which require that the same person who hears the case during the trial should deliver the judgment. Arguably, these institutional arrangements may infringe upon the independence of the judge, interfere with the impartial adjudication of disputes, and lower the standard of consistency in the application of the law. In conclusion, the activity of the judicial committees impairs an important aspect of the rule of law, as understood in Western jurisprudence, namely judicial independence.

A further limitation on judicial independence is provided by the system of individual case supervision, which consists of the possibility of supervising or removing the lawsuit from the judge in charge and assigning it to a senior judge for the purposes of revision and control, in a discretionary fashion. This constitutes a violation of the principle of the predetermination of the judge by law.

However, part of the Chinese doctrine contends that judicial committees do not exercise undue interference compromising the autonomy and independence of judges. A paradigmatic example of doctrinal theories that support a limitation on judicial independence, is the approach of Zhu Suli,[273] who does not deny the existence of factors that systematically interfere with the work of the court, including interference by the party, but holds that they are not pathological in the context of socialist law. In Zhu Suli's view, judicial committees support the activity of judges and represent an

---

[273] See Chen, AH (2004) 'Socio-legal Thought and Legal Modernization in Contemporary China: A Case Study of the Jurisprudence of Zhu Suli' in Doeker-Mach, G and Ziegert, KA (eds) *Law, Legal Culture and Politics in the Twenty First Century* Franz Steiner Verlag 227.

effective protection against external interference. In addition, Zhu argues, the committees have the function of harmonising the opinions on the case, [274] and for this reason many judges waive their responsibility to adjudicate. Along the same lines that conservative thinkers usually put forward to justify the practice as it is at present, Zhu puts forward two arguments, that will be here referred to as: the 'social acceptance' or 'social acceptability' argument, and the 'pragmatic-consequentialist' argument.

The social acceptance or acceptability argument is premised upon the idea of the ubiquitous influence of the Communist Party on society. The ideology of building the country is tightly linked with the role of the party: the party builds up the state, governs it and is above the state. Moreover, the CCP permeates every aspect of Chinese people's lives. [275] Zhu Suli contends that it is misleading to speak about the influence of the party upon the judiciary, and to differentiate it from the influence that the party exercises on society and administration: in so doing the Western model would be inappropriately applied to China. Zhu contends that according to the explicit provision of the Constitution and law, the judicial system is independent from any other power. The law attributes to courts and procuratorates [276] the necessary powers and instruments to resist external influence, which might come from individuals, associations, the party and the party members, but often the courts do not use the instruments provided by the law. The social acceptance or social acceptability argument affirms that even if the CCP exerts or has exerted a decisive influence upon the judicial system, the view of the party would not be incompatible with the general one shared by common people. Zhu holds that it is not only difficult to identify the influence of the party in everyday life, because it overlaps with the view of the common people, but it is also appropriate to understand that this influence possesses a remarkably pragmatic and opportunist character.

The pragmatic-consequentialist argument holds that the practice of asking the opinion of the party on the correct resolution should not be regarded as a way for the party to exercise unlawful interference in the adjudication of a case. By using counterfactual

---

[274] Ibid.

[275] In this sense, Zhu Suli does not differentiate the CCP from the Nationalist party or Kuomintang.

[276] The procuratorate is the office of the public prosecutor, exercising the functions of prosecution and investigation.

reasoning, the author affirms that even if the courts did not ask the opinions of party members, the decisions, which in fact are taken after they receive the advice and suggestions of the party members, would not differ from the ones they would have taken without consulting them. The reason is that all the parties in any dispute are under the leadership of the CCP, the economic and social elites are made up of party members, the CCP is accepted by the people and in fact controls and influences every aspect of Chinese social life, and it determines the direction of government and society. Moreover, the party sets up cells in every governmental organ and in citizens' associations. Bearing this in mind, the argument holds that it would be misleading to speak about the party's influence on the judiciary, because it would be difficult to distinguish this influence from other kinds of influence such as that of other administrative agencies and social organisations. The point of this argument is that the structure of thought, the hierarchy of values, the weight attributed to the competing arguments, and the orientation of the judiciary would reflect the policy dictated by the party, with the supreme goal of the construction of a developed socialist state.

Limitations on the independence of the judiciary are also supported by the thesis that judicial decision-making does not possess peculiar characteristics differentiating it from administrative or governmental decision-making. Judges do not differ significantly from civil servants, which is why they are called 'judgment officials'. Zhu argues against the preference accorded to law as a method to ensure justice and social solidarity. The political way or perspective in his opinion should be preferred to the separation of powers and the principle of the supremacy of law. In this view, party interference could be seen as the performance of its political functions of integration and social representation. On the basis of the arguments above, Zhu Suli argues that party interference with the courts' activity actually protects the activity from external influences. According to Zhu Suli, the supremacy of law, the principle of legality and the primacy of the parliament are not necessary to ensure justice and social solidarity.

Zhu advocates for the use of 'local resources' in the development of the Chinese legal system. He emphasises the importance of the informal mechanisms developed by society, and the prominence of networks and customary rules and habits as opposed to the emphasis on the supremacy of state-enacted law. In Zhu's opinion, the rule of law is constructed by the nation, and not by the state or by scholars, who can only explain, observe and understand the whole development of this process. A theory of Chinese rule of law in his opinion should be constructed as a social phenomenon, and therefore it should take into account the characteristics of Chinese society and the practice of self-regulation through customary rules and informal institutions. The informal practices, customs, conventions and institutions are, according to Zhu, the most valuable resources on which the Chinese rule of law should be constructed. The reason lies in the lack of confidence in human faculties: human reason is limited. Therefore, the design of legislation by the state cannot be considered to be able to direct social development in any way. According to Zhu, traditional and rational authority can both be based on the rule of law while charismatic authority is based upon the rule of man. The two have the same value and significance. Interestingly, he regards the history of China as a rotation of periods of rule of man/rule of law models of governance, due solely to the will of the emperors.

Recently, some Chinese scholars have rejected Zhu's position, advocating judicial independence and considering it a 'fundamental ingredient of the rule of law'.[277] They have argued that, even if one of the fundamental principles of the Chinese state is the leadership of the CCP, the party officials and organs should not interfere with the adjudication of individual cases.[278] In particular, Zhang Wenxian has proposed a theory of the socialist rule of law that includes two aspects.[279] The first is the relationship between law and society—

---

[277] Chen, AHY 'Toward A Legal Enlightenment' supra note 185 at 33; Li Buyun (2008) *Lun Fazhi* She hui ke xue wen xian chu ban she; Li Buyun, (2006) *Xianzheng Yu Zhongguo* [Constitutionalism and China] Falu Chubanshe, reprinted in Yu Keping (ed) (2010) *Democracy and the Rule of Law in China* Brill 197.

[278] Liu Hainian, Li Buyun and Li Lin (eds) (1996) *Yifa Zhiguo Jianshe Shehuizhuyi Fazhi Guojia* [Ruling the Country According to the Law Establishing a Socialist Nation Ruled According to Law] Zhongguo Fazhi Chubanshe at 196-197.

[279] Xu Xianming and Qi Yongpin (2007) 'Practicality' supra note 222 at 113-114. Zhang Wenxian (2014) 'Quanmian tuijin fazhi gaige, jiakuai fazhi zhongguo jianshe - Shiba jie san zhong quanhui jingshen de faxue jiedu' [Promoting Legal Reform in an All-round Way and Accelerating the Construction of the Rule of Law in China - A Legal Interpretation of the Spirit of the Third Plenary Session of the 18th CPC Central Committee] (1) *Fazhi yu shehui fazhan* [Law and Social Development];

including the CCP leadership, the people's democracy and the public function of the law—which is understood in a way that makes it consistent with the socialist orthodoxy, namely in the sense that the law has to align itself to social needs, as interpreted by the CCP. The second is the request for a 'generalised respect for the rule of law in the mind of the officials and the people at large, including the idea of respect for and protection of human rights, the concepts of fairness and justice, honesty and credit, the principle of due process of law, and the philosophy of harmonious good governance'.[280]

The Shift to Socialist Market Economy

In general, changes in the economy have been causally associated in various ways with institutional transitions to democratic systems of government, including a higher degree of protection for human rights. This assumption has not been verified in China. On the contrary, economic growth, accelerated enormously by the adoption of a quasi-capitalist system, seems to have reinforced authoritarian government. The legal reform, carried out under the tight political control of the single party and implemented as a means to maintain its power, initiated a profound process of change which, some hold,[281] may eventually lead to a change in the conception of law.

From 1978 onwards, there has been a progressive transition from an entirely planned economy to an economy that in 1992 has been defined as a 'socialist market economy', or 'multi-sectoral' or 'mixed regime' (socialism *and* market economy). There is no agreement upon the definition of the expression 'socialist market economy'.[282] The set of institutions, their actual functioning, and the

---

Zhang Wenxian (2014) 'Fazhi yu guojia zhili xiandaihua' [The Rule of Law and the Modernization of State Administration] (4) *Zhonguo Faxue* [China Legal Science].

[280] Xu Xianming and Qi Yaiping 'Practicality' supra note 257 at 114.

[281] Dowdle, MW 'Of Parliaments' supra note 230.

[282] The establishment of this system in China is due to the need to realise economic development. However, economic development is not a synonym for market economy. Moreover, it must be stated clearly that economic development is not necessarily generated by a particular system such as the capitalist market economy. To a certain extent economic development is not dependent on the economic model adopted. In other words, economic growth may occur either in the context of an economic system based on the capitalist market or in other systems, including a

94

rules and principles that are supposed to govern the socialist market economy as they developed in China are unprecedented, and their implementation is relatively recent. The characteristics of the Chinese socialist market economy represent a mixture of capitalist and socialist elements, and its nature is controversial also within the debate in China itself. Indeed, the expression 'socialist market economy' has several interpretations. A socialist market economy is different from a socialist economy with central planning because the government does not plan the entire economy, including investment, prices, the quantity and quality of goods to be produced and methods of production.[283] A socialist market economy is based on the view that the market is more efficient in allocating resources than the state, but it leaves a large role to the state, which is assumed to control and guide the macro-adjustment of the economy.[284]

Whether the Chinese socialist market economy conforms or not to the characteristics of a capitalist market is debatable. Alice Ehr-Soon Tay does not consider it either a pure socialist economy or a pure market economy. Linda Weiss defines the shift from planned to socialist market economy in China as an 'intra-systemic' passage rather than a change from a structure guided by the state to a structure guided by the market.[285] The economy is still guided by the state, but in a system in which the tasks have multiplied, together with the ways to fulfil them. According to Carty, the state has promoted, reinforced and maintained a social infrastructure, that is, a dense structure to organise industrial networks, trusts, commercial associations and other

---

planned economy. The term 'market economy system' must be also distinguished from the expression 'economic liberalisation', although the two terms are compatible.

[283] A socialist economic system has the following characteristics: the state owns the means of production and controls investments; there is a tendency to distribute income and wealth more equally than in capitalist systems, and the government officials responsible for economic decisions are designated through democratic election (Oxford Dictionary of Philosophy).

[284] Ehr-Soon Tay, A (1984) 'China and Legal Pluralism' (8) *Bull. Austl. Soc. Leg. Phil.* 23; see also Dernberger, RF (1991) 'China's Mixed Economic System: Properties and Consequences' in The Joint Economic Committee, Congress of the United States (ed) (1991) *China's Economic Dilemmas in the 1990s: The Problems of Reforms, Modernization, and Interdependence* Government Printing Office 89; Diamond, L (2003) 'The Rule of Law as Transition to Democracy in China' (12) *Journal of Contemporary China* 319.

[285] Weiss, L (2007) 'Guiding Globalization in East Asia: New Roles for Old Developmental States' in Weiss, L (ed) *States in the Global Economy* Cambridge University Press.

agencies of the same kind to pursue strategies in favour of a certain social sector.[286] While reducing direct control over the economy, the state kept the role to guide (*zhidao*), support and control (*jiandu*) the individual economy through administrative measures (Article 11 of the PRC Constitution).[287]

There is no doubt that the leaders and a group of intellectuals regarded the rationalisation of the legal system as the chief means to achieve a well-functioning market economy.[288] There is almost unanimous agreement that the 'call for a program of legal reforms explicitly intended to complement the economic reform policies'.[289] The slogans 'the market economy is a rule of law economy' or 'the market economy is the economy regulated by the law' (*shichang jingji shi fazhi jingji* 市场经济是法治经济) and 'rule the country according to the law and build a socialist rule of law country' (*yifa jianshe shehuizhuyi fazhi guojia* 依法建设社会主义法治国家), coined by politicians and intellectuals,[290] apparently affirmed the prevalence of

---

[286] Carty, A (2007) *Philosophy of International Law* Edinburgh University Press at 204.

[287] See Rinella, A and Piccinini, I (eds) (2010) *La Costituzione economica cinese* Il Mulino.

[288] See, for example, Clarke, DC (2007) 'China: Creating a Legal System for a Market Economy' available at <https://ssrn.com/abstract=1097587>; Clarke, DC (2007) 'Legislating for a Market Economy in China' (191) *The China Quarterly* 67. For a discussion on the role of law in economic growth see Dam, KW (2006) *China as a Test Case: Is the Rule of Law Essential for Economic Growth?* Law and economics working paper 275; Dam, KW (2006) *The Law-growth Nexus: The Rule of Law and Economic Development* Brookings Institution Press. See also Davis, KE and Trebilcock, MJ (2008) 'The Relationship between Law and Development: Optimists versus Sceptics' (56) *American Journal of Comparative Law* 895; Faundez, J (2000) 'Legal Reform in Developing and Transition Countries: Making Haste Slowly' in Faundez, J; Footer, M and Norton, J (eds) (2000) *Governance, Development and Globalization* Blackstone 396; Peerenboom, RP (2006) 'What Have We Learned About Law and Development? Describing, Predicting, and Assessing Legal Reforms in China' (27) *Mich. J. Int'l L.* 823.

[289] Potter, PB (2003) *From Leninist Discipline to Socialist Legalism: Peng Zhen on Law and Political Authority in the PRC* Stanford University Press at 108.

[290] Zhu Suli (1999) *Fazhi jiqi bentu ziyuan* [Rule of Law and its Local Resources] Zhongguo zhengfa daxue chubanshe.

law over politics and the adoption of a method of governance based on the authority and the autonomy of law.

During the 1980s there was not a clearly defined project for reforming the whole legal system in China. Many relevant legal innovations, such as the reform of state owned enterprises[291] (the only kind of enterprise recognised and allowed in the planned economy, and therefore operating in a regime of complete state monopoly), as well as the rules governing the private enterprises, were at first issued through governmental provisional decrees and only afterwards received proper legal discipline.[292] In the 1980s and '90s major reforming intervention concerned the areas of commercial and civil law.[293] These sectors of law are extremely relevant for the functioning of the market economy. A clear system of rules, attributing rights and effectively protecting them in practice, was issued in the area of commercial law to attract foreign investment. The foreign companies, from countries in Europe and the USA, would not have invested if they did not trust the capacity of the legal system in the absence of

---

[291] Shahid, Y; Kaoru, M and Dwight, P (1994) *Under New Ownership Privatizing China's State-owned Enterprises* Stanford University Press and The World Bank; Goldstein, J and Martin, L (2000) 'Legalization, Trade Liberalization and Domestic Politics: A Cautionary Note' (54) *International Organization* 603; Broadman, HG (1996) 'Reform of China's State-Owned Enterprises' in Schoepfle, GK (ed) *Changes in China's Labor Market: Implications for the Future* U.S. Department of Labor, Bureau of International Labor Affairs 4; Cao Siyuan (2007) 'Hibernation and the Revival of China's Privately Owned Economy' (40) *Chinese Law and Government* 89; Cao Siyuan (2007) 'The Homogenization and Decline of China's State-Owned Economy' (40) *Chinese Law and Government* 22; Cao Siyuan (2007) 'The Ownership System Reform of State-Owned Entrerprises' (40) *Chinese Law and Government* 71.

[292] Cavalieri, R (1999) *La legge e il rito. Lineamenti di storia del diritto cinese* Milano at 187-193.

[293] See generally Chen, AHY 'The Developing Theory' supra note 230; Erh-Soon Tay, A and Kamenka E (1985) 'Elevating Law in the PRC' (9) *Bull. Austl. Soc. Leg. Phil.* 69. On the Civil Law Reform more specifically, see Edward, E (1998) 'Codification of Civil Law in the PRC: Form and Substance in the Reception of Concepts and Elements of Western Private Law' 32 *U. Brit. Colum. L. Rev.* 153; Epstein, EJ (1989) 'The Theoretical System of Property Rights in China's General Principles of Civil Law: Theoretical Controversy in the Drafting Process and Beyond' (52) *Law and Contemporary Problems* 177; Hsu, BFC and Arner, D (2007) 'WTO accession, financial reform and the rule of law in China' (7) *China Review: An Interdisciplinary Journal on Greater China* Hong Kong 53; Lichtenstein, NG (1987) 'Legal Implications of China's Economic Reforms' (1) *ICSID Review – Foreign Investment Law Journal* 289.

formal legal dispositions stating the rules of the game,[294] and would not have trusted an environment which did not ensure even a minimum sufficient degree of predictability.

In 1998 the right to property was enshrined in the Constitution through the amendment to Article 13.[295] This major change in the provision for property rights in the context of the new legal framework was the object of scholarly debates. Both Chinese and non-Chinese literature analysed the theorisations by Chinese scholars on the relationship between law and the socialist market economy.[296] During the 1990s the 15th National Congress of the Communist Party[297] endorsed the principle of the rule of law state (*fazhi* 法治: rule through the law, rule by the law or rule of law, although the latter seems not to be the most faithful translation of the concept *fazhi* as it is now understood in China; or *fazhiguo* 法治国, considered the equivalent of *rechtsstaat*),[298] which was then enshrined in the Constitution by the 1999 Amendment. In the wording of Article 5 of the PRC Constitution: 'The state guarantees the coherence (or cohesion) and the dignity of the socialist legal system (*fazhi*)'.[299] After the Constitutional amendment of 1999, individual enterprises (*getihu*) and individual management (*getijingying*) were allowed to play a

---

[294] Cohen, JA and Lange, JE (1997) 'The Chinese Legal System: A Primer for Investors' (17) *New York Law School Journal of International and Comparative Law* 345; Huang, Y (1986) 'Foreign Investment in China – the Legal Requirements' (27) *South China Morning Post*; Potter, PB (1992) 'The Legal Framework for Security Markets in China: The Challenge of Maintaining State Control, and Inducing Investor's Confidence' (7) *China Law Reporter* 61.

[295] Cardinale, V and Rinella, A (2010) 'La costituzione economica' in Rinella, A and Piccinini, I (eds) *La Costituzione* supra note 285 at 24.

[296] See Chen, AH 'The Developing Theory' supra note 230; Keith, RC and Lin, Z *Law and Justice* supra note 263.

[297] The structure of the party parallels that of the institutional organisation of the state. The National People's Congress (NPC) is the organ endowed with legislative power according to the Constitution (Article 58). In the Constitution there is no explicit mention of the parallel party structure. The CCP has its own Constitution. Even though the NPC is formally the 'supreme organ of the state' (Article 57), the real place where political decisions are taken is the National Congress of the CCP.

[298] See General Secretary Jiang Zemin's keynote address at the 15th National Congress of the Chinese Communist Party in September 1997.

[299] Author's translation.

supplementary role in the Chinese economy according to the theory of planned economy with market adjustment, while they were considered 'capitalist evil' before. 81% of productive activities today are not carried out by the state owned enterprises but by privately owned enterprises. It is significant that the reform of private property preceded the proclamation of the rule of law state because it is a sign that the reform of the economy was the main objective. The legal reforms followed, along with the new importance attributed to the law by the Chinese leadership.

The new reality of the socialist market economy produced far-reaching consequences for both the theory of law and ideology.[300] The legal reforms initiated to support the economic changes have produced three interconnected effects. First, the reduction of the state's direct control over the economy implied a separation between the subject who makes the laws and the subject of the law, between the ruler and the ruled. In fact, in the socialist planned economy system, the holder of law making power and regulatory power in relation to economic activity coincided with the subject of these laws and regulations, both represented by the state.[301] The structure of the state also mirrors the structure of the single party. The party structure and the state structure were separated in 2000, in a process called the 'basic separation' between the state and the party. At present, the CCP's structure parallels that of the state.

Second, in order to function, the market needs individual subjects taking the initiative, running businesses, generating profits, investing and reinvesting capital. The new economic regime, therefore, attributed powers and subjective rights to the individual, transforming her into a legal subject. Moreover, it created an area in which the legal subjects can enjoy freedom of economic initiative free from direct intervention or intrusion by the state. The relevance of individual will or individual autonomy was legally very modest in the planned economy system. The 1981 Contract Law finally attributed a fundamental role to the will of the parties. Since then, the legal subjects, including also 'legal persons (法人 faren), regardless of their public, collective or private nature, and of their political and social characteristics', have been legally admitted to 'coexist on an equal basis and in a single normative system, with a plurality of different

---

[300] Chen, AHY 'Toward A Legal Enlightenment' supra note 185 at 14-15.
[301] This is usually supported by an ideology that assumes the coincidence of the interests of the governing and the governed.

(and competing) legal subjects'.[302] In the new context of the market economy (even if it is not a pure one), the benefits of economic activity, once almost entirely managed and reallocated by the state, remain, at least partially, at the disposal of the person who obtained them. Any individual who actively engages in business possesses some interests, which could be in conflict with those of other social categories, for example the category of employers and that of employees. Some scholars believe 'the differentiation of social interests to be the most important social issue in contemporary China'.[303]

Third, the new role of law is to coordinate, integrate and set the balance between competing interests.[304] Even if this may constitute the first step towards the legalisation and guarantee of the interests of the subjects, however, recognition that the subject has rights of an importance independent of and separated from the community of which the subject is a part still appears to be problematic.[305] However, by virtue of the Administrative Litigation Law, in force since 1989, it is now possible for citizens to act according to the law to protect their legitimate interests against the state. Scholars see this development as a significant and indeed a 'revolutionary' one due to its far-reaching consequences for the evolution of political culture in China. Indeed, the possibility to challenge the state was inconceivable before. Some believe that this innovation 'has begun to re-configure the psychological structure of the Chinese people'.[306] However, the impact of this law has not been

---

[302] Cavalieri, R *La legge e il rito* supra note 290 t 175-176.

[303] Chen, AHY 'Toward A Legal Enlightenment' supra note 185 at 30.

[304] Ibid; Keith, R and Lin, Z *Law and Justice* supra note 263. Interestingly the laws, for example those regulating the ending of the relationship between employer and employee, can be understood as a compromise between the opposed needs of the parties. For example, the law approved in 2010 prohibits firing the employee without a just reason, but allows downgrading of an employee to the trainee level.

[305] Xia Yong (2007) *Zou xiang quanli de shidai. Zhongguo gongmin quanli fa zhan yan jiu* [Toward an Age of Rights—A Research of the Civil Rights Development in China] Shehui kexue wenxian chubanshe [Social Sciences Academic Press] at 319.

[306] Chen, AHY 'Toward A Legal Enlightenment' supra note 185 at 36.

as far reaching as expected, and recent research demonstrates this point.[307]

The introduction of subjective rights[308] was therefore due to economic reasons, in order to permit the establishment and functioning of the market. Nevertheless, in the years following the initial reforms, the provision of rights spread into other contiguous areas of the legal system, as the Chinese legislator acquired confidence in the usage of the technique of law-making (Civil Law mainly at first, with the 1993 Contract Law and the 2007 Property Law, then administrative law and labour law, and the 2009 Tort Law). The idea of law as serving economic growth, boosting the functioning of the market economy, can be described as rule by law. 'The PRC has spent the last twenty years rebuilding its legal system and creating a modern administrative law regime as part of its efforts to adapt to the needs of a market economy and a political system that is moving away from its totalitarian past toward a new form of polity.'[309]

Clearly, the cooperation of different institutions is necessary for the law to acquire autonomy and authority, and for the norms providing fundamental rights and freedoms to be effectively applied. The authority and legitimacy of the autonomous legal reasoning by legal professionals is the main issue at stake. On one side, jurisprudence and judges, or legal practitioners, must have the authority and the power to elaborate and suggest normative premises different from those corresponding to and consistent with (or not contradicting) political directives. On the other side, the judiciary must be able to apply premises of that kind to actual cases. Indeed, the degree of autonomy of law depends to a great extent on what Silverstein calls the 'constitutional space'[310] of the courts. This expression refers to the range of judicial activities allowed within a constitutional space. Courts should be capable of using the principles elaborated to solve controversies in areas of law that are functional to economic development (civil and commercial law) in other areas of the law, operating an extension of their principles and reasoning. In their application of legal dispositions, courts should be able to issue judgments whose premises are different from political instructions and

---

[307] Biddulph, S *The Stability Imperative* supra note 13.
[308] Subjective rights are the rights attributed to the individuals. Human rights are provided by law in the form of subjective rights. The first category is broader than the second.
[309] Peerenboom, RP 'Globalization' supra note 184.
[310] Silverstein, G (2003) 'Globalization' supra note 10 at 442.

directives. However, the 'constitutional space' is defined also by the capacity that the courts possess to make sure other institutions and the holders of political power accept, respect and implement their judgments. The norms providing guarantees for rights and human rights are the kind of premises upon which the legal reasoning is grounded. If these premises cannot form the basis of the judges' reasoning because the other institutional actors prevent or resist this operation, the law might easily become a ductile instrument in the hands of power holders.[311] In those cases power tries to co-opt legal professionals by neutralising actions and ideas potentially conflicting with those held by the regime, and which are based on a different conception of law,[312] for example law as having a value per se. The analysis above supports the provisional conclusion that the courts are not likely to be the key institutions in a process that will eventually lead to the autonomy of the legal system. It seems correct to hypothesise that the developments in Chinese institutional and legal systems are likely to lead to an original institutional structure, a distinctive Chinese model.

Finally, the application of the law by the courts may be subject to direct interference by the CCP. In his recent study, Peerenboom argues that:

> Although the CCP still often fails to abide by the circumscribed role set forth in the state and Party constitutions, on a day-to-day level, direct interference by Party organs in administrative rulemaking or specific agency decisions is not common. Rather, the Party's main relevance to administrative law lies in its ability to promote or obstruct further political and legal reforms that would strengthen the legal system, but could also lead to the demise of the Party or to a drastic reduction in power.[313]

Legal Instrumentalism and the Rule of Law

In the context of the planned economy, the provisions regulating economic activities often blurred the line between politics and the law,

---

[311] Dowdle, MW (2002-2003) 'Of Parliaments' supra note 230 at 20.

[312] Ibid at 38-39.

[313] Peerenboom, RP (2001) 'Globalization' supra note 184 at 167-168.

because the main actor in the economy, the state, was also acting as the lawmaker. The decision taken and confirmed in the last decades of the 20th century, to follow the path towards government according to the law (*fazhi* 法治), was a political decision driven by the party from above. Seemingly, the proclamation of the superiority of law with respect to policy had the consequence of repudiating the socialist subordination of law to politics. The entire system of law and legal practice, however, could not be changed overnight. The question that will be discussed here is whether the declared commitment to law as a means to govern the country in the specific Chinese context acts for or against a higher degree of autonomy of law, stepping away from the model of the rule by law towards the rule of law.

The alleged modification in the conception of law in relation to party policy, towards greater autonomy of the legal system from political directives, was attributed to the need to put in place a legal system to support the emerging economic activities. Some scholars[314] argue that this shift represents a real change in the conception of law, which entails a higher degree of autonomy from politics. However, it is disputable. In this regard, the analysis by Trubek[315] is insightful. He argues that the idea implied by the political determination to follow the law and to build a country ruled according to the law is that 'law is the functional prerequisite of an industrial economy', and also that market institutions are necessary for economic development. As Trubek remarks: 'Modern law is a process by which rules governing social life are consciously formulated and consistently applied, the basic goal is to ensure that social life is effectively governed by universal and purposive rules'.[316]

Trubek notes that the core of this thesis, if developed, serves two different and potentially contradictory explanations. According to the first, the law is essential to the market economy because it confers predictability, needed for exchanges and transactions, and a set of universally applicable rules. Both the aforementioned requisites are sufficiently guaranteed by a formal legal system that possesses stability. The second explanation highlights what Trubek calls the

---

[314] Dowdle, MW 'Of Parliaments' supra note 230.

[315] The analysis by Trubek focuses upon the relationships between law and economic development and is a critical response to the thesis of the law and development movement. See Trubek, DM (1972) 'Toward a Social Theory of Law: An Essay on the Study of Law and Development' (821) *The Yale Law Journal* 1.

[316] Ibid at 9.

'purposiveness' of law, which places the law in a close relationship to power. According to this perspective:

> development is viewed as a consciously willed transformation of economic activity. The state is seen as the chief vehicle through which this conscious design is articulated and imposed upon the population; modern law is the instrument through which such development goals are translated into specific, enforceable norms. The more effectively these norms define and channel behaviour, the more likely economic growth will occur.[317]

The use of the law according to the second explanation can be inscribed in the paradigm of instrumental rationality: the use of a means to realise a certain end. This latter explanation of the core conception is less alien to traditional Chinese legal tradition, especially the Legalist conception, which defines the law as a 'tool' in the hands of the emperor,[318] and to the understanding of law as a means in the hands of the government (rule by law).

The second explanation suggested by Trubek seems to better describe the recent evolution of the conception and use of law fostered by the party in China over the last seventy years. Trubek concludes that an augmented level of legal instrumentalism, instead of causing an increase in the overall autonomy of the legal system, could reinforce the inter-dependence of the legal system and the state structure. In authoritarian systems like China, in which the state is firmly controlled by the CCP, the increased degree of legal instrumentalism can in turn strengthen the political control exerted by the elite in power. A similar argument is sustained by Jayasuriya,[319] who affirms that advocacy of the rule of law is more likely to provide political elites with the means to control society, while denying that the rule of law will go hand in hand with a transition to market-based

---

[317] Ibid at 7.

[318] Liang Zhiping (2002) *Fabian Zhongguo Fade Guoqu, Xianzai yu Weilai* [The Difference of Law: Chinese Law Past, Present and Future] Zhongguo zhengfa dazue chubanshe.

[319] Jayasuriya, K (ed) (1999) *Law, Capitalism and Power in Asia: The Rule of Law and Legal Institutions* Routledge.

economies and even democracy in East Asia, if not sustained by a serious ideological commitment to judicial independence.

Arguably, the new emphasis on the principle of 'ruling the country according to the law', instead of fostering the autonomy of the law, could reasonably be part of a strategy of the CCP to perpetuate its power.[320] Indeed, post-Mao elites, including Peng Zhen,[321] continued to regard the law as an instrument: under their leadership 'legislation and regulations were aimed primarily, if not exclusively, to implement policy goals'.[322]

While an instrumental conception of power and law is generally considered as being consistent with rule by law, some scholars have argued that the rule of law would not be compatible with such a conception. Tamanaha, among others, affirms that, since an instrumental conception of law is compatible with the idea that law can have any content, it is therefore not compatible with the idea of the rule of law, presupposing that law should always possess certain characteristics.[323] This view is shared by the advocates of the model of rule of law within the jurisprudential debate in China, such as Cheng Liaoyuan, Wang Renbo[324] and He Weifang, whose ideas were discussed in the previous chapter.

The advocacy for a power restrained by its own laws comes not only from legal theorists, but also from laymen, workers and peasants. According to Lubman, the unprecedented rights consciousness of Chinese citizens is consistent with Western ideas of equality, justice and legality, and in particular the idea that the government *should* be restrained by its own rules.[325] Lubman argues

---

[320] The argument draws on the analysis in Dowdle, MW 'Of Parliaments' supra note 230. See also Chen, J *Chinese Law* supra note 229.

[321] Peng Zhen was a prominent political figure during Mao's rule. As President of the National People's Congress he led this institution to gain stronger institutional authority due to his personal charisma vis-à-vis other high officials. In his work, Potter, PB *From Leninist Discipline* supra note 287, discusses the role of Peng Zhen at length.

[322] Ibid at 108.

[323] See generally Tamanaha, BZ (2006) *Law as a Means to an End: Threat to the Rule of Law* Cambridge University Press.

[324] See Cheng Liaoyuan and Wang Renbo *Fa zhi lun* supra note 215; and Lubman, SB *Bird in a Cage* supra note 73.

[325] Lubman emphasises the role legal consciousness plays in shaping concepts about vertical relationships between state and citizens and horizontal relationships between citizens. Protests and lawsuits brought by citizens against state law are, in Lubman's opinion, evidence of a changing idea of the correct relationship between state and citizens. Lubman, SB *Bird in a Cage* supra note 73 at 307. This argument is put

that the rule of law is an 'alternative ideology' whose generalised recognition is apt to 'legitimate a distinct form of power'[326] in China.

In this sense, the recent focus of the CCP on improving the rule of law, in particular in the area of public law, could be understood as aimed at maintaining the CCP's legitimacy as the ruling party. The fourth plenary session of the 18th Central Committee of the Communist Party of China was eminently dedicated to the rule of law. The final document individuated the goal of forming a system serving 'the socialist rule of law with Chinese characteristics' and to 'build a country under the 'socialist rule of law'.[327] The CCP attributed a pivotal new role to the Constitution. It committed itself to strengthening the Constitution's implementation, to promoting administration by law, and to building a law-abiding government. It also adopted the goals of reinforcing judicial fairness and judicial credibility, as major political objectives. The decision to institute a control mechanism to examine the legitimacy of government decision-making is significant because it represents an attempt to rationalise and proceduralise the exercise of power, limiting the executive power and constraining it under the law.

The CCP also committed to increase both officials' accountability for their major decisions and the transparency of governmental affairs.[328] The leadership's efforts to promote the rule of law are visible in the reform of the judiciary and in the anti-corruption campaign. The intention is to record and make public official interference in judicial cases. The policy reform contemplates the introduction of circuit courts set up by the Supreme People's Court, as well as cross-administrative regional courts and procuratorates, with the power to file public interest litigation cases. The CCP also manifested a commitment to enhance human rights protection in judicial procedures. However, in practice, the path traced by the

---

forward by Ke, Wei (2007) *Foundations of the Main Body of Rule of Law in Contemporary China: Study on Public Consciousness of Rule of Law* Falu Chubanshe.

[326] Lubman, SB Ibid at 307.

[327] Zhang Wenxian 'Promoting Legal Reform' supra note 277.

[328] For a thorough examination of the issue of transparency in contemporary China see Palmer, M; Fu, H and Zhang, X (eds) *Transparency Challenges* supra note 10.

official statements is not going to be straightforward, as the recent crackdown on lawyers and human rights defenders[329] unfortunately demonstrates. In addition, it seems that the recent reforms of the judiciary have the objective of enhancing speed and efficiency rather than respect for human rights and guaranteeing the defence of individuals from abuses of power in their many forms. The party member's encroachment on Chinese court is still pervasive.[330] The promise to upgrade the standards of the judicial system's transparency, thus allowing citizens to trust the courts and their work, as Susan Finder[331] demonstrates, was not upheld in full. The information regarding judges, their career, the interferences of the CCP, sensitive data, are still kept, at least partially, secret.

In continuity with the past, contemporary legal practice is still characterised by the coexistence of parallel systems of rules, the official and the unofficial. The latter comprises informal social rules and principles, such as the principle of *pao,* which form a strong base of customary norms.[332] Further research should be undertaken to

---

[329] Pils, EM (2016) 'If Anything Happens…:' Meeting the Now-detained Human Rights Lawyers' *China Change* available at <https://chinachange.org/2016/01/10/if-anything-happens-meeting-the-now-detained-human-rights-lawyers/>

[330] Ling Li (2016) 'The Chinese Communist Party and People's Courts: Judicial Dependence in China' (64) *American Journal of Comparative Law* 6.

[331] Finder, S (2019) 'China's Translucent Judicial Transparency' in Palmer, M; Fu, H and Zhang, X (eds) *Transparency Challenges Facing China* Wildy, Simmonds and Hill Publishing at 141.

[332] The word *pao* has a wide range of meanings but the core meaning is 'response' or 'return' (Lien Sheng Yang (1957) 'The Concept of Pao as a Basis for Social Relations in China' in Fairbank, JK (ed) (1957) *Chinese Thought and Institutions* University of Chicago Press 291 at 291-308). The notion of *pao* signifies a principle which regulated social interaction and still has paramount importance because it works as a normative principle of social organisation. The notion of *pao* is illuminating for understanding the way social relations work in China and the system they are apt to frame. 'The Chinese believed that reciprocity of actions (favour and hatred, reward and punishment) between man and man, and indeed between men and supernatural beings, should be as certain as a cause-and-effect relationship, and therefore, when a Chinese person acts, he normally anticipates a response or return. Favours done for others are often considered what may be termed "social investments", for which handsome returns are expected'. Lien-Sheng Yang acknowledges that in every society this happens to some extent, but points out that in China 'the principle is marked by its long history, the high degree of consciousness of its existence, and its wide application and tremendous influence in social institutions' (Ibid at 291). The principle of *pao,* the 'principle of reciprocal response', 'has been applied to social relations of all kinds, beginning with that between the ruler and his subjects, the first of the *Wu-lun,* or Five Relationships'

assess the relevance of customary principles, norms and rules for official law today. Given the strong and durable character of non-official social norms, their permanence has represented a fundamental factor at the base of the Chinese economic miracle. The solid set of rules governing the organisation and coordination of social family-based networks substituted for law in the early stages of the economic transition from a planned to a quasi-capitalist economic system.[333] Such rules have functioned as a coordinator and regulator of economic activities, in the place of a weak, incomplete legal system, whose

---

(Ibid. at 296). The principle of *pao* operates on the basis of family ties (for example between father and son) and in turn reinforces them. Yet its origin lies in the religious belief in a sort of cause-effect chain for human acts and heaven's response. The principle of *pao* may be considered universalistic in nature since it prescribes reciprocity for all social relationships. However, this principle is particularistic in its actual functioning, 'because a social response in China is often an additional entry in a long balance sheet which registers the personal relationships between two individuals or two families. Conditioned by already established personal relations, a given response can easily have an effect, or at least an appearance, of nepotism and favouritism. Generally speaking, personalised relations have a tendency to particularise even institutions which were intended to apply in a universalistic manner. Thus in traditional China, even in a case of fulfilment of an official duty, if it happened to be beneficial to a particular person, he would be expected to cherish a sense of indebtedness to the person who was instrumental in the outcome' Ibid. at 303. The coincidence of the notions of private personal relations and public duties is the cause of favouritism, nepotism and problems generated by the general overlapping of family bonds and institutional relationships. To some extent, it is a *structural* problem in Chinese society but it has played a role in the impressive economic growth of the last decades, in some ways subsidiary to the legal regulations of the market. The case of Chinese economic development deserves attention in the perspective of the studies about the role of culture as preventing or fostering economic development. The preference for the family interest over the public affairs of the collective echoes the thesis of 'amoral familism' elaborated by Banfield (Banfield, EC (1958) *The Moral Basis of a Backward Society* Free Press.) Amoral familism is assumed to be a hindrance to economic development. However, the case of China seems to disconfirm this hypothesis, at least partially. Further studies would be needed to shed some light on the topic.

[333] Clarke's persuasive research on 'the rights hypothesis' demonstrates that the Chinese economic miracle was due to the functioning of social networks ensuring predictability and certainty rather than an established legal system coupled with an authoritative judiciary. See Clarke, DC (2003) 'Economic Development and the Rights Hypothesis: The China Problem' (51) *The American Journal of Comparative Law* 89.

contents were largely inadequate for regulating an emerging market economy.

Conclusion

At the end of this analysis of the main ideas about the role and function of the law and the legal system, it seems appropriate to conclude with two points. The first is that the doctrines about the nature and purpose of the government by or through law differ remarkably and they range from positions supporting the idea of the value of law per se, and views supporting the idea of law as a means to an end. The second is that, at present, the dominant position could be interpreted as a version of the rule by law. In particular after the Constitutional amendment in 2018, it became clearer that the official position held by the regime is that 'socialist rule of law', or 'rule of law with Chinese characteristics' entails as a core element the CCP rule, and that the CCP is a law maker, and it is also above the law in most cases. However, the positions arguing the use of law as an instrument to govern paying equal respect for everyone's rights and equipped with means to restrict power abuses are not absent. Certainly, they have been silenced or marginalised by the official dominant position and by the rules of the CCP censorship. The relations between academic work and the holders of political power are complex, and they are the objects of the next chapter.

CHAPTER FIVE

Academic Discourses and Political Power

Introduction

Academic debate in China, as elsewhere, is relatively disconnected from the general public debate. It does influence the ideas used in the political debate, but this influence is usually indirect. In this chapter, I will consider the extent to which Chinese academia is free to formulate and discuss theories of human rights and equality. I will be arguing that, within specific limitations imposed on academic discourse, which have become increasingly significant since 2013, at least between the late 1990s and the first decade of the new millennium legal scholars have enjoyed a relative degree of autonomy. For a short period of time, this relative freedom enabled academic discourse on human rights to have some direct or indirect influence on law-making as well as on court decisions, at least in cases deemed to be apolitical. But what was the space of this freedom? To what extent can academics reach out and influence legal reforms and the broader political debate? When academic arguments came into conflict with the mainstream party view, to what extent could they be expressed? How strong was their influence? And how broad their reach? Could academia set its own research agenda? In answering these questions, I will also address the relationship between academia, the regime, and the broader public debate.

Any account of the evolution of the relationship between academia and the regime must consider the most recent development: the new leadership has recently restricted the scope of academic discussion by requiring scholars to limit the use of non-Chinese sources and reference to non-Chinese values. This is a very preoccupying twist for academic freedom, and it is coherent with the new political line adopted by Xi Jinping. At present, while academics enjoy some freedom, the debate is still subject to heavily increasing constraints. One of these remains ideology. The context however, has changed: since the early

1980s, the gradual shift to a market economy has loosened the grip of ideological dogmatism.[334] As a consequence, a plurality of arguments has been introduced in the academic debate, aside from the ones dictated by political authority. In general, even unorthodox views have been tolerated, provided that they are kept within academia without gaining political traction. The core of the new doctrine guiding academic research and debate is adherence to the method of historical materialism as the highest scientific method, in opposition to methods and values coming from the 'West', which are depicted as contrary to Chinese identity and potentially undermining the achievement of Xi Jinping's 'Chinese dream': a strong state with solid international leadership and stable economic development.

Finally, I will consider how effective these scholars' theories are, or the role they actually play in shaping the Chinese government's legal and political decision-making as concerns human rights. In particular, I will reconstruct the debate on efficiency versus fairness, and the implied question of which of these two values should be dominant in the context of a market economy. On the one hand, I will investigate the extent to which scholarly theorisations inform the government's framing or implementation of political and legal reforms designed to enhance the protection of individual rights in light of threats both old and new. On the other hand, I will investigate whether, and to what extent, scholars are able to influence the broader political debate and legal reforms. To this end, I will also explore the ways in which scholars critically engage with the 'orthodox views' held at the top by the CCP leadership on the efficiency *versus* fairness debate.

Jurisprudence in an Authoritarian State: Authoritarianism and Pluralism in China

Needless to say, the jurisprudential debate in authoritarian, semi-authoritarian and semi-totalitarian regimes suffers from the limitations imposed on public discourse by public powers. The scope of scholarly discussion is restricted to topics that do not pose threats to the regime; scholars are pressured to set up, formulate, and ground their arguments in a way that supports the

---

[334] Keith, R and Lin, Z *Law and Justice* supra note 263; Dowdle, MW 'Of Parliaments' supra note 230.

broader political action and expresses ideas fostering the legitimacy of the regime.

In the literature, the designation of China as a totalitarian, authoritarian or semi-authoritarian regime is controversial. In general, the notion of a *totalitarian regime* is that of a 'most extreme modern dictatorship possessing perfectionistic and utopian conceptions of humanity and society'. [335] As authoritatively held, 'totalitarianism', this 'new kind of tyranny', has never been realised in its fullness, and, especially during and after the cold war, it has been associated with communist systems, such as the former USSR, North Korea, and Vietnam.[336] On the other hand, the term *authoritarian regime* is generally understood to mean a political system in which an authority not accountable to the people exercises political power, or in which pluralism is limited and the political elites are not accountable for their own actions.[337] In authoritarian regimes, power is highly concentrated and there is no system of checks and balances, but social and political conflicts are not eliminated.

The People's Republic of China is sometimes defined as a mild dictatorship. Whilst authoritarian, it seems that the Chinese government does not have the elements of a totalitarian state understood as a state that aims to control every aspect of its society under a unifying ideology. Hence China is described as a *mild* or loose dictatorship, for instead of being absolutely monistic, the system allows for a degree of pluralism, with 'elements of a legally recognized society'[338] in a context where the state's power and administration are still monopolised by a single centralised power. While in a totalitarian state the state apparatus tends to become an empty framework in the hands of power holders, the single-party structure in China on the one hand parallels the

---

[335] Litwack, EB (2015) 'Totalitarianism' *Internet Encyclopedia of Philosophy* available at <https://www.iep.utm.edu/totalita/>.

[336] Walzer, M (1981) 'The theory of tyranny, the tyranny of theory. Totalitarianism vs. Authoritarianism' (185) *The New Republic* 21.

[337] Linz, JJ (2000) *Totalitarian and Authoritarian Regimes* Lynne Rienner Publishers at 156-157.

[338] Stawar, A (1973) *Liberi Saggi Marxisti* La Nuova Italia at 7.

structure of the state,[339] but at the same time does not fully coincide with it. The Chinese political elite appear to stand by the 'value of state order and sovereignty', ie to be concerned with *strengthening* the symbolic-representative function of the state, rather than being at one with it. Lastly, unlike what totalitarian regimes typically do, Chinese authoritarianism does not seek to elicit an emotional consensus from the people as a strategy by which to legitimate power.[340]

Chinese political and institutional future was the object of a vivacious debate especially after the 2008 global economical crisis.[341] Even though economic development was already ceasing to be a source of legitimacy for the CCP while nationalism was emerging as the new one, some scholars, mainly 'overseas Chinese democrats', optimistically affirmed that economic development was not sustainable and the political and institutional set would in a decade time change towards democracy. However, this thesis was not verified by subsequent historical fact. Instead, the opposite thesis was confirmed by the actual developments. The most recent evolution of the Chinese institutional and political regime has in fact been towards an authoritarian resilience,[342] rather than towards a higher

---

[339] Lubman, SB *Bird in a Cage* supra note 73; Gries, PH (2004) *China's New Nationalism: Pride, Politics, and Diplomacy* University of California Press; Lieberthal, K and Oksenberg, M (1998) *Policy Making in China: Leaders, Structures and Processes* Princeton University Press.

[340] Forti S (2005) *Il Totalitarismo* Laterza at 53-54.

[341] Consiglio, E (2018) 'Ipotesi Concorrenti sulla Futura Sostenibilità del Sistema Politico Cinese' (49) *Giornale di Bordo* 86.

[342] Authoritarian resilience has been theorised as the most likely trajectory of change for China by A. J. Nathan (Nathan, AJ (2003) 'China's Changing' supra note 15). According to this position the economic crisis faced by China could be overcome. Despite its boom in the early 2000s, the Chinese economy is still underdeveloped: more than half of the country has yet to be urbanised and this offers potential for future economic growth. There is strong evidence that the Chinese economy can grow constantly. So far, the process of privatisation has been driven in such a way as to avoid the negative effects that it had caused in the former Soviet Union, Central Europe and the Baltics. The way in which the remaining state-owned sector will be privatised is both an economic and political challenge and will have important consequences for China's future economic development and political cohesion (Walder, A 'The Party Elite and China's Trajectory of Change' supra note 15 at 195). According to A. Walder the most probable path of political change is 'a version of the principles employed in the governance of post British Hong Kong', that will most likely evolve into a 'stable system dominated by a single Party' rather than a multi-party system. Another argument is that current social unrest bolsters rather than weakens CCP leadership. The political elite needs the obedient

degree of democratisation and political pluralism. The 2018 Constitutional amendment has enshrined the leadership of the Chinese Communist Party[343] for the first time since the 1979 Constitution, and therefore implicitly wiped out any prospect of democratisation of the system and the very possibility of political pluralism. In this context, what is the space for academic discussion and what is the relationship between academia and political power?

As a matter of fact, in the recent past, the Chinese intellectual scene was very diversified and included a variety of opinions, which Albert Chen has grouped into two big camps, one of 'conservative' scholars, the other of 'liberal' ones. [344] Conservative intellectuals generally hold ideas and support methods of governance in line with a Marxist-Leninist-Maoist frame of thought. Liberal intellectuals, by contrast, call for democracy and civil liberties, though to varying degrees and urgency. Some ask for full democratisation of the Chinese political system, along with a full recognition and protection of freedom of speech, freedom of the press, freedom of assembly, and the right to protest. [345] Others embrace more moderate

---

cooperation of state bureaucracy (most of the cadres are party members) and also of the people that work outside the bureaucracy. These groups of people are the holders of real power; therefore, if they keep their discipline and loyalty to the party, economic and social troubles can be managed by the CCP itself without shifting to a different political organisation of power (Ibid at 197). The CCP has successfully institutionalised a method of selection of the new power elites but factionalism and regionalism remain major challenges for the tenure of the CCP's rule. There is a change from vertical and central authoritarianism to horizontal and fragmented nationalism: power centres are multiplying. According to Perry, the party should keep the capability to mobilise people in adherence to the policy objectives to create unity and cohesion among the population in the name of the national spirit (Perry, EJ (2007) 'Studying Chinese Politics' supra note 15 at 20).

[343] The 2018 amendment inserted a new sentence in article 1 (2) 'The defining feature of socialism with Chinese characteristics is the leadership of the Communist Party of China'.

[344] Chen, AHY 'Toward A Legal Enlightenment' supra note 185.

[345] Among them are Liu Xiaobo and the drafters of Charter 08, a petition to the government requesting a full democratisation of the system, coupled with a full recognition and guarantee of civil rights and political freedoms. In

114

positions, supporting a greater degree of democratisation but *within the single-party system.*[346]

A general distinction could be drawn: in the recent past, when academic theory fell into line with the official party positions, the party had an interest in bringing these voices to a public audience, beyond the small circle of academia. When academic theory supported the party view, this increased or reinforced the party's legitimacy and they were not silenced. On the other hand, when it did not support the official view, as long as it remained separate from the public debate, academia was not perceived as posing a direct political threat to the Chinese regime, and for this reason it enjoyed relative freedom. This is because the ideas that are liable to turn political are perceived as potential threats to the elite in power because they can attract a large following and support anti-establishment movements, which of course would have to be repressed.

The interference by the elite in power in the academic discussion have intensified in the recent years. While in the past the government used the tool of funding policy to shape the structure and identity of higher education institutions, and certainly to determine the capacity of academics to influence the intellectual debate,[347] the government today does not refrain from openly dictating the research guidelines for higher education institutions. In particular, the guidelines established by the Minister of Education Yuan Guiren aim at restricting the use of 'Western' textbooks and banning the books disseminating 'Western

---

December 2009, Liu Xiaobo, the leader of the movement, was found guilty of sedition and attempting to undermine the state's security: he was sentenced to a prison term of 11 years and six months. The trial was not open to the foreign press, and the decision was handed down in short order. Liu Xiaobo was awarded the 2010 Nobel Peace Prize. However, instead of providing the reformists with ammunition, this international recognition seems to have worsened their position.

[346] The contemporary leadership advocates reform within the single-party system. Lin, G (2004) 'Leadership Transition, Intra-Party Democracy, and Institution Building' (44) *China Asian Survey* 255.

[347] Since 2010 the central government started cutting funding to specialised higher education institutions called 'Universities of Political Science and Law'. The Universities of Political Science and Law, opened after the era of legal nihilism in the Cultural Revolution, formed excellent legal scholars and generations of practitioners trained in law. Perhaps for this reason the government decided to cut funding to these extremely successful institutions that were training lawyers and legal scholars.

values'. The ban is on ideas that are perceived to be threatening for the CCP leadership and vilifying socialism, labelled as 'Western' ideas. The political move is part of a broader project aimed at restoring the ideological orthodoxy under the label of 'sinicisation', a process of rendering any belief similar to the thought put forward by the CCP line. This is not limited to the academic sphere, but includes other areas where freedom of conscience and thought may be manifested, as in the regulation of religious activities, where important changes have also occurred in 2018.[348]

The elite identifies the higher education institutions as a strategic element in the ideological struggle and propaganda.[349] Universities are the outpost of ideological control on intellectual life and the new political guidelines aim at curtailing the spread of ideas such as 'human rights', 'the rule of law', and 'democracy' understood as pluralistic political competition. These concepts are deemed not in line with the official ideology and potentially harmful for the CCP's leadership. In particular, the guidelines[350] request all the higher education institutions to adhere to Marxism and Xi Jinping thought, which has been consecrated as part of the Constitution by the 2018 Constitutional amendment.[351] The primary objective of academia has become: 'Thoroughly develop instruction in the beliefs of Marxism and Communism, and in the stance, viewpoint and methods of Marxism', as affirmed by Zhu Shanlu, Communist Party secretary of Peking University. Addressing especially the faculties of humanities, including law, Xi Jinping gave a demonstration of how to apply

---

[348] The Religious Affairs Regulations first issued in 2005 were revised by the State Council on 7 September 2017. The New Religious Affairs Regulations entered into force on 1 February 2018.

[349] Chen Baosheng, Minister of Public Education, explained the importance of higher education institutions in his interview for Xinhua on 30 April 2019.

[350] The guidelines issued by the leadership on 19 January 2015 indicated the primary task of universities to ideological loyalty to the party, Marxism and Xi Jinping thought.

[351] The amendment to the Chinese 1982 Constitution was adopted by the National People's Congress of the PRC on 11 March 2018. See National People's Congress of the PRC (2018) *Zhonghua renmin gongheguo xianfa xiuzheng an* [Peoples Republic of China Constitutional Amendment] available at <http://www.npc.gov.cn/npc/xinwen/2018-03/12/content_2046540.htm>

Marxist-Leninist dialectical materialism to policy, as the best scientific method in order to understand reality and determine the lines of action in policy and law. Open academic research and inquiry are deemed compatible with strict adherence to dialectical materialism as the sole method, and with loyalty to the party line. In this sense, the room for free academic debate and research has reduced drastically.

The war declared by Xi Jinping on 'Western' textbooks and values is inherently contradictory. As noted by the prominent legal scholar He Weifang, the 'whole course of modernisation over the past century and more has been a process of absorbing Western influences. Marxist theory is also a Western theory'. He Weifang recalls how, 'In legal studies, in fact, the mainstream of thinking emerges from Western theories and traditions. [...] We should convene a conference to study how Premier Li Keqiang disseminated Western legal theories.'[352] In this opposition lies the new tension between higher education institutions and the party in power.

By examining the relationship between academia and the elite in power regarding the human rights debate, it will be proposed that the relationship between the regime and academia in China can be described as asymmetric and reciprocal. Firstly, this relationship is asymmetric because the regime can unilaterally determine the shape of the academic debate if it so wishes. In fact, throughout the history of the PRC, the political line set from the top by the CCP has not only drawn the boundaries of the academic debate but also framed its contents. In fact, when the rule of law (see Chapters Three and Four) and human rights (see Chapters Seven and Eight) flourished as fields of inquiry, from the end of the Cultural Revolution to the 1980s, academics were encouraged, and therefore freer, to discuss the select range of issues that were consistent with the party's new key political objectives. But within this constraint, the debates have always had to follow the party line, without criticising the CCP leadership, or calling the socialist way into question, or straying from Marxist-Leninist-Maoist thought.

Secondly, the relationship between the regime and academia is also one of reciprocal influence, in that the academic debate can influence political and legislative decision-making, as

---

[352] Buckley, C (2015) 'China Warns Against 'Western Values' in Imported Textbooks' *New York Times* January 30 2016 available at <https://cn.nytimes.com/china/20150130/c02textbook/en-us/>.

has happened on various occasions.[353] There are different reasons why academic research can exert such influence on the CCP and the regime. First, technical and theoretical legal analyses are needed to address complex problems, especially in the context of the new socialist market economy.[354] In fact, the ruling party is facing new challenges that require sophisticated expertise, and very often technical knowledge, that is hard to find among members of the party. Second, academic legal expertise is needed to develop adequate and sustainable strategies and solutions at the macro level. Legal scholars are increasingly being called on to translate party policy into legal frameworks, specifying the operational details of a policy line, balancing conflicting interests, and taking account of social needs. The academic proposals presented to the elites in power are only advisory, so they may be rejected, but they may also be accepted, and they often are when changes are made to them. In this lies the reciprocal nature of the relationship between academia and the party in power.

External Constraints on the Academic Debate and Ways to Evade Them

Even if the academic debate enjoyed phases of relative freedom, it is still subject to a number of constraints. These are both external and internal to the academic discussion. The external constraints are mainly due to the government's authoritarian control, influence, and censorship, while the internal ones pertain to the structure, methods, goals, and vision of academics themselves. Let us now briefly look at each of these constraints.

Perhaps the most evident obstacle to the flourishing and circulation of new ideas lies in the constraints imposed on the discussion in politically sensitive matters. There are still topics off limits to academic debate, forbidden zones or concepts immune to critique. Thus, there can be no criticism of the four fundamental principles forming the basis of the Chinese material constitution, including adherence to the socialist road and

---

[353] Keith, RC and Lin, Z (2005) *New Crime in China. Public Order and Human Rights* London at 244-245.
[354] Dowdle, MW 'Of Parliaments' supra note 230.

118

submission to the party's leadership. No argument can be made challenging China's designation as a 'developing' country rather than a 'developed' one. Also subject to political constraints is any discussion of human rights in the academic debate. In fact, some of the most significant and innovative ideas on human rights are watered down, silenced, or delegitimised. The degree of control and the scope of the constraints on academic discussion vary over time. While in the 1980s the Chinese leadership was comparatively receptive to outside ideas on the rule of law and human rights, the tide turned in the early 2010s, when tighter controls began to be placed on this discussion. There is in particular an outright suspicion of ideas labelled as 'Western'.[355] The general consensus, in accord with the party line, is that these ideas should be not promoted or endorsed by Chinese scholars. The guidelines from the top are that scholars ought to rely on the theoretical tools of Marxism, especially dialectical materialism.

Academics have reacted in different ways to the top-down control to which the ruling elite subject their work by limiting the scope of topics that are open to discussion and fixing the basic presuppositions from which research must proceed. The most common response is precisely the one the elite want: silence and self-censorship. Another consists in aligning one's thinking with the mainstream. However, there is another kind of reaction, more subtle and interesting. Some scholars still manage to present ideas that are not in line with political directives or with orthodoxy: ideas that reflect their own thought and beliefs, including support for 'Western' values and theories. To this end they practise an artful craft that consists in couching original arguments in a language and style that makes them appear to be advancing establishment views when in fact, on closer inspection, they are not. Thus, 'Western' theories can be presented with dry detachment, apparently to undermine them but actually to present them to the public and to promote their circulation. Using this

---

[355]Xi Jinping banned Western ideas as they purportedly corrupt the Chinese identity. The first question is whether it is possible to identify a 'Chinese identity' before even asking if some ideas can in fact corrupt this identity.
25 Gao Wei and Chang Xuemei (2015) 'Xi Jinping: Persist in Applying the Dialectical Materialism World Outlook Methodology to Improve the Basic Problems of China's Reform and Development' *People's Daily Online* available at <http://cpc.people.cn/n/2015/0125/c64094-26445123.html>.

strategy, Chinese scholars will refrain from expressing their opinion on the theories they are presenting, so as to focus instead on articulating their content, often in a very simple and plain style.

Still another component of this strategy is to use an orthodox vocabulary to express unorthodox ideas or views. Authors may use a kind of language that would normally be used in support of a view opposite to the author's own, making it possible to challenge the mainstream view while appearing to work within the mainstream. Another strategy is to revisit the most essential orthodox authors on the basis of these orthodox authors' own premises. Thus a scholar might proceed on a Marxist basis to argue that Marx was actually more interested in the individual than in the collective, and that he was not arguing against civil rights but was rather saying that they should be woven into the very fabric of society and the economy.

The attitudes and strategies that dissenting Chinese scholars use to pass the test of censorship without renouncing their own ideas are similar to those that Leo Strauss described in his famous book *Persecution and the Art of Writing.* [356] Intellectuals holding heterodox views do not refrain from expressing their ideas and criticism or calling establishment views into question, but rather resort to strategies enabling them to make their arguments obliquely. In this way, their work can be understood by those who are capable and receptive, while remaining hidden from the censor's view.

Internal Constraints on the Social Impact of the Academic Debate
Internal constraints are so termed because they are inherent in the very nature of the scholarly debate, thus acting from within to reduce its ability to influence the broader socio-political debate. In particular, as some scholars have argued, certain aspects of the Chinese method of researching and studying the law limit the social impact of Chinese legal scholarship and jurisprudence. The academic professionalisation of young legal scholars is sometimes criticised by arguing that it isolates research from legal practice.

---

[356] Strauss, Leo (1952) *Persecution and the Art of Writing* Free Press.

Academic education should in principle advance the scholarly debate, but the Chinese legal education and research system has also been harshly criticised by Chinese scholars themselves for stressing quantity over quality, the latter sacrificed to the former in the vast literature that young researchers are asked to produce.[357]

Also perceived as a fault of contemporary legal research in China is the lack of a focus on Chinese issues: in the eyes of Chinese scholars there does not seem to be any clear direction in this regard, and as a result they feel unable to answer the question 'where does China's jurisprudence go?'[358] Other important limitations come from the already mentioned self-restraint of scholars and from shortcomings inherent in the research methods used.

In the opinion of some Chinese scholars, the main reason why Chinese jurisprudence has been unable to guide the development of China's own legal system lies not so much in the party's ideology and censorship as in an uncritical adoption of a 'modernising model' based on the ideal of Western developed society as a blueprint for Chinese development. This model has been faulted for promoting a 'Western legal ambition' to the detriment of any 'Chinese legal ambition'.[359] The latter is a perspective that takes into account of long-established ideas rooted in the Chinese legal tradition (as has not been done to any significant extent in the contemporary scene), while setting a legal agenda specifically tailored to the Chinese context today, rather than pursuing a research programme set out by jurists seeking to address the concerns of an earlier time by drawing on ideas from their own cultures. While this made sense for those jurists, it does not make sense for Chinese jurists working to address the problems of contemporary China: to this end, the argument goes, it is necessary to find solutions using a Chinese legal toolkit,

---

[357] Deng Yungcheng, Hu Xiyan (2012) 'An Empirical Analysis of Students' Scientific Research Stimulated by Existing Scholarship System in China' (7) *Legal Education Research* 267. Young scholars looking to get promoted or confirmed are in large part evaluated on the quantity of work they do, and women who are expecting a baby or have just given birth are subject to the same quantitative requirements as their male counterparts.

[358] Xu Xianming and Qi Yaiping 'Practicality' supra note 257.

[359] Ibid.

perhaps through a happy synthesis with Western ideas, but not discounting that which is distinctive to China itself.[360]

To overcome the impasse, Chinese jurisprudence has assumed a new attitude over the past two decades, taking a second look at its own resources and its role in the broader construction of a 'more prosperous future for China'.[361] This new attitude is the result of a critical reflection that took hold in the late 1970s with a focus on Chinese identity, culture, and tradition. As earlier mentioned, part of the recent legal literature looks at the Chinese legal tradition as an important and neglected source of inspiration, rather than as an unwanted legacy of no use in the effort to solve present problems. Some scholars distinguish those aspects of the Chinese tradition that would hold back the effort to establish a modern system of law protective of citizens' rights from those aspects that, on the contrary, may be used to fashion a model serving as inspiration not only for China but also for the rest of the world.[362]

The recovery of traditional values and ideas, however, is itself not independent of the elite's broader political project, a project initiated by Hu Jintao and carried on by Xi Jinping. The communist ideology sponsored by the CCP to some extent functioned as the moral cement of society, providing a shared framework for public debate and political decision-making. Thus, conflicts between competing stakeholders have been addressed, at least on the surface, by appealing to ideology. The shift to a socialist market economy has eroded the effectiveness of the

---

[360] Among others: Chang, W (1986) 'Traditional Chinese Attitudes Toward Law and Authority' Paper presented at the Symposium on Chinese and European Concepts of Law, University of Hong Kong (20-25 Mar); Chen, AHY *An introduction* supra note 34; He Weifang (1999) 'Realizing social justice through the judicial system: A perspective on Chinese judges situation' in Yong Xia (ed) (1999) *Toward an age of rights* China University of Political Sciences and Law Press 179.

[361] The expression is used by Xi Jinping in describing the 'Chinese dream' (*Zhong guo meng,* 中国梦).

[362] Cheng Liaoyuan and Wang Renbo (2014) *Quan li lun* supra note 2.

122

appeal to ideology as a way to solve conflicts and maintain the CCP's legitimacy.[363]

In 2013, President Xi Jinping proclaimed in his inaugural address what has come to be known as the 'Chinese dream', making specific reference to the leadership's project to build up a strong and stable Chinese state: this marked the transition from a pragmatic attitude to ideology to a strong Chinese presence in the world's geopolitical system. The leadership appealed to the 'essential genes of Chinese culture' (*jiben de wenhua jiyin*, 基本 的文化基因)—its traditional, cultural, and philosophical ideas and values—in a bid to foster China's internal renaissance. In the leaders' view, then, China's renaissance needs to start from the recovery of traditional values, including harmony, filial piety, loyalty, and humaneness. These values are viewed as the basis on which a morality shared by Chinese citizens can be reconstructed. In the name of these values, efforts have been made to counter corruption in the party and in the administration. The question arises of the extent to which contemporary jurisprudence takes account of this political project to foster traditional values, and whether or not the scholarly discussion is in line with the leadership's policy goals. As is discussed in the following section, the overlap between the official government view and the jurisprudential account of the significance of cultural and traditional values is only partial.

The Significance of the Chinese Academic Debate on Human Rights

Notwithstanding the previously described internal and external constraints, in the last two decades of the 20th century especially, the Chinese jurisprudential debate had on the whole gained a stronger significance. [364] This is partly because ideological dogmas, beliefs, and assumptions—hitherto acting to undercut the debate—had lost their strength. Thus, legal theorists enjoyed greater autonomy, and at least in some cases their ideas managed to influence political decision and law-making, even if some constraints remained in place. However, an argument can be made

---

[363] Dowdle, MW 'Of Parliaments' supra note 230.
[364] Keith, R and Lin, Z *Law and Justice* supra note 263, Dowdle, MW 'Of Parliaments' supra note 230; Weatherley, R *The Discourse of Humam Rights* supra note 22.

that legal theory in China still tends to hew closely to the trajectory of the political leadership. On the one hand, the party allowed discussion on certain topics, and even promoted it. In fact the official support for certain research topics, such as human rights,[365] made possible an impassioned debate. At the same time, however, the party also specifically redlines certain topics of discussion: it will not countenance unorthodox opinions challenging current political priorities or dogmatic definitions (such as the status of China as a developing country) or cornerstone principles (such as the four fundamental principles).

The import of academic debate lies in its capacity to operate within the constraints explicitly stated by the party and to advance innovative ideas that can then spill out into the public at large. In China, the extent to which jurisprudential conceptions are accepted and integrated into the legal system depends on a mixture of elements. One of these, as previously discussed, lies in the degree to which a scholar adheres to Marxist ideology: the closer the adherence, the more likely the scholar is to enjoy a good reputation. However, even unorthodox scholarly positions in tension with orthodox party views can have a social impact and contribute to legal change. But to this end, as past experience teaches us, they need to first break out into the open, for once they reach a broader public audience they are in a better position to resist attempts to silence them. The dynamic of this interaction between the party and academia is reflected in the trajectory that human rights discourse has been taking since the foundation of the new state.

Since the PRC was founded in 1949, jurisprudential speculation has closely reflected changes in official ideology and

---

[365] On 17 September 1990, the Research Centre for Social Science Development of the State Education Commission inaugurated a series of conferences and seminars dedicated to human rights in China (see Chen, AHY 'Developing Theories' supra note 39 at 134). Chen argues that, in part, the interest in human rights was at least initially promoted by government authorities themselves (Ibid).

the development of institutions.[366] In the early decades of the new republic, Chinese jurisprudence proceeded under the strong influence of Soviet theory of law and the state, especially as developed by Vishinski. Official Chinese ideology endorsed the Soviet idea of socialist legality, namely, the idea that the legal form (the enactment and enforcement of statutory provisions) could serve as an instrument for managing socialist society so as to bring about the dictatorship of the proletariat. This idea would later lose favour when the use of statutory law came under suspicion and thus began to face aversion, beginning with the anti-rightist campaign of 1957, namely, the movement against those intellectuals who appeared to oppose collectivisation by favouring the market economy—a movement that culminated in the legal nihilism of the Cultural Revolution.[367] As Chen observes, legal nihilism is to be understood as a severe and complete distrust of law as a method of government. The law and legal scholarship, along with any form of legal theorising, were accused of being a 'bourgeois form of restraint on revolutionary activities', [368] and were accordingly despised and abandoned during the Cultural Revolution and in the decade that followed. Socialist legality and legal nihilism conspired to suck the air out of any human rights discourse, with the consequence that human rights were rejected and labelled as 'bourgeois patent'.[369] Only in 1978 were the law schools reopened, and Chinese jurisprudence started to develop new approaches to the law, overcoming both legal nihilism and socialist legality.

The subsequent shift in the attitude to human rights discourse was driven from the top, as other major changes have been in Chinese history. In fact, at the end of the 1980s, the CCP leaders themselves strategically promoted and encouraged research on human rights in response to the international critiques of China's human rights practice.[370] In the 1990s, the general

---

[366] Ibid at 123 breaks down the history of legal philosophy in the PRC into four periods: initial development, from 1949 to 1956; decline, from 1957 to 1965; downfall, from 1966 to 1977; and rapid revival, from 1978 onward.
[367] Ibid.
[368] Ibid.
[369] Zhenghui, L and Zhenmin, W (2002) 'Diritti dell'uomo e Stato di diritto nella teoria e nella pratica della Cina contemporanea' in Costa P, Zolo D (eds) *Lo Stato di diritto. Storia, teoria e critica*, Feltrinelli available at <https://www.juragentium.org/topics/rol/it/wang.htm>.
[370] Ibid.

jurisprudential paradigm started to shift: Soviet theories of law were discarded in favour of other Western (European and American) influences. In the 1990s, to be sure, Marxism still stood as the de facto standard, but it was being reinterpreted in a way that responded to new priorities: it was claimed that Marxist thought would provide the best definition of the idea of human rights, since a 'socialist society should be a society in which human rights are taken into consideration and respected'.[371]

Chinese jurisprudence on human rights has since shown a considerable degree of autonomy from political directives, and has proven capable of influencing political and legislative choices. In fact, notwithstanding the (still penetrating) constraints on the contents of jurisprudential discourse, in some cases the pressure that legal scholars put on political leaders has proved an effective force of change.[372] For example, as has been persuasively argued by Keith and Lin, the broad consensus in jurisprudential opinion has played a significant role in the advancement of three principles of criminal law: those of legality, presumption of innocence, and non-retroactivity of criminal law.[373]

Advanced jurisprudential theories have increasingly worked their way into academic debate, as well as into legal practice, in the context of a shift to a market economy, because in such an economy complex legal problems emerge that can only be solved with highly technical legal skills.[374] To address such problems jurisprudential syntheses have been taken into account in policy- and law-making, as has been the case with the drafting of the Chinese Civil Code.[375] In particular, recent Chinese scholarship has shown an interest in working out new approaches to human rights in the context of a reassessment of the very idea of the law. As Keith and Lin have argued, the shift to a socialist

---

[371] Interview with Cheng Liaoyuan, legal philosopher and leading contemporary Chinese intellectual. Chongqing, December 2009.
[372] Keith, R and Lin, Z *Law and Justice* supra note 263.
[373] Keith, R and Lin, Z (2005) *New Crime* supra note 351 at 244-245.
[374] Dowdle, MW 'Of Parliaments' supra note 230.
[375] Lei Chen and van Rhee, CH (eds) (2012) *Towards a Chinese Civil Code: Comparative and Historical Perspective* Martinus Nijhoff.

market economy indirectly brought about an internal push towards a more sophisticated debate on human rights, emphasising in particular the need for their adequate theoretical justification.[376] At the same time, the change in the economic system and the social changes brought about by the very same process have in turn led to a change in the jurisprudential understanding of the aims and values attached to law as a method of governance. In these discussions on human rights and the law, normative and socio-economic considerations combine and influence each other.

In addition, Chinese jurisprudence becomes influential when very important and controversial judicial cases,[377] or cases of national interest, play out in the Chinese media. On such occasions, the debate among scholars and their contrasting reasons, opinions, arguments, and perspectives on disputed matters resonate with the audience. This kind of engagement takes on legal significance, since broad public support for a scholarly position, according to the socialist idea of justice, adds weight and legitimacy to it.

The Italian legal theorist Giovanni Tarello offered an analysis of the concept of legal culture that may be useful in understanding the interaction between legal scholars and political authorities. A country's 'legal culture' is defined by him as 'the set of interpretive techniques used by legal professionals, both practical and theoretical, and the complex of the ideologies

---

[376] Keith, RC and Lin, Z *Law and Justice* supra note 263.

[377] See He Weifang (2010) 'He Bin, He Weifang deng Beijing faxue mingjia yantao Li Zhuangan' [Discussion on Li Zhuang case by He Weifang, He Bin and other Beijing famous jurists] available at <http://news.mylegist.com/1605/2010-01-05/18658_2.html>. The doctrinal discussion triggered by the case of Qi Yuling, regarding the direct application by the judges of rights conferring constitutional provisions also became part of the national public debate. The Supreme People's Court of the PRC initially issued instructions for the lower court handling the case indicating that it had to protect the constitutional right to education even lacking a specific law regulating this right. The decision, however, was later officially revoked. The case of Sun Zhigang, who died in custody, also triggered much debate and discussion on the issue of administrative detention under the 2003 State Council Regulation on Custody and Repatriation. A group of scholars, including Teng Biao, requested the supreme legislative authority to repeal the law. As a result of this pressure, the law was repealed. See Teng Biao (2013) 'The Sun Zhigang incident and the Future of Constitutionalism: Does the Chinese Constitution Have a Future?' Centre for Rights and Justice Occasional Paper available at <https://www.law.cuhk.edu.hk/en/research/crj/download/papers/2013-tb-szg-constitutionalism.pdf>.

pertaining to the function of the law that are presupposed by such techniques'. [378] Different kinds of legal professionals (legal scholars, judges, lawyers, and legal practitioners) can be distinguished by the specific cultural approach they each take to the law and by the way the legal profession is structured and organised in each national legal system. [379] Tarello also distinguishes between an 'internal' legal culture and an 'external' one. The internal legal culture consists of the whole system of values, principles, ideologies, and technical terminology distinctively used by legal professionals. The external legal culture consists of the ideas about law held by laypeople, or the popular understanding of law rather than the experts' construal of it. The analysis that can be offered on the basis of Tarello's insights is that scholarly approaches begin to play a role in the political system to the extent that they affect the culture of practising lawyers, scholars and practitioners and they exert an actual shaping influence when, through the mediation of legal practice or of social movements, they gain a foothold in the popular legal mind (the external culture), thereby triggering a critical engagement with current legal-political arrangements.

Jurisprudential conceptions are particularly likely to influence political debates on human rights and their application. This is because human rights practice is discursive: jurisprudence can therefore contribute to human rights practice by supplying a language with which to assert legal claims as well as arguments on which basis to substantiate such claims. So, too, jurisprudential arguments can play a role in human rights protection by shaping the framing of statutory provisions or by finding an established use in judicial practice. By the same token, jurisprudential conceptions of human rights can also easily be adopted by or integrated into political movements.[380]

---

[378] Tarello, G (1988) *Cultura giuridica e politica del diritto* Il Mulino at 24.

[379] Ibid at 24-25. The distinction between internal legal culture and lay legal culture was already made by Friedman, LM (1997) 'The Concept of Legal Culture: A Reply' in Nelken, D (ed) (1997) *Comparing Legal Cultures* Dartmouth 33.

[380] See Angle, SC *Human Rights and Chinese Thought* supra note 2.

In the specific case of China, the role of jurisprudence has gained significant relevance and authoritativeness since the late 1980s. The debate on efficiency vs fairness is one example of how academia has proved capable of influencing the political agenda and law-making during the first decade of the new millennium. The following section will describe the debate and specify how scholars' arguments were received outside the restricted academic circle. As mentioned above, however, the most recent political turn has silenced non-orthodox voices and reduced pluralism in the academic debate, which must now adhere to strict ideological guidelines. Most probably, the vibrant debate on legal issues that occurred in the past few decades will not easily be replicated in the contemporary political climate.

The Debate on Efficiency and Fairness
The scholarly debate regarding efficiency and fairness in the law shows that the arguments advanced by legal scholars had a positive influence on legal reform and law-making. This debate has formed the background to the new ways to address forms of poverty and social marginalisation that have accompanied the transition to a socialist market economy, and that will be described in the next chapter in more detail. Since 1978, the Chinese government has been single-mindedly pursuing economic growth as its top policy objective, and this push has engendered serious social problems and conflicts. At the root of some of the most troublesome human rights issues currently besetting the country is the dual economic system in which 'the old machinery of social economic security had yet to be replaced by coherent mechanisms reflecting the new social and economic circumstances'.[381]

As Potter[382] observes, while traditional social conflicts in China have been concerned with labour relations, healthcare, education, and the rights of women and ethnicities, further conflicts have recently emerged relating to the media, the internet, environmental protection, and corporate social responsibility. Whilst granting that the government has made efforts to regulate these fields, Potter questions the continuity and consistency of the

---

[381] Kent, A (1993) *Between Freedom and Subsistence. China and Human Rights* Oxford University Press at 132.
[382] Potter, PB (2013) *China's Legal System* Polity Press.

government's commitment to ensuring the practical implementation of such norms. It is a crucial role that is attributed to law and human rights in addressing social conflicts both traditional and emergent: in responding to the serious, deeply felt, and still largely unresolved disconnect between the goal of economic growth and the need to guarantee a fair society, effort also needs to be devoted to the protection of legal rights.

In the Chinese marathon for economic development, 'efficiency' has been a primary political goal for the Chinese government. Broadly understood as productivity, or the capacity to achieve the greatest economic output per unit of input, making the most of available resources, including time and money, and aiming for faster economic growth at a lower cost,[383] efficiency has been prioritised in that it was necessary for economic growth. Nowhere, perhaps, is the CCP's overriding emphasis on economic development more aptly captured than in the motto 'efficiency is primary, fairness supplementary' (*xiaoyi weizhu, gongping weifu*): it seemed that any other value or social goal could be sacrificed to the aim of economic growth.

However, the need to make efficiency compatible with individual rights has emerged in scholarly theory on the relationship between efficiency and fairness: scholars who attribute a comparatively higher importance to fairness affirmed the pivotal importance of protecting legal rights from government interference. In fact, fairness is usually understood in a broad sense in the Chinese debate, and it includes two main concerns. The first of these concerns is distributional, that is a concern with equality, which can be understood in either of two ways: as equality of resources (an equal entitlement to a minimum standard

---

[383] The notion of efficiency has been used in technical ways in Law & Economics. In one sense, under the so-called Kaldor-Hick criterion, resources are efficiently used when allocated to the highest bidder: that is counted as a way to maximise wealth. Another criterion is that of Pareto efficiency, under which an allocation of resources is efficient if no change can be made to it without making somebody worse off. Here I will use the term in its broadest sense, the one mentioned a moment ago, meaning the ability to make optimal use of available economic resources.

of living) or as equality of opportunity. The second is a concern with equality before the law, which includes the uniform application of legal rules, but also an equal enjoyment of fundamental rights.

There are two ways in which this idea of fairness has been interpreted in the Chinese doctrinal debate in relation to the question of efficiency, with some scholars arguing that fairness is to be pursued only as long as it contributes to efficiency, and others, in contrast, making a case for fairness as an inherently valuable principle which has to be balanced with efficiency and which, to that extent, may limit the scope of what may be undertaken in the name of the latter.

The Instrumental Approach to Fairness

In the Chinese debate, fairness has often been supported as instrumental to the 'efficiency' of the socio-economic system. In particular, it has been argued that an impartial application of the law and an effective legal guarantee of individual rights contribute to making business activity and the market itself more predictable. Legal certainty favours investment and exchange, and thus contributes to an environment supportive of the socialist market economy. Moreover, the fluidity of business transactions and the free flow of capital, and more generally the smooth running of the economy, require that disputes be resolved expeditiously. Zhu Suli, a noted professor at Peking University, argues that the efficiency of the legal system is 'paramount in the process of economic construction'.[384] He points out the problem that many laws lack any effective oversight and enforcement mechanisms. In his view, more investment should be devoted to ensuring the effectiveness of the law, since the cost of enacting legislation is sensibly inferior to the cost of enforcement.[385] He also observes that an efficient market economy requires a rapid and reliable dispute-resolution method.

Another scholar, Kang Xinhai, similarly argues that efficiency is primary but needs to be coupled with due consideration for fairness. This means that the allocation of resources should promote the productivity and efficiency of the

---

[384] Zhu, M (2004) 'Stability and Democracy' (4) *Human Rights* 1 at 103.
[385] Ibid at 105. See also Chen, J; Li, Y and Otto, JM (eds) (2002) *Implementation of Law in the PRC* Kluwer Law International.

market until 'social wealth has increased and people can enjoy more social fairness'.[386] This also means that efficiency needs to be pursued consistently with fairness, not because fairness is inherently good but because it is instrumental to efficiency: unfair treatment will make workers unhappy, and this will in turn undercut efficiency and the ability of the market to generate wealth.

The idea that rights need to be protected if efficiency is to be promoted seems to sit poorly with the fact that China's impressive economic growth initially took place without any robust legal and judicial system. This apparent paradox Clarke[387] proposes to resolve by his 'rights hypothesis', stating that, while the market does need certainty and predictability—a system in which expectations are satisfied and promises kept—these functions of a market economy could initially be performed in China by social networks rather than by the legal system, which was still young and fragile. Only after the economic reform and opening up policy did China put in place and strengthen an 'efficient' and professionalised judicial system for resolving disputes.

It bears pointing out, however, that the concept of judicial efficiency is often understood in a limited way in China. The research that Stephanie Balme [388]has carried out over the last fifteen years shows that judicial efficiency tends to mean speedy dispute resolution, not necessarily with an interest in ensuring the substantive and procedural correctness of judgments required by the due process of law. As Balme emphasises, the Chinese government makes it a high priority to control judicial activity in the face of the growing number of cases—a priority justified under the fundamental political premise that the judiciary needs to support the goal of ensuring that the economy can grow smoothly

---

[386] Kang Xinhai (2009) 'Qian xi pingdeng yu xiaolu de guanxi ji qi chuli duice' [Analysis of the Relationship between Equality and Efficiency and Its Countermeasures] (1) *Zhongxiao qiye guanli yu keji* [Management and Technology of SME] 80.

[387] Clarke, DC 'Economic Development' supra note 331 at 89.

[388] Balme, S *Chine* supra note 10.

without encumbrance. In this context, the ruling elite sets the political agenda and implements it through legislation. As Perenboom has noted commenting on Jayasuriya, 'statist ideology [...] rejects the liberal notion of a neutral state in favour of a paternalist state that grounds its legitimacy in its superior ability to fathom what constitutes "the good" for society; therefore, courts are more likely to serve as instruments for the implementation of the policy objectives of the state and the ruling elite'.[389] Adjudication may therefore be inclined to 'decide cases in light of a substantive normative agenda for society, as determined by the ruling elite'.[390]

This view subordinates the protection of individual interests and rights to the achievement of collective goals like that of economic growth and maintaining social stability. According to the April 2012 White Paper on Intellectual Property Protection issued by the Supreme People's Court, the courts' primary focus in 2001 was the 'delivery of justice', which in turn consists in adjudication according to the law. The Supreme People's Court stated that the focus of judicial activities is on ensuring that 'facts are properly determined, laws correctly applied and decisions complied with judicial policies', trying to 'balance legal outcomes and social effect, improve the quality and efficiency of adjudication and increase public confidence in intellectual property adjudication'.[391] However, according to the prevailing conception as expressed by the Supreme People's Court, the fairness and efficiency of the judicial system consists in expeditious adjudication and respect for official policy. Legal correctness receives little attention in the 2012 White Paper, especially as concerns the protection of individual rights.[392]

Recent research shows that an instrumental approach to human rights still prevails in contemporary Chinese legal practice, a case in point being the protection of the right to private property

---

[389] Peerenboom, R 'Globalization' supra note 184 at 186, in reference to Jayasuriya, K (1999) 'Corporatism and judicial independence within statist institutions in East Asia' in Jayasuriya, K (ed) *Law, Capitalism and Power in Asia: The Rule of Law and Legal Institutions* Routledge at 173.
[390] Ibid.
[391] Supreme People's Court of the PRC (2012) 'Intellectual Property Protection by Chinese Courts in 2012' available at <http://www.court.gov.cn/zscq/bhcg/201304/t20130426_183662.html>.
[392] Ibid.

and the right to be protected from unlawful evictions.[393] Political views seem indeed to coincide with the scholarly views just described, namely, the idea that the protection of individual rights is justified, but primarily insofar as it contributes to the socioeconomic goal of wellbeing and economic growth. Even in the early reflection on human rights in China, especially in the works of Liang Qichao and Yan Fu, it was argued that individual rights could be used as means to realise the collective goals of the state.[394]

Beginning in the early 1990s, however, many Chinese legal scholars have embraced the idea that human rights should be viewed not only as instruments with which to achieve collective goals, but also as ends in themselves.[395] To these theories we now turn.

Fairness as a Value in Itself, and Necessary to Achieve Efficiency

According to Keith and Lin, part of contemporary Chinese jurisprudence is indeed committed to effectively balancing the values of efficiency, justice, and social stability.[396] At the core of the contemporary debate is the idea that a proper balance between efficiency and fairness (justice) requires a strong legal protection of individual rights. Chinese legal scholars who welcome the idea of human rights are committed to developing a synthesis between fairness and efficiency, claiming that the two values are equally important and thus deserve equal stress. Keith and Lin observe that for Chinese scholars striking the right balance may make it

---

[393]Pils, EM 'If Anything Happens' supra note 317.

[394] Weatherley, R *The Discourse of Human Rights* supra note 22 at 147.

[395] Han Depei (ed) (1995) *Renquan de Lilun Yu Shijian* [The theory and practice of Human Rights] Wuhan University Publishing House; Xia Yong (1992) *Renuquan Gainian Qiyuan* [The Origin of the Theory of Human Rights] China University of Politics and Law Printing House at 26.

[396] Keith, R and Lin, Z *Law and Justice* supra note 263 49. See also Keith, RC (1998) 'Post-Deng Jurisprudence: Justice and Efficiency in a 'Rule of Law Economy'' (45) *Problems of Post-Communism* 48; and Keith, RC (1997) 'Legislating Women's and Children's Rights and Interests in the PRC' (149) *The China Quarterly* 29.

necessary to distinguish 'special groups' of rights-holders—women, children, the disabled, and the elderly—ensuring special guarantees specific to each. This idea has found an implementation in the law, with legislation tailored to each of these groups, recognising special rights and interests and providing a means to protect them[397] (see Chapter Eight for a discussion on the nature and justification of group rights).

Other scholars understand efficiency and fairness as interconnected and interdependent principles, such that to achieve one does not mean crowding out the other. On the contrary, there is a mutual implication between them, such that the two principles need to be put into effect at the same time. In other words, to balance the two principles is to achieve a synergy between them, even when a trade-off is necessary. Thus, for example, as Hu Angang argues,[398] it would not be feasible to accord priority to efficiency without bringing fairness into the picture, just as it would be self-defeating to make fairness primary without taking account of efficiency, in such a way as to support the market and promote the economy. Thus, in his view, efficiency and fairness are not opposite concepts but are complementary and mutually reinforcing, because that is the nature of the two objectives they are meant to achieve: efficiency provides the material foundation for social fairness and public services, and depends on the market, while fairness promotes social stability and is entrusted to the government. As Hu argues: 'In socialism it is possible to gain economic efficiency and social fairness at the same time'. If the wellbeing of the people as a whole is to be secured, the government needs to 'coordinate efficiency and fairness in a uniform way'. According to Hu Angang, 'sacrificing social fairness'[399]—which has to do with income distribution and social development—is neither necessary nor beneficial to the goal of greater efficiency. In fact, in his opinion, Deng's opening-up reform was designed with two main goals in mind: to make the economic system more efficient, while making for a fairer

---

[397] Keith, R and Lin, Z *Law and Justice* supra note 263. See also Keith, RC (1997) 'Legislating Women's and Children's Rights and Interests in the PRC' (149) *The China Quarterly* 29-55.

[398] Hu Angang (2000) *Jingji xiaolu yu shehui gongping hu angang* [Economy efficiency and social fairness, Society and Development] Zhejiang People's Publishing House at 349.

[399] Ibid.

socialist economy and social system. Only in combination can these two goals constitute the whole content of the socialist market economy.

Yin Jicheng and Song Rufeng [400] distinguish market fairness (fairness *in* the market) and social fairness (fairness *outside* the market). Market fairness is the fairness of the economic process: it requires that markets function in such a way as to ensure the economic equality of participants in the market. Competitors in the market should enjoy equal opportunities, be subject to the same rules, and operate under the same labour costs. The principles of equivalent exchange, even bargaining, and equal competition should be applied. Social fairness is implemented through social adjustment measures. These measures are meant to ensure basic survival and social stability. In this way they set the stage for steady development. They are also aimed at mitigating the inequality inherent in the primary distribution due to competition in the market: this is achieved by redistribution through taxation and further redistribution through political and ethical measures. These measures need to be adopted at the national level, so as to bring back into balance inequalities caused by externalities as a result of which some citizens lag behind.

In a similar way, Qin Xuan recalls that Deng's socialism was aimed at combining efficiency and fairness: 'In view of the fact that China's productivity is lagging behind, Deng stressed that poverty is never socialism, and slow development is not socialism either. The basic task of socialism is to develop productive forces, in order to achieve efficiency. Socialism is neither egalitarianism nor polarisation, and its ultimate goal should be common prosperity'.[401]

Another voice in the debate on efficiency vs fairness concerns the specific question of the alienability of rights in the

---

[400] Yin Jicheng and Song Rufeng (2003) 'Shichang jingji xia de xiaolu yu gongping ji qi shixian jili' [The Efficiency and Equity in Market Economy and its Mechanism of Realization] (1) *Jinan daxue xuebao* [Journal of Jinan University] 52.
[401] Qin Xuan (2003) 'Pingdeng yu xiaolu: Shehui zhuyi de liang da jiazhi mubiao' [Equality and Efficiency: Two Values of Socialism] (1) *Wenshi zhe* [Journal of Literature, History & Philosophy] 152.

market. The dominant role of the market mechanism in Chinese society has led to the view that all legal entitlements, including basic human rights, are commodities to be traded in the market. Some Chinese scholars have challenged this approach, bringing the issue of the alienability of rights to bear on the debate on the balance between efficiency and fairness. The argument is that the alienability of rights may contribute to efficiency by providing additional or cheaper resources for economic growth, while enhancing competition and flexibility. On the other hand, limitations on alienability may contribute to fairness, ensuring that individuals subject to unfavourable market conditions are not forced to completely surrender their fundamental rights.

Cheng and Wang analyse the issue of the alienability of rights with reference to the Law & Economics approach developed in the United States, which has introduced the term *rights trading*, understood as the alienation of rights in exchange for money or other advantages. Cheng and Wang explain that with the creation of a market without clear legal rules establishing what rights exist, how individuals can alienate these rights, and within what limits, the conditions are in place for the systematic devaluation of human rights. According to Cheng and Wang, when everybody places their rights on the market and sets a price through heated arguments and intense negotiation, rights can no longer be part of dignity and cannot give citizens the power to resist encroachment by the state.

The two legal scholars hold that the fact that even fundamental human rights can be alienated without legal limitations devalues and impoverishes the very notion of a human right. In rights trading, the holders of rights simply 'calculate the economic return on the rights they are trading, for example the rights of land use. They then decide if they really want to do the exchange'.[402] Therefore, a decision as to whether to alienate one's rights depends on a consideration of costs and gains. In this way, human rights are reduced to commodities on the open market, and when this happens, human rights become empty shells and lose their ability to act as effective individual safeguards. In particular, poor people may be forced to give up their basic rights in situations of hardship: a person will happily take a job waiving some of the associated rights and freedoms, and will even resort

---

[402] Cheng Liaoyuan and Wang Renbo (2014) *Quan li lun* supra note 2 at 273.

to theft, if the alternative is to starve.[403] In order to remedy this situation, Cheng and Wang argue, the law needs to exhaustively define individual rights, their contents, and the legal ways to transfer them, and needs to set limits on the alienability of individual rights.

Overall, the new significance ascribed to law and rights has not yet given rise to systematic or long-term initiatives to address social injustice. Indeed, pragmatic reasons seem to count more than normative ones in shifting the balance between justice and efficiency, for they are more likely to influence the official response to social injustice. The government's ability to address social issues and satisfy the demands for justice (or to give that impression) is an important element on which the CCP bases its legitimacy to govern. [404] Increasingly significant among the demands raised by the population are those involving the protection of rights. Therefore, it may be argued that part of the government's strategy for maintaining social stability will lie in the effort to appearing as a guarantor of certain human rights, as well as committing to the rule of law.[405]

The local governments' top priority to maintain stability downgrades the same governments' capacity to guarantee citizens' rights, preventing, addressing, and repressing their violation.[406] In a context where the prevailing conception of stability is the government led one, that characterises any form of social unrest as a threat to political stability, law does not become a means to protect aggrieved citizens' rights.[407] This is at the same time a

---

[403] Ibid.

[404] Together with the emerging nationalism, the attempt to build up a strong Chinese state, with heavy geopolitical weight, strong cultural heritage, and supporting fellow developing countries in a position of leadership among them.

[405] The Third Session of the 12th National People's Congress on 8 March 2015 put reinforcement of the rule of law at the centre of the party's future actions.

[406] Biddulph, S *The Stability Imperative* supra note 13.

[407] Biddulph indicates two different concepts of stability: 'Professor Yu Jianrong, one the best-known scholars of petitioning and mass incidents in China, sets out two ideal types: rigid stability and resilient stability. Rigid stability tends to view society as inherently unstable and therefore in need of active state intervention to maintain

central issue for the domestic legitimation of the CCP and its ability to maintain power.

In general, legal debates and legislative initiatives aimed at addressing social inequality are characterised by a convergence of normative and pragmatic considerations. Firstly, it is often argued or assumed that the principle of equality has a moral justification. Each person has a moral right to equal respect, and the law should consequently treat all citizens as equals, regardless of differences in talent, wealth, education, religion, age, sex, and so on. The differential treatment of certain individuals or groups needs to be justified by relevant circumstances (as in the case of affirmative action, where differential treatment is instrumental to the goal of achieving substantive equality). As the following chapter will discuss, the normative idea of equality has been at the centre of the doctrinal debate and has been enshrined in the Chinese Constitution, at least in the sense of equality before the law. Secondly, as already mentioned, it is often argued that equality has an instrumental significance, in that it can serve both economic efficiency and political legitimacy. Therefore, even those scholars who set much store by efficiency, embracing the government's perspective, tend to argue that equality (or fairness) should also be taken into account, being both synergetic to and supportive of legitimacy. Indeed, for one thing, unequal distribution of resources and distorted competition would in the long run generate inefficiency. And, for another, the citizens' perception of injustice could deepen and become widespread, leading to a loss of legitimacy detrimental to power holders.

---

order. It is centred on maintenance of the CCP's monopoly over political power and requires absolute social order. This view of stability tends to construe any disruption of social order as undermining political stability and requiring intervention. ... Resilient stability, on the other hand, requires that more sustainable long-term stability be based on observance of the law and the Constitution. Stability is constituted through stability of the stability of the political system and institutions of state based on the rule of law. This model sees stability as being based on norms of justice and equity, or at least mitigating injustices such as an insecure and unfair employment market, unequal opportunities and access to education and health care, and expropriation of land, especially rural land, without proper procedures and compensation. ... Such a model of stability would not be so quick to construe all socially disruptive conduct as constituting a fundamental threat to stability. The problem, according to Professor Yu, is how to move from a model of rigid stability to one of resilient stability.' Biddulph, S *The Stability Imperative* supra note 13 at 8-9.

In the following chapter it will be shown that when the demand for equality is supported by a convergence of normative and instrumental considerations, it can influence legislation and legal practice. The emerging significance of equality in Chinese law will be illustrated by looking at the imbalance between rural and urban zones, particularly in connection with the internal mass migration from rural to urban areas, involving a group initially referred to as *nongmingong* (农民工, literally 'population of farm workers') and now more gently designated as *xinshimin* (新市民 or 'new urban population').

CHAPTER SIX

The Debate Over Equality and The Rural-Urban Divide

Introduction

In this chapter, the new scholarly reinterpretations of the principle of equality will be compared to the interpretations of the same principle that were prevalent in the past. It will be argued that, to some extent, the new understanding of equality has influenced legislation over the past two decades. The focus will be on one of the deepest and most longstanding factors of inequality, namely, the urban-rural divide. To show how legislation has evolved in light of the principle of equality, three case studies will be analysed: the reform of tort law; the reform of electoral law; and the reform of the household registration system (*hukou zhidu* 户口制度).

The Rural-Urban Divide and the Issue of Migrant Workers

While the economic reforms have generated economic growth, they have widened the perennial gap between rural and urban areas: as economic development has mostly taken place in the coastal urban areas, rural areas have by comparison become much poorer. Thus, in the rural-urban divide lies a deep-rooted inequality problem in China, with a disparity that rural Chinese citizens are well accustomed to. The difference in the development of rural and urban areas is perceived as a serious injustice, and it leads to severe social discontent. In addition, the economic difficulties encountered by the rural population have caused the phenomenon of the 'floating population', consisting of people who live in places where they do not have an official residence status, such as a *hukou* or a temporary residence permit.

The *hukou*, already in use in imperial times, is a form of administrative control of the population. Each Chinese citizen has a fixed *hukou* assigned from birth: the *hukou* has either a 'rural' or 'urban' designation, inherited from the individual's mother or father, and a fixed location. The *hukou* includes personal and family data such as marriages, births, deaths, and divorces. The social services a person is entitled to receive are tied to the area where the person has her *hukou*. Moreover, the *hukou* registration is necessary in order to receive identification documents such as a passport and identity cards. As such, the Chinese *hukou* ties access to local welfare and public services to one's place of residence. It is the key to access basic rights, starting from the attribution of citizenship. Without *hukou* a person does not legally exist, is not recognised as a Chinese citizen, cannot request identification documents, and cannot enjoy public healthcare and education.

The 'floating' population of internal migrants lives in large cities and mostly consists of migrant workers with rural *hukou*. The government's attention has only recently turned to migrant workers from the countryside, who in the meantime came to be known as *nongmingong*, or rural workers in the cities. These migrants are not entitled to any public services or social security benefits in the cities where they live, because their *hukou* has a rural designation. Their children are often left behind in the countryside, where they can access public education and healthcare. The family or rural community in the villages have often cared for the children when parents migrate. These workers are often employed without any protection for their fundamental rights, or any guarantee of social security, such as access to healthcare. Their work is usually poorly paid, and they end up living in precarious conditions. The *nongmingong*, now referred to as *xinshimin* have for the most part borne the human cost of the Chinese economic miracle: they are numerous but often politically invisible.[408]

Over the years this phenomenon has ballooned into an increasingly conspicuous problem of social justice, recognised by scholars but also by society at large. Public discontent has become a problem for the government, which has launched initiatives for legal reform. It will be argued here that the government's recent reforms of the *hukou* system are primarily aimed at restoring the rights of the internal migrants within China, including the

---

[408] Li, L (2001) 'Towards a More Civil Society: Mingong and Expanding Social Space in Reform-Era China' (33) *Columbia Human Rights Law Review* 149.

nongmingong, reducing the rural-urban inequalities and allowing for more fluid internal mobility for the whole population. The change in attitude to migrant workers is reflected in the fact that they are now called *xinshimin*, or 'new urban population', which does not carry the same pejorative overtones, and to some extent expresses an inclusive approach.

It seems that the debate on the rural-urban divide reflects a change in the way the principle of equality is conceived, in Chinese society as well as in the government, in that the principle is now understood to include substantive criteria of equality in addition to the merely formal criterion whereby legal provisions need to be general, applying equally to all the members of the class to which they are addressed. To understand this dynamic of change, I will analyse three case studies, all linked to the rural-urban divide. First, I will discuss the way the principle of equality before the law has evolved to include the idea of equal respect and a rejection of unjustified discrimination, arguing that this development has influenced the reforms made to both tort law and electoral law. Second, I will address equality of opportunity, arguing that the scholarly interpretation of equal market opportunities has supported and promoted the reform made to the household registration system for migrant workers.

Equality Before the Law
In discussing the concept of equality, it seems relevant to recall the imperial age regime of 'legalised inequality' between members of the family (father and son; husband and wife) and between government officials and commoners. This regime sanctifying inequality was in place for two millennia before the fall of the empire and the subsequent political turmoil that led to the establishment of the PRC, when the CCP under the leadership of Mao Zedong defeated the Nationalist Party and the Republic of China. While the post-1949 ideology strongly emphasised equality, in opposition to the past regime, the idea of legalised inequality was maintained on the grounds that the socialist struggle in the permanent revolution to communism is class-based. This meant that the 'enemies' of the revolution were subject to a different (harsher) treatment than its 'friends'. The designation of groups as part of the proletarian class was different from that of Marxist ideology, for it was not confined to the proletariat but also included other groups such as the petty

bourgeoisie, [409] and sometimes the intellectuals. A form of legalised inequality could also be observed in the legally sanctioned differential treatment of urban and rural residents, which was premised on a 'structural difference' between the urban and rural populations in terms of wealth, education, opportunities, and level of economic development.

Under the Maoist regime, people were considered 'enemies' on the basis of such criteria as their family history and socio-economic background (the term 'feudal' was associated with exploitation, and persons labelled as 'feudal' were therefore persecuted). This outlook changed with the proclamation of the principle of equality, whereby 'the rights of citizens were made dependent on behaviour rather than class, and the notion of class struggle itself came to be reconstructed'.[410] It was accordingly claimed that the focus of state coercion shifted from 'class' to the 'behavioural manifestation of class'. The principle of equality before the law—a principle of *formal* equality— is enshrined in the 1982 Chinese Constitution at Article 33, stating that citizens of the PRC are 'all in the same way equal' before the law. In the official ideology, the constitutional proclamation of this principle is justified as 'a shift in the character of class struggle, testifying to the transition to a law-based system of governance which replaced the campaign style of rules associated with Mao and the doctrine of permanent revolution'.[411]

There are, however, two major issues in the wording of the Chinese Constitution. Firstly, it explicitly proclaims the equality of Chinese *citizens*. Even if some scholars argue that the only coherent interpretation of this expression is that 'all *people* are equal before the law',[412] equality seems to be reserved for Chinese

---

[409] The petty bourgeoisie were considered proletarians according to Deng's theory of the 'Three Represents'.

[410] Potter, PB *From Leninist Discipline* supra note 287 at 124.

[411] Ibid.

[412] Chen, J (2004) 'The Revision of the Constitution in the PRC. A Great Leap Forward or a Symbolic Gesture' (33) *China Perspectives* 250.

citizens,[413] raising the suspicion that some classes of non-citizens may enjoy better treatment. The wording of the Constitution reflects the Marxist conception of rights as created by law and granted by the state only to its *citizens*. This was formerly the mainstream position among legal scholars, and will be discussed in more detail in Chapter Seven. However, there now seems to be a generalised acceptance of the universality of human rights, which are now predominantly viewed as human rights belonging to all individuals.[414] The second issue, brought into focus by Chen Jianfu, is that in the Chinese Constitution 'equality before the law apparently refers to equality in implementing laws, not in law-making'.[415] In this sense, the law could also establish different regimes for different classes of persons without violating the principle of formal equality. Only a different application of the same law to different individuals would violate formal equality so understood.

This limited conception of equality has recently come under challenge, since the idea of equal entitlement to fundamental rights in virtue of the equal moral standing of human beings supports a deeper understanding of the principle of equality before the law as also entailing a rejection of differential legal regimes unless a justification is offered for such differential treatment. In this sense, equality has increasingly become a normative law-making criterion complementing those of efficiency and economic development. In particular, the idea of equality has effectively influenced law-making when coupled with considerations pertaining to political legitimacy, as has happened in regard to migrant workers. I will now illustrate the point with two examples.

The first example comes from civil law. On 26 December 2009, the Standing Committee of the National People's Congress amended the General Principles of Civil Law promulgated in 1986. This amendment changed Chinese tort law. Article 2 of the amended law, in force as of 1 July 2010, provides that 'if civil rights have been violated, tort liability is regulated by this law', and proceeds to lay out a non-exhaustive list of rights that

---

[413] See for example Chang Jian and Liu Kun (2004) 'On Equal and Special Protection of Human Rights' (4) *Human Rights* 20-23.

[414] Weatherley, R *The Discourse of Human Rights* supra note 22; Chen, AHY 'Developing Theories' supra note 39 at 123.

[415] Chen, J 'The Revision' supra note 410.

includes the right to life and health; the right to one's name, reputation, honour, and image; the right to privacy; the right to marriage; the rights to property and usufruct; copyright and patent and trademark rights; and the right to inheritance and other personal and property rights. In case of violation, these rights receive legal protection through the remedies specified by the same law. The list of the protected rights is wide-ranging, and it ends with a clause conferring on the judge the power to also recognise rights that, while not expressly included in the list, can be construed by reasoning from other legal provisions contained in the legal system. However, the remedies provided by the new civil law only apply to violations committed by other private citizens; they do not apply to public officials or government agencies. Under the law previously in force, in the event of death caused by a traffic accident the victims' families were entitled to receive damages, a money award in an amount tied to whether the victim's *hukou* was designated as rural or urban, or to whether he or she had a permanent residence permit: people with an urban designation were entitled to higher damages than those with a rural one. The amount of the damages varied depending on factors of an eminently economic nature. In particular, the 'cost' and the 'productivity' of a citizen with a rural *hukou* were deemed comparatively lower than those of citizens having urban *hukou*, in that they were living and working in a richer and more developed urban area. The new law modified these provisions by stating that when the same accident causes the death of different individuals, the damages have to be for the same amount regardless of their residence (Article 17).

The second example is drawn from public law, as it concerns the reform made to the electoral law, which on 15 March 2010 was amended by introducing a number of important changes.[416] Article 38 of the new law explicitly established that

---

[416] The decision approving the amendment can be found in Chinese at the following website: <http://www.npc.gov.cn/npc/xinwen/2010-03/14/content _1563772.htm, last accessed on 15.03.2010>. The text of the new electoral law can be found at <http:/www.npc.gov.cn/npc/xinwen/2010-03/14/content_1563869.htm>.

146

the vote is secret; even before the amendment the vote was secret, but the provision was scarcely enforced in practice. The new electoral law also provides that all citizens of full age who have not lost their political rights can elect members to the People's Assemblies (legislative organs) in their place of residence, and may also stand for election themselves. Universal suffrage and open electoral lists were initially restricted to village elections,[417] and only subsequently were they extended to municipal and district elections. All other higher-level legislative organs are elected by a second-level election: the representatives of the basic-level People's Congresses elect members of the legislative organ at the next higher level; members of the National People's Congress are elected by the People's Congresses of Provinces and Municipalities directly under the control of the central government (Shanghai, Chongqing, Beijing, Nanjing). As described, this mechanism seems to ensure a bottom-up election, with full popular legitimation for the elected representatives. However, it is the party that controls the list of candidates from the top before they can run for office and be elected under the bottom-up mechanism just described. The most remarkable change introduced by the 2010 reform consisted in making the rural vote equal to the urban vote. Under the 1953 Electoral Law, as amended in 1979, it was only in the cities that every vote counted equally: in rural areas it took four, five, or eight individual votes to count as a single urban vote, depending on whether the election was being held at the municipal, provincial or national level. On 2 February 1995, this tiered system was replaced with a system under which it uniformly took four rural votes to count as a single urban vote, regardless of the electoral level. The law now in force, amended on 15 March 2010, finally introduced the 'one head one vote' rule by making all votes count equally for every Chinese citizen (urban or rural) in application of

---

[417] Jacobson, L (2004) 'Local Government, Village and Township Direct Election' in Howell, J (ed) (2004) *Governance in China* Rowman and Littlefield 97; Hsu, SC (ed) (2003) *Understanding China's Legal System: Essays in Honor of Jerome A. Cohen* New York University at 319. Manion, M (2000) 'Chinese Democratization in Perspective: Electorates and Selectorates at the Township Level' (163) *The China Quarterly* 764 shows that township elections are designed to align the popular vote with the preferences of CCP committees: 'local party committees want to select candidates who will win, ideally with a margin of victory big enough to legitimate party choice' (ibid at 765).

the principle of equality. Even if the right to vote and stand for election does not mean as much in a single-party state as it may in a multi-party system, there is an important message that is conveyed by providing that every citizen's vote counts equally.

A New Understanding of the Principle of Equality

The legal and economic reforms initiated under Deng Xiaoping were based on the idea that the market economy can bring prosperity to the whole country. The new economic system has deeply influenced the theories of equality developed by legal scholars. The new theorisations counter at least in part the ideological theories elaborated in the early 1990s. Albert Chen examined the theories developed in the early 1990s, in which, under Marxist orthodoxy, formal equality was analysed to have little significance in capitalist society. Thus, Zheng Chengliang (Jilin University) argued that 'feudal' society did not respect the principle of equality, which in his view was for the first time applied in capitalist societies. While recognising this progress, he criticised this kind of equality as merely formal, and hence empty, since in a capitalist society all citizens have the same rights (or can gain rights in the same ways), but the underlying economic inequalities remain in place. The idea widely shared by legal scholars was that the socialist society 'opposed the division in classes that divides society into rich and poor, exploitation and oppression that render illusory the rights promised by the capitalist system'.[418] In this lay the superiority of the socialist system. The Chinese scholars' subsequent thinking on equality and efficiency in the socialist market economy was aimed at reconciling the two principles of economic growth and justice in a comprehensive and consistent theoretical framework.

In the new context of a market economy, the idea of equality as 'equal distribution of income', which has always been a cornerstone of planned economies, had to be abandoned. The shared premise is that economic growth is a necessary prerequisite if the people's material and cultural needs are to be met. In this

---

[418] Chen, A 'Developing Theories' supra note 39 at 128-129

sense, scholars argue that the market economy serves the socialist purpose of enhancing justice. On the contrary, they regard the lack of competition and low level of efficiency that characterised the traditional planned economy as symptomatic of a lack of justice.[419]

Legal scholars started theorising a new notion of equality, linked to fairness and justice. Equality is now understood, first and foremost, as, or equal *opportunity* (*gongping de jihui pingdeng* 公平的机会平等). This replaced the earlier stress on *income* equality. In fact, equal opportunity leads to competition and justifies an unequal distribution of income. It is premised on the view of procedural justice that the inequalities generated by competition in the market are fair so long as everyone starts out with the same opportunities and has equal access to the market. On this new understanding, equality implies that every individual in the socialist market should be in a position to meaningfully exercise their rights to improve their position and should have an equal possibility to obtain income or property.[420] The possibility to obtain new income and property, to enhance one's economic position, is seen as an incentive for individuals to exercise economic initiative. The earlier understanding of equality as equal distribution of income is rejected on the reasoning that by removing economic incentives it hampers market efficiency. Consequently, inequality of outcomes is not regarded as unfair but as the fair outcome of different individuals exercising this initiative. This doctrine is embodied in the slogan 'to become rich is glorious'.

In this theoretical framework based on a market-economy model, efficiency and fairness are viewed as complementary (as Cheng Lixiang characterises their relation) or as mutually reinforcing, as Teng Jianhua characterises it, arguing that efficiency and equality need to be in balance if the global market is to give rise to widespread prosperity, which in turn he considers a necessary prerequisite of equality, as greater wealth also means that the government can provide social welfare programmes and support low-income citizens. The first goal is therefore to increase

---

[419] Cheng Lixian (1999) 'Lun shehui gongzheng, pingdeng yu xiaolu' [On Social Justice, Equality and Efficiency] (9) *Zhexue dongtai* [Philosophical Trends] 3.
[420] Li Yining (1997) *Ethical Issues in Economics* Peking University Publishing House at 12-13.

the overall wealth and quality of life. Thus, macro-economic rules can be put into place to correct the inequalities created by the market and to guarantee competition through education and job training. Equality of opportunity supports economic efficiency, and the way to solve this problem, Teng argues, is to find the right system of incentives that will make it seem worthwhile for individuals to pursue their economic interest: 'Currently the inequality of opportunity accounts for a large part of the unfair income distribution. In order to address this problem, we should enhance legal construction to modify people's economic behaviour and contribute to a fair and reasonable competition process.'[421]

In reinterpreting the idea of equality, these scholars maintain a strong connection between equality, fairness, and efficiency.[422] The majority believes that an unfair society—in which competition is distorted and there are no guarantees for essential goods and services or for such resources as the environment—cannot be efficient. In the long run, the pursuit of growth without taking into account the background condition of substantive and procedural fairness may have negative consequences, such as depletion of resources, environmental pollution, and corruption, 'which could jeopardise efficiency

---

[421] Teng Jianhua (1997) 'How to balance the relationship between efficiency and equality in social market economy' (1) *Academic Exchange* 6

[422] Li Songling believes that equality includes every aspect of the social economy, as it is the exercise of rights by every member of the society. However, effective equal enjoyment of rights may not be beneficial for the functioning of the market economy. Li suggests realising the reciprocity of economic rights rather than equality (see Li Songling (1993) 'Lun shichang jingji de pingdeng yu xiaolu' ['On the equality and efficiency of market economy'] (5) *Qiusuo* [Seeking] 3. Zhao Zhenjiang admits that equal income distribution does not guarantee a high level of efficiency and productivity, so the equal income distribution project must be abandoned and the pursuit of efficiency should take its place: equal competition, equal opportunities, and improvement of efficiency, recognising inequality as a result of income distribution as well as taking the respective adjustment measures that could control the inequality within acceptable limits (see Zhao Zhenjiang (1994) 'On the principle of efficiency and equality in market economy context and its legal solution' (5) *Peking University Law Journal*.

fundamentally'.[423] Cheng Lixian argues that 'in no case should we sacrifice justice for external high efficiency',[424] and he links the theory of social justice to the theory of the unity of rights and obligations (a classical Marxist position on rights that will be explained in detail in Chapter Seven). Cheng and Wang quote Rawls,[425] and affirm that: 'social justice is "the first virtue of social institutions" it would guarantee the unity of rights and obligations on the basis of political equality and thus help to achieve the optimum union of equality and efficiency, which is a moral prerequisite for China's socialist market economy'.

Chinese theorists[426] broadly subscribe to the view that promoting competition against a background of equal opportunities is conducive to economic efficiency and reduces the income gap between citizens, but also prevalent is the view that this can be achieved by relying on the 'invisible hand' operating in the market. At the same time, however, there is also an awareness among Chinese scholars that the market economy can produce negative effects (externalities) and can even widen the wealth gap. For instance, Hu Angang[427] highlights that already in 1997, a well-known political scientist by the name of Tsou Tang predicted that the economic reform would increase social and economic inequality, and he accordingly developed a strategy that would benefit the disadvantaged. He argued that the principle of justice required that the economic reform should be undertaken in such a way that it works as far as possible to the benefit of the disadvantaged. Many scholars advocate mechanisms for the correction of market inequalities. One such mechanism consists in progressive taxation coupled with redistribution of tax revenues, under a system of transfer payments to aid the poorest.[428]

Hu and Shen suggest that in both a planned and a socialist market economy, two principles should be applied at the same time: equal opportunity and efficiency. Both principles may

---

[423] Cheng Lixian 'On Social Justice' supra note 417.
[424] Ibid.
[425] Cheng Liaoyuan and Wang Renbo (2014) *Quan li lun* supra note 2 at 115; Rawls, J (1971) *A Theory of Justice* Columbia Univesity Press.
[426] Hu Jian and Shen Guang (1993) 'Lue lun shichang jingji zhong de pingdeng yu xiaolu' [A Brief Discussion on Equality and Efficiency in Market Economy] (4) *Renwen zazhi* [The Journal of Humanities] 50.
[427] Hu Angang *Jingji xiaolu* supra note 396 at 349
[428] Hu Jian and Shen Guang 'Lue lun shichang' supra note 424.

justify unequal income, but only so long as both are respected. Under the first principle, everyone should be given an equal opportunity put their skills and talents to use, without any hindrance or discrimination other than the natural lottery whereby some are naturally more talented than others. This means that not everyone will have the same capacity to take advantage of the equal opportunities recognised for all, and that all unequal income resulting from such differences is fair (so long as there is no other factor causing such inequality). The principle of efficiency instead requires that income be distributed in such a way as to incentivise efficiency. Unequal income is fair so long as it results from an efficient allocation of resources.[429] By contrast, no income or wealth inequality is fair if it results from either unequal opportunities or inefficient allocations.

Hu Angang advocates three basic principles in the development of social fairness:

> The first is *fair equality of opportunity*, which means that every person, whatever his or her initial status, is entitled to have an equal chance to participate in social development, including education or employment and other basic rights given by the constitution and the law. The second principle is the *public relief* principle: public initiatives should aim at improving social fairness as well as at providing or stimulating investment to increase future productivity. The third one is the *common development* principle, including an increase in district income and progression in the level of social culture. Given the fact that the level of development in China varies from region to region, only through a common development of both economy and society could common prosperity finally be realised.[430]

While recognising that both equality in distribution and equality of opportunity may contribute to efficiency, Zhang Renshou argues that the right balance between efficiency and

---

[429] Ibid
[430] Hu Angang *Jingji xiaolu* supra note 396 at 349.

fairness cannot be reached when there is income equality, nor can it be reached when there is a huge income gap. In his view, the factors of production cannot be rearranged with a view to a reasonable allocation of resources except against a background of resource fluidity, and in particular of labour mobility:

> it is labour mobility that promotes the transfer of capital, technique, and other economic resources among departments and enterprises, and also reduces industry restructure. Without equal opportunity for labour forces to choose their occupations, it is impossible to realise labour mobility, thus making the improvement of resource allocation impossible to achieve. Moreover, when competition in the labour market is limited or excluded, the efficient operation of enterprises is impaired.[431]

Equality of Opportunity and the *Hukou* System
The theoretical debate laid out in the previous sections has emphasised how efficiency and equality of opportunity can, and should, come into synergy, especially in dealing with migrant workers: if discrimination against migrant workers is overcome, it will not only be possible to achieve the internal mobility and freedom of movement needed to ensure a flexible and dynamic movement of labourers in accordance with market needs, but there will also be a basis on which to ensure equal opportunities for Chinese citizens. These theories tying equality of opportunity to efficiency have had a practical effect, contributing to the reform of the household registration system for migrant workers. This programme will be explored in the final part of the chapter.

As mentioned earlier, the household registration system assigns to every Chinese citizen a *hukou* (戶口) with a 'rural' or 'urban' designation and a fixed location. The social services an individual has access to are tied to the location of his or her *hukou*. In March 2013,[432] Premier Wen Jiabao announced that a 'unified

---

[431] Zhang Renshou (1994) 'Lun shichang jingji zhong de pingdeng yu xiaolu' [On equality and efficiency in market economy] (6) *Guancha yu sikao* [Observation and Ponderation] 7 at 12.

[432] See Huwitch, J and Hui Li (2013) 'China eyes residence permits to replace divisive hukou system' available at <http://www.reuters.com/article/2013/03/06/us-china-parliament-urbanisation-idUSBRE92509020130306>; China Daily (2013) 'Reform of hukou system'

national residence permit system' was going to be adopted as part of a ten-year urbanisation plan. The main goals of the reform were to reduce the gap between the rural and urban populations, to strengthen the right to freedom of movement and residence, and to secure greater equality of opportunity for urban and rural residents. The new policy makes benefits and entitlements 'basically equal' in rural and urban areas, although the changes would be phased in gradually.

On 30 July 2014, the State Council officially announced the 'Opinions on further reform of the household registration system'. By 2020, a 'people-oriented, scientific and efficient, standardised and orderly new household registration system should be achieved to support the basic establishment and completion of a comprehensive well-off society [*xiaokangshehu*i, 小康社会] and 100 million people in rural areas should succeed in settling in the town'.[433] Among the goals of the reform was to unify the urban and rural household registration system, and in the long term to create a parallel system based on residence permits.

The reform created four kinds of settlement areas: small cities, medium-sized cities, major cities, and megacities. The basic requirements were a stable residence, a steady job, and a minimum period of enrolment in urban social security. The settlement requirements varied widely depending on the size of the city. The requirements for megacities like Beijing and Shanghai were not relaxed; for major cities (with a population of three to five million) they were slightly relaxed, with a plan to resettle 17% of the highly educated floating population there; for medium-sized cities (with a population of one to three million) they were relaxed even more, with a plan to resettle 35% of the floating population there; and in small towns and cities they were the least stringent, with a plan to resettle 10% of the floating population there. The reform is currently being implemented by

---

available at <http://usa.chinadaily.com.cn/opinion/2013-03/08/content_16290371.htm>.

[433] Office of The State Council of the People's Republic of China (2014) *Guowuyuan guanyu jìnyibu huji gaige de yijian* [State's Council Opinions on Further Promoting Reform of the Household Registration System] People's Press.

local governments, and in particular by 20 provinces and autonomous regions including Anhui, Fujian, Guangdong, Guangxi, Guizhou, Hebei, Henan, Heilongjiang, Hunan, Jilin, Jiangsu, Jiangxi, Liaoning, Qinghai, Shandong, Shangxi, Sichuan, Xinjiang and Yunnan, which published provincial regulations implementing the household registration system reform. Throughout 2015, the Beijing government collected suggestions from citizens. Until specific regulations are implemented it is unclear how the plan will work in practice.

In December 2015, the government announced further reforms of the *hukou* system, followed by Opinion of the State Council 96, published on 14 January 2016, with the aim of 'further improving the household registration policy and eliminating any pre-existing conditions that previously disqualified individuals from obtaining registration, strengthening the management of household registration'.[434] The Opinion stresses that no unlawful requirements can be imposed as conditions for registration: the *hukou* must be granted to any child, including those born outside of wedlock.

The huge problem is how to implement the new policy at the local level, where there is widespread abuse through unlawful practices. The State Council itself acknowledges the obstacles lying in 'local and departmental policy', which is 'not conducive to the protection of the legitimate rights and interests of citizens, and directly affects the establishment of the new national household registration system'.[435] This quote from the Opinion shows that the concrete obstacles to the successful implementation of the policy are well known to the supreme executive organ of the PRC. These problems lie in administrative inertia at the local and grassroots levels, an inertia that is difficult to tackle even for the Chinese central government. The goal of the reform seems to be to 'redirect urbanization, relieve pressure on first-tier cities and

---

[434] Office of The State Council of the People's Republic of China (2015) *Guowuyuan bangong ting guanyu jiejue wu hukou renyuan. Dengji hukou wenti de yijian* [The General Office of the State Council on the settlement of non-*hukou* personnel. Opinions on the problem of *hukou* registration] available at <http://www.gov.cn/zhengce/content/2016-01/14/content_10595.htm>. See also Chan, KW (2019) 'China's Hukou System at 60: Continuity and Reform' in Ray Yep; Jun Wang and Johnson, T (eds) (2019) *Edward Elgar Handbook on Urban Development in China* Edward Elgar 59.
[435] Ibid.

redirect migrant flows to second and third tier cities where they need development, they need labour, and can actually absorb a significant number of migrants'.[436]

There are some problems with the implementation of the reform. Some provinces and municipalities abolished the urban/rural designation. However, an application to change the *hukou* is necessary in order to obtain permanent residence status in a city, and thus be entitled to the same rights and benefits as those who were born urban residents. In principle, it is possible to change one's *hukou,* but there are certain standards to be met and no guarantees that a request to be registered in another area will be granted. The most important requirements are related to employment and housing. The fundamental principles are that someone requesting a *hukou* must have a steady job and a stable place of residence in the new city or town where the *hukou* is going to be issued. The person applying for a *hukou* must also show proof of the following: her level of education; an employment contract; and either a home-purchase or a rent contract, depending on whether the applicant meets the 'steady' job criterion: those who do not must show proof of home ownership (no matter how many other criteria they meet); those who do need only show that they are renting. The success of a *hukou* application therefore hinges on the type of employment contract one has. Special attention is paid to what is called 'company ranking': a person with a job in a 'high-ranking company' is more likely to be granted a *hukou* than one working for a 'low-ranking company'. Two factors that go into this ranking are a company's size and its ties to the government. So the principle is that the more 'steady' and government-connected one's job is, and the bigger and more prestigious or international the company one is working for is, the better one's chances of obtaining a *hukou*. Civil servants (*gong wu yuan*) are usually

---

[436] See interview with professor Lu: Martines, J (2016) 'Despite Policy Reforms, Barriers to Obtaining Hukou Persist' *The Diplomat* available at <https://thediplomat.com/2016/02/despite-policy-reforms-barriers-to-obtaining-hukou-persist/>.

issued a *hukou* easily. People working for state institutions (*shiye danwei*) and state-owned enterprises (*guoyou qiye*) also stand a good chance if they have a permanent contract, and fewer chances if their contract is temporary. However, senior managers with temporary contracts are likely to be granted a *hukou* as well. People with a rural *hukou* are at a disadvantage relative to urban *hukou* holders, and so are generally less likely to obtain an urban *hukou*.

There are greater chances, but no guarantees, to obtain a *hukou* in smaller cities, provided that the residential and employment requirements are met. In big cities, such as Shanghai or Beijing, the combination of limited resources and an expanding population imposes stricter criteria for people to obtain a *hukou*. Thus, a person holding an MA degree will find it easier to obtain a *hukou* in Tianjin than in Beijing. However, an overseas higher education degree (from the UK, Europe, the United States or Canada, for example) will significantly increase one's chances of obtaining a *hukou*. Chinese citizens with overseas higher education degrees do not have to meet strict requirements related to the company they work for: if they have an employment and a residential contract, they will usually obtain a *hukou* even in big cities, such as Beijing. By contrast, people with a lower level of education and a temporary contract may be subject to additional residential requirements. Big cities, such as Shanghai, require additional residential requirements such as 'to have held a TRP [Temporary Residence Permit] and have been in the city's social insurance programme for seven years, to have paid taxes, to have intermediate to high vocational qualifications, and to have clean credit and criminal records'.[437]

Official discrimination against migrants on the basis of their *hukou* status affects the provision of other public services as well. Many local regulations require a local *hukou* registration in order to access the local health insurance programmes. Social benefits (such as unemployment insurance) and pensions are linked to *hukou*. In developed urban areas the standard of the services provided with a *hukou* is higher. Other legal aspects related to *hukou* include the issuing of ID documents such as passports and visas, including the visa to enter Hong Kong and

[437]   AX   §   81   (c)   available   at <https://tribunalsdecisions.service.gov.uk/utiac/2012-ukut-97>.

Taiwan. These documents are issued by the local administrative agency of the place of residence (*hukou*). Migrants lacking a local *hukou* are often required to vote in their place of registration. Some cities, including Beijing, have introduced reforms aimed at allowing migrants to vote in their place of actual residence. However, these reforms generally require migrants to first return to their place of *hukou* registration and obtain official approval to vote in their place of actual residence.

Children and adults without a *hukou* are devoid of any legal identity. Without a *hukou* it is impossible to gain access to public education, healthcare, employment, transportation, or public housing.

The *hukou* reforms appear to be driven by a will to achieve grater recognition and application of the principle of equality and the right to freedom of movement. However, there are still a number of practical concerns and shortcomings in the way the reform is being implemented. The criteria for changing one's *hukou* appear to favour the mobility of the wealthy and the well-educated (including students), rather than guaranteeing the right to freedom of movement equally for all. Progress is being made in addressing differential treatment and the resulting inequalities, but the problems have not yet been fully resolved at the local level.

The Involuntary Political Consequences of a Pragmatic Approach to Human Rights

Keith and Lin have claimed that the jurisprudential debate on efficiency and fairness in the context of the market economy has contributed to a shift towards a stronger recognition and guarantee of individual rights in the socialist market economy. In the last two decades a more significant shift has taken place: the logics of modernisation and the socialist market economy have forced legal scholars to adopt a new paradigm, one that sits uncomfortably with the former one. The new paradigm has been implemented in Chinese legal institutions to an extent that is determined by the political elite in line with its main goals.

The main characteristic of the CCP's approach to rights— to be distinguished from the plurality of views on rights debated in Chinese contemporary jurisprudence—lies in its *pragmatism*.[438] Rights are recognised, legalised, and applied only to the extent necessary to further the regime's agenda, and so long as they do not threaten the party's monopoly on power. Yet there may be unintended consequences of the limited recognition of rights, owing to some characteristics of the rights themselves. One such consequence results from what Caney terms 'rights holism', the phenomenon whereby 'the acceptance of some specific rights implies the acceptance of some other specific rights'.[439] The holist view sees rights as interconnected, and this perspective can be contrasted with an atomistic approach in which there is a cultural-institutional distinctness to each individual right that makes it independent from other rights.

There are at least four reasons why an interconnection may hold among rights. Three are highlighted by Cécile Fabre in her observation that two rights may be linked by (*i*) a *logical* relation, under which one *entails* the other; (*ii*) an *empirical* relation, such that the best way to protect one may be to recognise the other; or (*iii*) a *normative* one, in that they may be grounded in the same rationale.[440] If any of these relations hold, then one cannot coherently affirm one right and deny the other. There is also a fourth relation, one of overall *completeness*, based on the reasoning that one right will not be complete unless the other is also recognised and effective.[441] It thus follows from these relations overall that it would be difficult for the Chinese government to recognise and guarantee one right without sooner or later being forced to expressly recognise other ones that relate to it logically, empirically, normatively, or by completeness.

This interconnectedness and non-severability of rights has also been put forward to support the idea that civil and political rights cannot be protected without also protecting economic, social, and cultural rights. But it can be used the other way around

---

[438] Pils, EM 'If Anything Happens' supra note 327.

[439] Caney, S (2005) *Justice Beyond Borders. A Global Political Theory* Oxford University Press at 83.

[440] Fabre, C (1998) 'Constitutionalising Social Rights' (6, 3) *The Journal of Political Philosophy* 263.

[441] Caney, S *Justice* supra note 437 at 83, emphasis added. On this basis Caney challenges the exclusion of some rights in Rawls's *Law of Peoples*, arguing that since the rights in this list *do not hang together well*, it would be a mistake to include some rights and exclude others.

if different rights are in fact interdependent.[442] The indivisibility and interdependence of rights has been affirmed both in the Bangkok Declaration on Human Rights of 1993, ratified by more than 30 Asian states, and in the Vienna Declaration adopted in the same year by the World Conference on Human Rights. The interpretation of these declarations offered by human rights advocates is that civil and political rights may not be traded off for economic and social rights. The interpretation preferred by the Chinese government is that there should not be an overemphasis on civil and political rights, but sufficient weight should be given to economic and social rights. [443] If indivisibility and interdependence are interpreted as Caney and Fabre do, it seems to follow that the protection of one right entails the protection of other rights. Therefore, the introduction of some rights and not others in the Chinese legal system may eventually make it necessary to provide other rights in order to protect the ones already in place.

The introduction of the concept of individual human rights in China could be defined as 'pragmatic adaptation' to external, irresistible factors. However, as previously explored, it is also the result of a serious and conscious effort by jurisprudence to reshape and adapt this concept to the existing Chinese reality, perceived as an internal need and not as an external imposition. As Zhu Suli[444] comments, recourse to legal provisions and legal theory as a guide to legal practice cannot entirely take the place of trial and error in the effort to overcome conceptual and theoretical

---

[442] Viola, F (2000) *Etica e metaetica dei diritti umani* Gisppichelli at 82. Viola argues that this reasoning holds up so long as no hierarchies are understood to exist among rights, but not if some rights are allowed to trump others, as when, in the face of scarce resources, public policies can promote economic growth without any of the institutional constraints in place to protect the worst off—a scenario that leads to poverty.

[443] Chen, AHY 'Conclusion' supra note 21 at 508. See also Davis, MC (1995) 'Chinese Perspectives on the Bangkok Declaration and the Development of Human Rights in Asia' (89) *Am. Soc'y Int'l L. Proc.* 157.

[444] Zhu Suli (2004) *Daolu tongxiang chengshi - zhuanxing zhongguo de fazhi* [All Roads Lead to Cities - Rule of Law in China's Transformation] Falu chubanshe at 94-95.

challenges, to which end it is also essential to draw on the resources that can be found in Chinese legal tradition itself.

The number of rights that have been legalised is remarkable and, since the 1990s, the government has redoubled its effort to increase awareness of legal rights among the population. The rhetoric of the slogans,[445] along with the broader effort to educate people about the law, which is deemed necessary for the market to function properly,[446] ended up having long-term consequences that national policy had not intended or predicted. The working theory was that by instilling a greater legal consciousness in citizens, the government could also increase their demand that the law be complied with and enforced. But the same consciousness also generated a whole menu of other demands: citizens demanded legal recognition of new rights and guarantees,[447] coupled with greater accountability in the form of legal compliance by bureaucrats and officials themselves, as well as a fuller scheme of laws regulating their action and more clearly setting out their relation to citizens.[448]

The protection of human rights is also supported by an argument highlighting another set of unintended consequences of recognising a limited range of rights and protections: these are consequences deemed undesirable from the standpoint of the single party in power, and the argument is based on the perceived meaning of public promises,[449] which is to say that the

---

[445] In the Mao Zedong era, slogans were used to spread political messages in every corner of the state and to drum up general support and adhesion to the mass mobilisation, or 'campaign'. Slogans are now used as effective means to keep people informed about public policy, while garnering wide support for the same policies.

[446] The idea here is that the law cannot function properly without broad spontaneous compliance with it (hence the need to educate people about its content, methods, and purpose), and that such compliance in turn supports the functioning of the market.

[447] A similar argument is put forward in Alford, WP (1993) 'Double-Edged Swords Cut Both Ways: Law and Legitimacy in the PRC' (122) *Daedalus* 45.

[448] For recent developments in administrative law and administrative litigation law, see Palmer, M (2006-2007) 'Controlling the State? Mediation in Administrative Litigation in the PRC' (16) *Transnational Law and Contemporary Problems* 165.

[449] A similar argument can be found in Elster, J (2000) 'Arguing and Bargaining in Two Constituent Assemblies' (2) *U. Pa. J. Const. L.* 345 available at <https://scholarship.law.upenn.edu/jcl/vol2/iss2/1>; and in Elster, J (2000) *Ulisses Unbound. Studies in Rationality, Precommitment and Constraints* Cambridge

government's commitment to the protection of human rights may come to be viewed as a promise. Regardless of whether the officials who make a promise actually *believe* what they say or actually want to keep their word, making a promise gives rise to an attitude of trust in the person who makes the promise, and an expectation that the promise will be kept, while failure to fulfil the promise gives rise to discontent and distrust, which in turn undermines the legitimacy of the power holder. In short, *the very action of promising* generates an *expectation of fulfilment*, such that unfulfilled promises deprive the promisor of public support. This is not to say that the CCP will keep its promise to respect human rights, lest its legitimacy should be undermined, but rather that it has a strong reason to do so.

Even so, it doesn't seem that the Chinese people see it as a priority to democratise their system of government (by demanding political pluralism and democratic competition in choosing their representatives). On the one hand, their expectations of material wealth have to a sufficient extent been met by way of economic growth. Moreover, pluralism is in large part still viewed by the Chinese as synonymous with 'chaos' and 'instability', and hence with 'danger'. It is considered a danger not in itself but as a potential source of conflict (absent a trusted and reliable procedure for resolving conflicts), or at least this is what emerges from the public discussion. It is difficult to assess the nature of the general support for one-party rule. This support may not be so widespread or genuine. Serious concerns that such support is in fact manufactured on a mass scale come from the state's practice of 'spiritual socialist education' under Article 19 of the 1982 Constitution of the PRC. The imbalance of power, concentrated in

---

University Press; Elster analyses the dynamics of discussion amongst members of the American and the French Constituent Assemblies. Elster suggests that the public nature of the debates forced the various parties within the assemblies to frame their specific parochial interests as matters of public interest. Paradoxically, Elster argues, this hypocritical stance had positive effects: it made it difficult to sustain self-interested strategies without taking public interest into due consideration. Elster describes this process as the civilising force of hypocrisy. Doubtless, this is not the case when the negotiation and deal-making happen behind closed doors.

the hands of the government, makes the official voice seem stronger than it is, all the while isolating intellectuals and the common people. The channels through which different ideas and opinions are discussed are mainly unofficial; among them, an important role is played by online forums and discussion groups.[450] This engagement therefore takes place on the third level of discussion on human rights within China: not that of the state or that of the intelligentsia but that of public opinion at large.[451]

---

[450] Chase, MS (2002) *You've got dissent! Chinese dissident use of the internet and Bejing's counter-strategies* Rand. See also Cheung, ASY (2007) 'Public Opinion Supervision: A Case Study of Media Freedom in China' (20) *Columbia Journal of Asian Law* 357; Liebman, BL (2005) 'Watchdog or Demagogue? The Media in the Chinese Legal System' (105) *Columbia Law Review* 1.

[451] Of great importance in this respect is the activity of NGOs. See Lee, DC (2000) 'Legal Reform in China: A Role for Nongovernmental Organizations' (25) *Yale J. Int'l L.* 363; Cf. Liu Meng, Yanhong Hu and Minli Liao (2009) 'Traveling theory in China: contextualization, compromise and combination' (9, 4) *Global Networks* 529.

CHAPTER SEVEN

Theorising About Rights: The Orthodox Position

Introduction

The previous chapters explained how legal scholars critically engage with the official views of the Chinese leadership within the limitations imposed by the government on academic discussion. The analysis demonstrated that Chinese scholarship is capable of exerting a moderate influence on public discussion and legal reforms despite censorship by the authorities. Having defined the context in which scholars work, the remaining two chapters further explore how they engage both with official Marxist theories, and with liberal theories of human rights. The discussion will highlight the ways in which the scholars belonging to different currents make use of and interpret traditional arguments elaborated by Confucian scholars.

The party holds an orthodox view on human rights rooted in its theoretical and political tradition, that of Marxism, Leninism, and Maoism. The remaining two chapters discuss academics' engagement with the latter in different embryonic or mature theories of rights.

After the Chinese government's publication of the first white paper on human rights in 1991[452]—and following the Bangkok declaration on human rights by the Asian countries in 1993—the Chinese government endorsed the idea of human rights in response to criticism from the West. However, the post-Cultural Revolution debate on human rights had already started in the 1980s, when the government began to advance the claim of a Chinese view on human rights in opposition to Western theories. This idea of rights put forward by the government claims to reject Western individualism and

---

[452] The 1991 White Paper on Human Rights was issued by the Information Office of the State Council of the PRC and describes the overall approach to human rights. See Information Office of the State Council of the PRC (1991) 'White Paper on Human Rights in China' available at <http://www.china.org.cn/e-white/7/index.htm>. Since then, the Chinese government issued several white papers and three action plans on human rights (in 2009, 2012 and in 2016).

to focus instead on distinctively Chinese notions of social acceptance and harmony as criteria to identify the scope and the limitations of individual rights.[453]

Some legal scholars in China have embraced these views, and claimed that, since conceptions of human rights are country-specific, it is important to produce discourses of 'human rights with Chinese characteristics'. The debate on the 'Chinese characteristics' of human rights was picked up by academics but it did not develop into a fully-fledged and coherent theory of rights. A similar, parallel debate initiated at the political level by the former prime minister of Singapore Lee Kuan Yew concerned Asian values. The Asian values supporters affirmed that there is an 'Asian' preference for collective harmony, subsistence and solidarity, and this identity is opposed to the Western emphasis on the individual and the pursuit of her interests, desires, etc at the expense of the collective. Among the most persuasive critics of the Asian values approach is Amartya Sen.[454]

The position in line with the governmental view is inspired by Marxist-Maoist-Leninist thought, according to the different interpretations of this thought given by the subsequent leaderships of Deng Xiaoping, Jiang Jemin, Hu Jintao, and, most recently, Xi Jinping. The Marxist perspective in China is influenced by Leninist views developed by Mao Zedong: an interpretation which focuses on revolution, class struggle, dictatorship of the proletariat, and the role of the state as an instrument of that dictatorship, even if the most recent Marxist scholarship has lessened the emphasis on class struggle and dictatorship of the proletariat.

To better grasp this complex process of evolution, it is also important to clarify that some Maoist notions resemble Confucian ideas of society, law and rights. According to Weatherley the influence of the Confucian heritage on Chinese Marxist thinkers in formulating certain ideas about rights is direct. [455] As Cheng Liaoyuan and Wang Renbo noted and as others [456] argue, contemporary Chinese conceptions of human rights are built upon

---

[453] Bangkok declaration on human rights 1993; Shih, CY (1993) 'Contending Theories of Human Rights with Chinese Characteristics' (29) *Issues and Studies* 42.

[454] Sen, A (1997) 'Human Rights and Asian Values' *Sixteenth Morgenthau Memorial Lecture on Ethics and Foreign Policy* Carnegie Council on Ethics and International Affairs.

[455] Weatherley, R *The Discourse of Human Rights* supra note 22 at 102.

[456] Ibid. Edwards, RR; Henkin, L and Natan, AJ (1986) *Human Rights in Contemporary China* Columbia University Press.

foundations laid by late-Qing and Republican thinkers. Such foundations reflect a Confucian imprint which is visible in the primacy of the collective, in the idea that human rights serve the needs of the state rather than the individual, and in the positive evaluation of selflessness. In the following, it will be discussed how the Confucian premises and ideas influenced Marxist thinkers. For example, the thesis of the prevalence of duties over rights resembles the Confucian idea, explored in Chapter Two, that individuals are defined by their duties in social relationships. The analysis in the next chapter will show how Confucian philosophical premises influence liberal Chinese scholars as well. Bearing this in mind, one realises how contemporary Chinese theories of rights, not only those based on Marxist views, but also those inspired by liberal approaches, are influenced by cultural premises originating within the Chinese intellectual tradition.[457] As the analysis progresses, it will become clear that the interpretations and the theoretical implications of arguments elaborated by traditional Confucian authors and neo-Confucian authors are in fact very different, and to what extent they differ from the view upheld by Marxist scholars and backed up by the elite in power.

The Orthodoxy: Marxist Approaches to Human Rights

The Marxist view on human rights, which dominated the debate until the end of the 20th century, is referred to here as the 'orthodox view'. The theory of human rights elaborated by orthodox Chinese Marxist legal scholars is in open ideological opposition to the alleged characteristics and assumptions of the so-called 'bourgeois theory of rights'. The critique pivots on the claim that capitalist societies are divided between rich and poor, exploiters and exploited. According to Marxist intellectuals, capitalism has grave moral flaws: not only inequalities in wealth, income and opportunities, but also excessive individualism, competition and materialism. Bearing this in mind, Chinese Marxist intellectuals advance several arguments to show the alleged superiority of socialist societies with regard to human rights in respect to liberal accounts.

---

[457] Cheng Liaoyuan and Wang Renbo *Quan li lun* supra note 2; Weatherley, R *The Discourse of Human Rights* supra note 22.

Some scholars stress that, even though the idea of human rights originated in capitalist societies, only socialist societies provide the economic conditions for the full and universal enjoyment of rights. Others maintain that the natural rights[458] upheld by the bourgeoisie are historical products of the past, and that socialist rights 'represent a higher level of human rights'. Still others hold that while in a capitalist society one class enjoys all the rights and the other bears all the duties because of the separation of the workers from the means of production, in the socialist system every person has equal human rights and duties, and it is by fulfilling their duties that citizens partake in the common wellbeing. According to this view, human rights achieve full equality among people through the realisation of the public ownership of the means of production and the principle of equal distribution to all workers.

To better assess the present significance of these orthodox Marxist theories it is important to further unpack the context of China's transition towards a socialist market economy which gives more space to privatisation. By the end of the 20th century, 81% of the market was already privately owned,[459] and there is now a consolidated consensus, in the party as well as in society, in favour of the realisation of a market economy. Nevertheless, there are visible tensions concerning the way in which this economy is governed. The general perception amongst a number of scholars is that in order to make the Marxist critique consistent with the market economy, its focus would have to change. In this perspective, Marxist theorists should no longer maintain that all social evils are intrinsically linked to the market. On the contrary, their approach should be framed as a normative critique of the effects of an unregulated—or badly regulated—capitalism, which can be addressed in a way that is consistent with a market economy. Such a criticism could then be viewed as attacking those ideologies that accept any outcome of market exchanges as inherently justified from a normative point of view.[460]

---

[458] Natural rights can be considered the origin of subjective rights in the modern sense, but the link between natural rights and human rights is at least problematic.

[459] Cavalieri, R *La legge e il rito* supra note 290 at 127 (translation of the author).

[460] Theories of this kind were advanced, for instance, by libertarian thinkers such as Hayek, F (1973) *Law, Legislation, and Liberty* University of Chicago Press; Hayek, F (1976) The Mirage of Social Justice University of Chicago Press; Hayek, F (1979) *The Political Order of a Free People* University of Chicago Press; Nozick, R (1974) *Anarchy, State and Utopia* Basic Books.

Doubtless, this criticism has its merits, particularly for what concerns the application and balancing of the principles of equality and freedom within market-driven states.[461] One could argue that liberal states often fail to adequately establish these principles. Furthermore, the case of India has shown that democracy and rights protection can exist even in a developing country that has a mostly socialist economy. Even though India has now endorsed a market economy, the Indian experience provides evidence against the argument that collective rights as well as social, economic and cultural rights, should be emphasised by socialist regimes at the expense of the enjoyment of civil and political rights.[462]

These arguments are certainly valid. However, in the context of China, the Marxist approach has to face the competition of other interpretations that also criticise unregulated capitalism and that affirm the *normative* relevance of the principle of equality, broadly understood as including substantive and economic equality. Those liberal theories argue not only for the equal enjoyment of the so-called negative freedoms, but also for equal entitlement to primary goods (Rawls) or resources (Dworkin), or for the equal enjoyment of substantive freedoms or capabilities (Sen). Furthermore, among liberals there are scholars who argue for the intrinsic value of economic equality, besides the instrumental one.[463]

The Main Tenets of the Orthodox Position

A number of Chinese Marxist legal scholars have recognised that human rights have a role to play in the Chinese legal system. However, they specify that in the context of a legal system in a developing socialist society, these rights cannot be considered

---

[461] For a reconstruction of the debate see Schiavello, A (2000) 'Principio di eguaglianza: breve analisi a livello concettuale e filosofico politico' (14) *Ragion Pratica* 65.

[462] Sharma, A (2006) *Are Human Rights Western? A Contribution to the Dialogue of Civilizations* Oxford University Press at 108 stresses that even if the Indian experience may have partially failed, it is still a valid argument against the association of a hierarchy of rights with a specific economic regime. I should also add that the Indian experiment has been less successful than China in remedying the most severe forms of destitution, and in providing security to its citizens.

[463] Marmor, A (2007) *Law in the Age of Pluralism* Oxford University Press at 260.

equivalent to those rights which exist in a capitalist society. Consequently, they argue that in China human rights are to be understood in a different way. A general description of the Marxist approach to human rights is provided by Albert Chen, who argues that this approach is characterised by the combination of the following views: 1) an economic view; 2) an historical view; 3) a class view;[464] 4) a state view; 6) a developmental view; 5) a view on the unity of rights and duties; 6) an emancipatory view.[465]

Similarly, Nathan lists six major characteristics that make Chinese rights different from those enshrined in the US Constitution: (1) Chinese rights are granted only to progressive classes; (2) their provision varies from one Constitution to the next; (3) they are programmatic, open-ended, and reflective of emerging goals; (4) they are always malleable, ie open to legislation that reflects changing cultural and socio-political values; (5) they are enforced by social practice rather than through formal judicial institutions; (6) their implementation is dependent upon hierarchical patterns of deference to achieve worth rather than upon ideals of popular sovereignty. According to Nathan, while in the US rights are understood as being universal and unchangeable, a-historical and a-cultural, in the Chinese context the idea of eternal human rights has been substituted with a view of rights as evolving social constructions, reflecting the conditions of Chinese society and the attitudes of Chinese citizens.

One of the core ideas of the 'orthodox view' is that rights are linked to the economy, development, and history. This evolutive-historical approach acquires a specific direction by linking human rights to levels of development. The link has both a factual and a normative component. The factual component consists in the idea that economic conditions characterising the level of development of a country determine the conceptions of human rights that are elaborated in that country. This is reflective of the Marxist view that economic conditions determine laws and ideologies, and especially that economic relations determine the content of human rights within those specific circumstances brought about by particular historical developments. The connection between rights and development also supports a normative approach. This holds it wrong to introduce the same rights in societies which have different levels of development.

---

[464] 'The importance attached to class status in early Soviet rights thinking had a significant influence on the Chinese Marxist understanding of rights' Weatherley, R *The Discourse of Human Rights* supra note 22 at 91.
[465] Chen, A 'Developing Theories' supra note 39 at 140.

The normative approach therefore posits that introducing rights in an underdeveloped society only pertinent to those societies with a higher level of development could hinder development in the former, negatively affecting societal welfare and security. It therefore proposes the realisation of those specific human rights appropriate to the level of development of that society. Here are some examples of how these notions influence Chinese scholars.

Lin Han and Li Lin,[466] for instance, refer to the Marxist view that 'the essence of man lies in his true social connections, and yet human rights are no more than the rights of the egoistic man separated from his human essence and from the community'.[467] Similarly, Shen Zhonglin[468] argues that although human rights are moral in nature, they are products of historical development and have a basis in class, according to the theory of dialectical materialism.[469] Focusing on the implication of Marxist texts, Guo Daohui[470] also argues that rights have a class nature, since their actual enjoyment is class-dependent. However, Guo Daohui adds that human rights also have a general nature in that they are rights that all ought to have as human beings. In his opinion, history is a progression toward the generalisation of human rights. In the course of history, human rights have expanded to higher levels.[471] Nevertheless, for Guo Daohui, the struggle for historical progress, while leading in the long term to the expansion and generalisation of rights, may in the short term negatively affect some classes and their rights: 'The inevitable price for progress in human society (including progress in human rights) is the suppression of the human rights of certain classes. Such historical injustice may

---

[466] Li Lin（李林）is a professor at the Chinese Academy of Social Sciences. Chen, AH 'Developing Theories' supra note 39 at 135.

[467] Sun Guo Hua (ed) (1998) *Basic Theory of Law* Tianjin Renmin Chubanshe; Chen, AH 'Developing Theories' supra note 39 at 139.

[468] Shen Zhonglin (1991) 'Human Rights: Rights in Which Sense?' (5) *Chinese Legal Science* 22.

[469] Ibid.

[470] Guo Daohui, ((郭道晖) eminent legal scholar and professor of the China Law Society. Guo Daohui (2009) 'Renquan de Guojia Baozhang Yiwu' [State Responsibility for Human Rights Protection] (27, 8) *Hebei Faxue* 10.

[471] Guo Daohui quoted in Chen, AH 'Developing Theories' supra note 39 at 138-139

only be balanced by the overall interest of historical development'.[472] In his opinion, therefore, revolution and class struggle are the sole methods through which more rights are obtained.

Another fundamental tenet of the 'orthodox view is that human rights are created by the state through law. It is important to note that the emphasis on the economic-developmental foundation of human rights does not exclude the statist perspective, which also characterises the orthodox Marxist approach. This perspective holds that legal institutions and in particular rights are linked to economic conditions, but only through the power of the state can they become effective realities. Critically, in this perspective rights are not entitlements against the state, but rather goods provided by the state: only when the state ensures the effectiveness of everybody's rights, providing everyone with equal material means for their enjoyment, can rights become concrete; until then they remain merely abstract or ideological.

The statist perspective therefore holds that rights are bestowed by the state through legislation. Is it also often claimed that the legal system in capitalist societies ensures that rights protect the interest of the ruling class, maintaining a structure of exploitation of the subordinate classes through the illusion of equality and liberty. One of the most representative scholars upholding this theory is Zhang Guangbo.[473] Zhang argues that socialist human rights represent an evolution with respect to capitalist human rights. He argues that while the latter have the objective of protecting capital and property, the former protect public ownership of the means of production and the principle of distribution according to work. Bearing this contextualisation in mind, one realises that Chinese orthodox theories hold that individual rights are not absolute[474] but determined by the material, historical and cultural conditions of each country. It therefore follows that rights are country-specific. However, in the theories proposed by these scholars there is notably no specification of what these arguments imply with regard to specific cases.

Another key aspect of the Marxist approach is the subordination of human rights to collective needs, implying that

---

[472] Ibid.

[473] Zhang Guangbo (1990) 'Jianchi makesi zhuyi de renquan guan' [Adhere to the Marxist View of Human Rights] (4) *Zhongguo faxue* [Chinese Law] 10. Chen, AH 'Developing Theories' supra note 39 at 136.

[474] The question of the absolute nature of human rights is debated by jurisprudence and has to be distinguished from the problem of their universality.

individual rights can be waived for the sake of the state's interest. According to this view, collective rights trump individual rights. As Weatherley notes:

> First of all, since rights are provided by the state, when the state is threatened, the fundamental task to implement human rights consists in defending state sovereignty, even when this requires sacrificing the rights of some individuals. Therefore, rights can be compressed and even sacrificed completely in case it is necessary to do so. Moreover, according to the Marxist perspective the conditions under which individual rights are removed do not have to be exceptional. On the contrary, any right which is seen as harmful to the interest of the state and society can be duly rescinded.[475]

Following Weatherley's first point, it can be added that secondly, and more generally, the Marxist approach holds that when there appears to be a conflict between individual rights and collective interests, the latter should prevail. From the Marxist perspective, this subordination of individual rights to collective interests contributes to the realisation of rights, since it is assumed that the realisation of rights can only be achieved when collective interests are realised. The relationship between individual rights and collective interest is framed in the following way: by exercising one's rights in ways that harm the collective welfare or interest one would also harm the equal realisation of human rights, while waiving one's rights for the sake of the collective welfare guarantees the maximum enjoyment of individual rights—as available under the prevailing socio-economic conditions—even if the person concerned does not exercise these rights directly.

This understanding rests on the Marxist definition of the human being as a 'social animal' who only realises herself within society. Therefore, collective development is a pre-condition of each individual's development, and individual flourishing is dependent on collective development. Significantly, Nathan argues that this subordination of individual rights to collective aims reflects not only the Marxist approach, but also the Confucian tradition. He states that

---

[475] Weatherley, R *The Discourse of Human* supra note 22 at 95.

'the Confucian understanding of the empirical and ethical relationship between the individual and society continues to inform Chinese political thought this century - the factual proposition that properly understood the individual's interests are inseparable from those of society, and the ethical injunction to place the interest of society first'. [476] Notably, as we shall see later in the chapter, this subordination of human rights to collective interests may lead to very different outcomes depending on the way in which collective goods are characterised.

Another important aspect common to all the Marxist views of human rights within China is the relatively higher importance attributed to social, cultural and economic rights over civil and political rights (including all the liberties and freedoms associated with the second group of rights). Marxist approaches, both in China and elsewhere, have tended to downplay the significance of individual rights and, in particular, liberty rights. These include the so-called negative liberties, ie freedom against interference from others (most importantly the state), which encompass the freedom of expression, information, association, movement, property, etc (see, among others, Waldron 1987). Following Marx (1843), Marxist scholars whether within or outside China often claimed that these rights do not belong to humans per se, but rather reflect the interests and social positions of bourgeois individuals in a capitalist society. These bourgeois individuals are identified as egoists who see fellow humans only as obstacles or instruments in the pursuit of their individual goals. Marx (1843) argued that people in capitalist societies live double lives within which are reflected different normative entitlements. People in capitalist societies are self-centred economic and social actors entitled with property and liberty rights, yet they are also supposed to be cooperative members of their community, namely, citizens (*citoyens*) entitled with rights to political participation.

This schizophrenic social and normative framework is considered to have arisen as a result of particular historical circumstances, in that the law reflects economic relations. This framework, Marx argues, did not exist before capitalism, and it will be overcome when a communist society is constructed. Marx assumed that in a future communist society law itself is overcome, and in any case a different kind of normative arrangement will be needed. Therein, since individuals will become species-beings, they will

---

[476] Nathan AJ 'Sources' supra note 43 at 141-143.

abandon egoistic perspectives and will instead become collaborative members of a just community, to which each will contribute according to their capacities and from which they all receive according to their needs.

Marxist approaches dismiss liberty rights as legal instruments of egoist individuals. Furthermore, they also reject them as being formal or abstract. Specifically, Marxist approaches claim that liberty rights have little practical significance for large parts of the population, namely, for all those who do not have the material means for the effective enjoyment of the liberties formally attributed to them. Consequently, Marxist thinkers argue that the universal conferral of some abstract rights—without the provision of equal means for the exercise of these rights—may contribute to inequality and injustice.

Marxist approaches also argue that the abstract conception of rights, typical of liberal theories, overlooks the particular social circumstances which characterise the environment where people live. For this reason, Chinese orthodox views preferred the expression 'citizens' basic rights and duties', because it was considered less abstract than 'human rights'. This expression was also favoured because of the link between rights and duties which accords with the theory of the unity of rights and duties proposed by orthodox Marxist ideology (see section below). However, the tendency of Chinese scholars to downplay the significance of the attribution of abstract rights may be linked not only to Marxist approaches, but also to legal thinking in imperial China.[477] According to the latter, each situation should be regulated by a rule specific to the specific case, emerging from the very circumstances of that case, rather than being regulated by a rule that is abstract and general.[478]

---

[477] Consiglio, E 'Early Confucian Legal Thought' supra note 197; Peerenboom, RP (1990) 'Confucian Jurisprudence: Beyond Natural Law' (36) *Asian Culture Quarterly* 12; Peerenboom, RP (1993) 'What's Wrong with Chinese Rights? Toward a Theory of Rights with Chinese Characteristics' (6) *Harvard Human Rights J.* 29; MacCormack, G *The Spirit* supra note 199.

[478] In the Chinese context, 'the changing and fluid constitutions register an emergent, empathetic order rather than a set of given criteria around which order can be effected.' Hall, DL and Ames, RT (1991) *Thinking through Confucius* State University of New York Press at 166.

Finally, Marxist orthodoxy also criticises liberty rights for having an ideological function. Liberty rights are criticised for creating an illusion that individuals are free. On the contrary, from the Marxist perspective all individuals in a capitalist society, even those who benefit from social inequality, are unfree, being subject to the impersonal laws of the capitalist market economy. Only in a socialist-communist social framework, which overcomes the market, can individuals be really free; their freedom consists in their active participation in a community.

These ideological premises explain why orthodox Marxist legal theorists have generally viewed civil and political liberty rights (freedoms of speech, assembly, movement, economic initiative, personal property, etc) with scepticism, and why they have emphasised the significance of economic and social rights (the right to food, education, employment, etc). It is true however that liberty rights have occasionally also been affirmed from a Marxist perspective. These affirmations have been proposed under the premise that despite being a historical achievement of capitalist societies, these rights could be relevant for the working classes and are therefore potentially possible under the conditions of socialism. Nonetheless, even in these occasional affirmations, the point is maintained that the focus must be on economic equality and development, without which formal rights remain ineffective. Based on these arguments, China has signed but not yet ratified the International Covenant on Civil and Political Rights (ICCPR), although it has ratified the International Covenant on Economic, Social and Cultural Rights (ICESCR).[479]

Historically, the PRC has showed a preference for economic, social and cultural rights over civil and political rights and freedoms. The reasons for that preference are political and ideological, but they are also tightly linked to the differences between the two categories of rights. The distinction between civil and political rights and economic, social and cultural rights corresponds—in the classification generally accepted—to that between first and second generation rights,[480] sanctioned by their provision in two different international documents: the ICCPR and the ICESCR.[481]

---

[479] Notably, this latter covenant has not yet been ratified by the United States.

[480] Bobbio, N (1991) *The Age of Rights* Wiley.

[481] The provision in two different international documents was strongly advocated by the US representative, who argued that the realisation of economic, social and cultural rights was only a long-term goal, while civil and political rights could be immediately realised. See Beitz, Charles R (2011) *The Idea of Human Rights*

This distinction between the two categories of rights has been the subject of an ongoing debate.[482] Those who doubt that economic, social and cultural rights can be classified as such usually put forward one or many of the following arguments. First of all, only civil and political rights would be rights as properly defined, while social rights have been considered 'fake rights' or 'non-rights'. The reason commonly adduced to support this affirmation is related to the high costs necessary for their realisation. Their recognition in law is in the majority of cases regarded as *flatus vocis*. Secondly, if rights are defined as valid claims with a certain content and enjoyed by certain subjects, determined by legal norms, and if to every right must correspond a specific obligation for a given subject, either public or private, in the case of social rights it would not be possible to determine their content for each subject entitled to them before their institutionalisation.

Furthermore, social rights would not be enforceable because their content and the entitled subject are not universal, and because they possess politico-constitutional value rather than legal-constitutional value, thus being more similar to political intentions. Moreover, social and economic rights would be directly influenced by circumstances of fact. The argument pivoting on the difference between positive and negative obligations holds that 'rights in any defensible sense depend upon the autonomy, freedom, and will of each person to develop what he already is. We do not have to show ourselves that we "deserve" them. Positive rights ought to be considered a matter of policy, of results of choice, work and enterprise'.[483] However, the protection of civil and political rights also entails costs for their realisation. For example, a functioning judicial

---

Oxford University Press and also Roberston, R (1994) 'Measuring State Compliance with the Obligation to Devote the "Maximum Available Resources" to Realising Economic, Social and Cultural Rights' (16) *Human Rights Quarterly* 693. China has signed both Covenants but has ratified only the ICESCR.

[482] Economic, social and cultural rights are not alien to the liberal tradition, but it is generally assumed that this tradition prefers civil and political rights, contrary to socialist tradition. For a synthesis of the debate see Diciotti, E (2006) *Il Mercato delle Libertà* Il Mulino at 73.

[483] Schall, JV (1987) 'Human Rights as an Ideological Project' (32) *Am. J. Juris.* 47 at 59.

system has to be established in order to ensure actual protection for freedoms and civil rights. It follows that, from a theoretical point of view, it is reasonable to exclude that cultural, social and economic rights are a weaker category of rights[484]: the differences between the two classes of rights concern the content of the obligation rather than the structure of the rights.[485]

An obvious reason for the preference for economic and social rights is the scarce interest an authoritarian regime has in expanding the scope of personal civil and political freedoms, such as freedom of expression and freedom of conscience. Article 35 of the 1982 PRC Constitution enshrined the rights of freedom of speech, press and assembly.[486] Nevertheless, these freedoms cannot be exercised if they conflict with the goals and the four cardinal principles expressed in the Preamble to the Constitution: the leadership of the Communist party, the socialist road, Marxist-Leninist-Mao Zedong thought and the democratic dictatorship (democratic centralism). For these reasons these freedoms have been subject to systematic repression.

According to the prevailing jurisprudence (coinciding in this case with the official position of the government), the right to development[487] is given logical and substantial pre-eminence over all the other rights.[488] The content of the right to development is broad, but Chinese intellectuals generally indicate that its core contents are economic and social development. This right would not be separable from other human rights, because it would offer the conditions of material stability in the absence of which no other rights can be realised. Understood as 'the right to subsistence', this right has been considered as comparable with some ideas of traditional Chinese legal

---

[484] Trujillo (2000) 'La Questione dei Diritti Sociali' (14) *Ragion Pratica* 43 at 44.

[485] Ibid at 44.

[486] 'Citizens of the PRC enjoy freedom of speech, of the press, of assembly, of association, of procession and of demonstration' (Article 35 of the PRC Constitution).

[487] For a discussion on the right to development as a human right see Alston, P (1988) 'Making Space for New Human Rights: The Case of the Right to Development' (1) *Harvard Human Rights Y.B.* 3 and Marks, S (2004) 'The Human Right to Development: Between Rhetoric and Reality' (17) *Harvard Human Rights J.* 137.

[488] For a discussion on the right to development in relation to other human rights see Sethi, JD (1981) 'Human Rights and Development. Symposium South Asian Perspectives on Human Rights' (3) *Human Rights Quarterly* 11.

thought,[489] and consistent with the Mencian theory of 'people as the basis' discussed in Chapter Three.

The pre-eminence of the right to development was officially stated by the Chinese representatives at the Vienna Conference on human rights in 1993. The Chinese delegates affirmed that the government has the duty to guarantee the full realisation of the right to subsistence and development. They also affirmed that the realisation of all the other rights is conditioned by the full guarantee and fulfilment of the right to development. According to this view, the elimination of hunger and extreme poverty and the provision of basic medical care and other services are functional to the realisation of freedom. Security, understood as 'the existential state of freedom from fear', is also considered a basic human right providing protection from threats coming from within and outside the country.[490] Following this reasoning, the protection of economic, social and cultural rights would be functional to development and should therefore be elevated above the realisation of civil and political rights.[491] Once the level of development is increased (up to a certain threshold which is not analytically specified), then it would be possible to give protection to

---

[489] Classical legal doctrines, and that of Mencius in particular, provided a legal justification for rebellion against the emperor. If the emperor failed to guarantee a minimum standard of material wealth sufficient for the survival of the population, or to secure the conditions of stability, peace and order, the people could legitimately rebel. The rebellion would have been legitimate and therefore successful, because at the same time Heaven would have withdrawn his mandate, the Tian Ming 天命 (see discussion in Chapter II). If carefully examined, though, the idea of a duty on the part of the emperor to guarantee certain living or welfare standards to his subjects has not been framed as a right to which the people are entitled. The seemingly religious character of the idea of the mandate of Heaven was probably present at the beginning, but was lost in later developments, while the pragmatic character of this justification of legitimacy remained.

[490] Luo, Haocai (2008) 'China Embarks a Road towards Human Rights Progress with Chinese Characteristics' (3) *Human Rights* 2 at 2.

[491] For a discussion of this argument see Howard, R (1983) 'The Fully-Belly Thesis: Should Economic Rights Take Priority Over Civil and Political Rights? Evidence from Sub-Saharian Africa' (5) *Hum. Rts. Q.* 467; Sen, A (1993) *Markets and Freedoms* Oxford Economic Papers.

civil and political rights.[492] This argument shows that the protection of rights is associated with and determined in relation to their pragmatic value. However, as explained in the next chapter, some scholars today strongly advocate for increased protection of the freedom of expression.[493] These scholars disentangle the realisation of this right from pragmatic considerations, and affirm the need to realise freedom of expression as a necessary step for the state to be legitimate.

Another point worth mentioning with regard to the basic tenets of the Chinese orthodox view of human rights has to do with the relationship between domestic and international human rights standards. This point is related to the understanding of sovereignty and international relations by Chinese scholars. Chen Zhonglin argues that the determination of the content of human rights should vary in different times and in different countries. The guiding principle is 'not to discuss human rights without giving due consideration to national conditions and not to abandon tradition when discussing human rights'.[494] Drawing a distinction between national and international legal domains, Chen argues that at the domestic level human rights should take precedence over sovereignty, while at the international level sovereignty should take precedence over human rights. This is because at the national level, government exists to protect the interests of the people and therefore the state must respect human rights.

At the international level, however, according to Chen, the principle of self-determination must be respected and must prevail over other principles that could open the way to foreign intervention. At the international level, respect for the right to self-determination therefore prevails over the right of intervention by other states to guarantee the human rights of the people in a certain country. Following the principle of self-determination, Chen argues that the people of a particular country should freely determine the content of human rights.[495] Thus, while Chen considers human rights to be absolute in principle, he sees them as being relative in their

---

[492] The political guidelines dictate that China must still be considered a developing country and no argument in support of the opposite claim is accepted.

[493] Among others: Chen Zhonglin 'Guanyu renqua' supra note 195; Li Buyun (2004) *New Constitutionalism in China* Falu Chubanshe; Cheng Liaoyuan and Wang Renbo *Quan li lun* supra note 2; Liang Zhiping (2006) 'Mingyu quan yu yanlun ziyou: Xuan ke an zhong de shifei yu qingzhong' [Reputation Right and Freedom of Speech: the Right and Wrong in Xuan Ke Case] (2) *Zhongguo Faxue* [China Legal Science] 143.

[494] Chen Zhonglin Ibid.

[495] Ibid.

realisation. In case of conflict between the abstract rights of one person and the beliefs held by the majority, the rights of that person should succumb.[496]

Chen's position is therefore consistent with dominant Marxist views. While acknowledging that there are common standards of human rights, Chen limits these commonalities by arguing that the area of consensus[497] is very restricted, usually regarding minimum levels of respect for human dignity (including for instance the prohibition of torture, inhumane and degrading treatment). For Chen, violations of such rights constitute a breach of 'international law and mankind's public morality, and the international community has the right to impose legitimate sanctions in response'. A general exception to this, as explicitly theorised, occurs when the state signs and ratifies international treaties, conventions, or agreements. States parties who sign and ratify international agreements should abide by the clauses of the convention or treaty, and implement the relevant human rights standards. This is a powerful statement to make because China has signed and ratified a number of international covenants, treaties, conventions and agreements.[498]

Having given a general introduction to Chinese Marxist approaches to human rights, in the following section I will focus on two more basic tenets of these approaches: the dialectical unity between rights and duties, and the fundamental harmony of interests between the state and the individual. As described below, both theories have potential implications for the actual enjoyment of rights, the definition of their limits, and the conditions for their enjoyment by their holders.

The Dialectical Unity of Rights and Duties and the Harmony of Interests between Individuals and the State

According to Marxist-Leninist theory, as interpreted in the thought of Mao Zedong, rights and duties constitute a dialectical unity. This

---

[496] Ibid.
[497] The definition of the nature of this consensus is unclear.
[498] For a non exhaustive list of the internationally binding documents signed by China, see note 2 in the Introduction.

thesis has been sustained by Shen Zhonglin, [499] whose conceptualisation resonates with the famous position of W.N. Hohfeld. Hohfeld sees fundamental legal positions, including rights and powers, as having correlatives and opposites.[500] While rights and duties appear to be opposite—the right being an advantage and the duty a disadvantage for the concerned individual—the thesis of the dialectical unity posits that they constitute a fundamental unity as complementary parts of the social position of the individual. By complying with their duties, citizens contribute to bring about a society where rights can be protected. Thus, a person is entitled to the protection of her rights only as long as she performs her duties towards the common good.

The conception of duty as the prevailing element in the dialectical unity is reflected in the formulation of rights in the Chinese Constitution. Here, the content of the duties and their hierarchy are specified as duties towards the state, society and the collective. Substantially however, the most important duties are those which are specified with reference to the state. In particular, the articles of the PRC 1982 Constitution prescribing citizens' rights and duties (Article 51 et seq) are modelled upon this theory of dialectical unity. To implement this, Article 51 of the Chinese Constitution sets clear limits upon the free exercise of rights: 'in exercising freedoms and rights, citizens of the PRC may not infringe upon the interest of the state, of society or of the collective or upon the lawful freedoms and rights of other citizens'. As explained by Gillespie, human rights are provided by the law, but must be applied 'in conformity with the interests of socialism and the people'. In other words, in the Chinese constitutional order, 'civil rights must conform to state-sponsored socio-political obligations.'[501] Other limitations are also found in the

---

[499] Shen Zhonglin 'Human Rights' supra note 466.

[500] 'Recognizing, as we must, the very broad and indiscriminate use of the term "right", what clue do we find, in ordinary legal discourse, toward limiting the word in question to a definite and appropriate meaning? That clue lies in the correlative "duty", for it is certain that even those who use the word and the conception "right" in the broadest possible way are accustomed to thinking of "duty" as the invariable correlative' (...) 'In other words if X has a right against Y that he shall stay off the former's land, the correlative (and equivalent) is that Y is under a duty toward X to stay off the place' Hohfeld, WN (1913) 'Some Fundamental Legal Conceptions as Applied in Judicial Reasoning' (23) *Yale L. J.* 16 at 31.

[501] Gillespie, J (2006) 'Evolving Concepts of Human Rights in Vietnam' in Peerenboom, R; Petersen, CJ and Chen, AHY (eds) (2006) *Human Rights in Asia: A*

Preamble to the Constitution, referring to the socialist spirit and socialist morality as a criterion for interpreting the scope and content of rights.

Significantly, while the subordination of the individual to the community corresponds to characteristics of communist orthodoxy, the unity of duties and rights also fits with notions inherent to classical Chinese Confucian philosophy as described in Chapter Two. Confucian legal philosophy holds that duties imposed by social roles can be understood as 'the correct action to perform in virtue of the right of the other subject'.[502] In this sense, the notion of 'correct action' or 'duty' encompasses that of 'rights'. Duties furthermore entail a particular significance and moral weight with respect to the notion of a right as being entitled to receive a certain treatment.[503] However, this is not the only resemblance between Marxist approaches and Chinese tradition.

Another core postulate of the orthodox Chinese Marxist doctrine of human rights is the fundamental harmony of interests between individuals and the state. In its Chinese variant,[504] the

---

Comparative Legal Study of Twelve Asian Jurisdictions, France and the USA Routledge 452 at 455-456.

[502] Kim, HI *Fundamental Legal Concepts* supra note 197 at 121

[503] In this regard, it is important to note Norberto Bobbio's argument that the conception of 'duties' in relation to 'rights' is a dominant feature of the moral history of mankind. Bobbio emphatically argues that the advent of the 'age of rights' is a 'Copernican revolution' in the field of morals. Accordingly, he argues that duty and right are correlative terms and that it is a matter of perspective as to which should be regarded as predominant. But interestingly, he adds that the reason why law first emerged as a list or codex of duties stemmed from the need to protect the social collective or group. Therefore, law originates from a social or collective perspective rather than a perspective based on the point of view of the individual (Bobbio, N (1999) *Teoria generale della politica* Einaudi at 432-440; see also Bobbio, N *The Age of Rights* supra note 478.

[504] This theory is derived from Marxist-Leninist doctrine. It sets the criteria for the just balance between individual interests and the general needs of the state. Priority is given to the needs of the state and national harmony, and individuals are therefore expected to subordinate their needs to those of the state. This theory has never been applied in full because the interests of the individual are still considered to some extent by Marxist-Leninist states. Both in China and Vietnam, 'In the mixed market-economy the state is increasingly using rights-based language to balance the public good against individual, civil, political and economic rights.' Art. 38 of the 1959

identifications and definitions of interests, as well as their syntheses, are determined by power holders. They are furthermore considered objective and legitimate and therefore 'scientific'. It is thus assumed that the party, as the vanguard of the people, determines both the individual and the collective good through scientific judgments. Such scientific judgments or syntheses are considered to be endowed with public normativity, and are sufficient to provide the criteria for authoritative decisions and for political action. In this perspective, the individual and the state constitute a moral unity, superior to the individual: a proposition which resembles, though on a larger scale, the Confucian idea—presented in Chapter Two—that the family is the fundamental unit of human relationships, and the state is analogous to the family.

From the Marxist-Leninist perspective, the negation of any real contraposition of interests between the state, society and the individual is based on the following reasoning: (1) the only source of power is the people; (2) the elite is the vanguard of the people; (3) the elite is capable of grasping and best representing the interests of the people, upon which the entire constitutional system of the Chinese state is organised. This reasoning is accepted within the framework of Marxism-Leninism but it is much criticised, and rightly, outside of this framework. However, the logical consequence of this reasoning on the organisation of power and the mechanisms set for its control is that there is no need to set up institutional checks on the persons and organs exercising power. This view is consistent with the idea that rights are granted by the state, created by law and in the same way can be negated by the state. Consequently, the Chinese theory of fundamental rights inspired by Marxist ideas downplays the role of human rights as limits to public powers. It affirms that the protection of human rights is only guaranteed through the Constitution[505] and the laws and it considers collective rights as progress in the understanding of human rights.

Once again, this view of a fundamental coincidence of interest between individuals and the state has ancient roots that can be traced

---

Vietnamese Constitution declared that 'the state forbids any person from using democratic freedoms to the detriment of the interests of the state and the people' (Gillespie, J 'Evolving Concepts' supra note 499 at 455).
[505] The Constitution, however, is not directly enforceable: the norms contained in it must be enacted in law in order to be applied by the judge.

back to Confucian thinking and to the ideal of 'harmony',[506] a 'principle of peaceful coexistence' that, once 'accepted by the whole society, will become the ritual and custom of that region'.[507] Conflict, as opposed to harmony, is considered an ethical and ontological evil, to be drastically eliminated though a reasonable distribution of benefits through consultation and argument.[508] The implications of the idea of the necessary harmony between individual and communal interests are highlighted particularly by Joseph Chan.[509] Simply put, when the justification of rights is a 'legitimate benefit', any benefit which is not defined as legitimate cannot be the ground for rights. In addition, the limitation and scope of each right is defined with reference to ethical principles.

In the analysis of the relationship between the state and the individual it is useful to distinguish the public sphere from the private domain. In the public domain the government has the duty to guide the citizens 'not to deviate', and its tools are persuasion and admonition. In fact, according to the Confucian ideal of harmony, one of the criteria to judge what is right is conformity to the natural path, which is harmonious. Thus, in this perspective correct order is coincident with the moral order, and the law, being the institutional protection of this moral order, is subject to ethics. At the level of private morality, the general principle of Confucian ethics is to prevent conflict, but the method is different because the actor is different. The moral agent, coinciding with the 'good' citizen, is expected to practise an 'inward psychological adjustment' with a 'subjective initiative'.[510] This practice of self-cultivation 'allows people to open the mind, to be willing to give up what they own with humanity, pure-heartedly and voluntarily, and this makes them reluctant to fight with others and invisibly eliminates the various

---

[506] On the idea of harmony and its relevance in ethical and legal thought see Delury, J (2008) 'Harmonious in China' (148) *Policy Review* 35; Hermann, M 'A Critical Evaluation' supra note 201; and Wei Yan 'Zhongguo gu dai' supra note 201.

[507] Ibid at 505.

[508] Ibid at 507.

[509] Chan, Joseph 'A Confucian Perspective' supra note 76 at 212.

[510] Wei Yan 'Zhongguo gu dai' supra note 201 at 508.

184

conflicts invisibly'.[511] This conception is still widespread amongst Chinese officials and laymen. To a degree these normative assumptions can be also found in the everyday interaction of Chinese people as internalised social norms. Internalised social norms can be defined as 'maxims that people want to obey because the maxims have been inculcated in them or are inborn'.[512]

Even though both Marxist and Confucian approaches assume the harmonious convergence of the individual and the common interest, there are some significant differences between the two. In the Marxist revolutionary perspective, the common interest pertains only to the proletarian class, and its interpretation is a prerogative of the vanguard. The proletariat is viewed as the universal class, namely, the class whose interest coincides with the interest of humanity in proceeding in its historical development toward the harmony of communism. Therefore, from the Marxist perspective, the long-term coincidence of interests between individuals and society does not exclude class struggle and the elimination of the 'reactionary' classes enacted, in the Maoist framework, through the permanent revolution. From the Confucian perspective, in contrast, harmony already characterises traditional social relations that are to be preserved and restored when they have been endangered or damaged.

Significantly, however, the revolutionary perspective has been progressively abandoned with the advent of the socialist semi-capitalist market economy, and has now become a view held by the minority. In addition, in the last few years the official understanding of harmony has absorbed and explicitly re-articulated aspects of the Confucian approach. The Chinese leadership has recently put forward the doctrine of harmony as the overarching ethical-political ideal for Chinese society. The rehabilitation and promotion of values and ethical ideas from the Confucian past is meant to provide an ethical background to contemporary Chinese society. The idea of class struggle has thus been substituted with the emphasis on the fundamental unity and integration of the different components of society, under a shared moral order and vision of the common good. In this perspective, the ideal of harmony supports the conception of a

---

[511] Ibid.

[512] 'These social norms appear attractive (…) to us not only because they are internalized, but also because they possess instrumental social value: they the guide individual's decisions and curb opportunistic behaviour in everyday life' Shavell, S and Kaplow, L (2000-2001) 'Fairness versus Welfare' (114) *Harv. L. Rev.* 961 at 973.

morally homogeneous society where there is no room for pluralism. The simultaneous presence of different views on good and evil, right and wrong,[513] is thus qualified as 'temporary imperfections that may occasionally cause problems, but they are ultimately accommodated making reference to a universal agreement upon what is right and good for society'.[514]

The Chinese leadership is aware that, following the changes in the economy, the Marxist-Leninist-Mao Zedong revolutionary ideology cannot provide a moral foundation for contemporary Chinese society. The Cultural Revolution—which discredited traditional values and tried to substitute them with Marxist ideology—is now regarded by the leadership of the CCP as a tragic mistake. The strategy of recovering traditional models—inaugurated by Hu Jintao and continued by Xi Jinping—is an attempt to fill the ethical vacuum created by the failure of the Cultural Revolution, and to maintain the legitimacy of the CCP. The attempt to define what ethical principles should dominate social interaction, and how they should be applied, by defining what is a 'legitimate interest', is in turn able to influence the determination of the actual scope of rights.[515] The appreciation of traditional virtues such as filial piety, loyalty and humaneness is presented as a reinforcement of the Chinese cultural identity, as a synthesis between socialism and humaneness (*ren*, a paramount Confucian principle and virtue, discussed in Chapter Two), and as a tool against widespread corruption.[516] However, one may wonder to what extent this emphasis on a shared tradition can deliver a political

---

[513] Lai, KL (2006) *Learning from Chinese Philosophies. Ethics of Interdependent and Contextualised Self* Ashgate
at 365-374.

[514] Clarke, DC and Feinerman, JV (1996) 'Antagonistic Contradictions: Criminal Law and Human Rights' in Lubman, S (ed) (1996) *China's Legal Reforms* Oxford University Press 135 at 135. Even if it is not possible to compare perfectionist theories with the one articulated here, it is possible to say that the notion of public morality entailed by this conception is similar to a 'perfectionist' notion; Dowdle, MW 'Of Parliaments' supra note 230 at 96; see also (Bobbio, N *The Age of Rights* supra note 478 at 124.

[515] In this way, as a matter of fact, the CCP is at present the ultimate authority with the power to determine the scope of rights.

[516] See Scarpari, M (2015) *Ritorno a Confucio* supra note 23 at 115-141.

morality that suits today's China, since the social atmosphere has profoundly changed. Pluralism of opinion is manifest and visible in Chinese society, and the public ideology does not provide solutions to the problem of the necessary cooperation between groups holding different views. However, it seems that even if the idea of revolutionary class struggle has been substituted by that of harmony, and the Cultural Revolution officially rejected, the other elements and fundamental assumptions of the Chinese orthodox conception of human rights, as described by Nathan and Chen, are still upheld in the Chinese human rights discourse. Let us now go on to describe this scenario.

CHAPTER EIGHT

The Incipit of New Theorisations

Introduction

This chapter explores the theories of rights by Chinese scholars that go beyond or challenge the orthodox view. It will be argued that some Chinese theories of human rights diverge remarkably from the official discourse of the government. More specifically, I will demonstrate that assuming that Chinese theories of rights are defined solely, or mainly, by their opposition to Western theories is inaccurate. Not all of the Chinese scholars have regarded differentiation from the West as a value in itself. After all, as the scholar He Weifang noted, Marxism is also a theory that originated in the West. In this chapter, some selected theories of rights will be analysed, in particular the ones that successfully integrated aspects from Western discourses as well as from their own tradition. In doing so, they see themselves as participating in global debates, and are interested in finding innovative Chinese contributions to the global debate on rights.

In the first decade of the 21st century, some legal scholars have articulated their own distinct views and have thus begun to 'own' their ideas and to develop a distinct Chinese perspective. Even though Marxist vocabulary still impregnates the current debate on human rights, a tension has progressively emerged between this ideological legacy and the need to consider liberal notions of individual autonomy and interests. Nevertheless, we will see how Chinese legal scholars reinterpret liberal theories or develop new justifications, drawing from a conception of the human person and society based on Chinese tradition. The result is an unprecedented hybridisation and new syntheses with justifications similar but not fully identical to the liberal ones.

To be sure, there is not a unitary, distinctively Chinese, uniform conception of rights, but rather a plurality of views. In the midst of these different positions, however, some distinctive elements can be identified, and these elements, it is argued here, can bring a valuable and meaningful contribution towards a global consensus on human rights.

The momentum gained by the scholarship upholding views different from the orthodox position, however, was drastically interrupted by the new guidelines provided for academic research since the beginning of 2015, described in Chapter Five. However, it is very important not to forget about the theories that the regime wants to silence, wipe out or minimise.

Human Rights Scholarship Beyond Marxist Jurisprudence

The orthodox Marxist positions described in the previous chapter dominated the scene until the end of the 20th century. Since the new millennium a new scholarship has emerged, debating and discussing the Marxist orthodoxy and, as a result, rejecting some of its core ideas. The emerging jurisprudence on human rights reflects the critical engagement with other theories of rights, for example the theories of natural law or the liberal accounts. In particular, at the core of the new jurisprudence is the idea that human rights originate from shared human nature. However, the expression 'human nature' should not be interpreted with reference to the theories of natural law, and human rights are in general, with the exception of some theorisations, not regarded as deriving from natural rights. Moreover, the conception of the human being embraced by Chinese scholars is not the classic liberal representation of the sovereign individual.

Following the premise that human rights derive from human nature, Chinese scholars identified the following defining characteristics of human rights: they are necessary (*buke huoque* 不可或缺) because they are related to the essential characteristics of human beings; they are non-transferable/non-negotiable (*buke zhuanrang* 不可转让) as they cannot be waived or sold; they are irreplaceable (*buke tidai* 不可替代) because they cannot be substituted; they possess mother nature or matrix (*muti* 母体) because they are capable of generating other rights; they are universal (普遍 *pubian*) because they pertain to every human being; they have common nature (*gongshi* 共似) because they are based on the characteristics that all human beings share; and they are stable (*wending* 穩定) because they do not change, as they are linked to human nature.[517]

---

[517] Xu Xianming *Principles* supra note 49 at 79-81.

The current Chinese jurisprudence theorises political rights and liberties as the core of human rights based on the social nature of human beings and on their self-determination in the political sphere. Given that the most general and essential expression of people's social nature and of their collective autonomy is participation in political society, these rights are particularly important because they guarantee the participation of each person in social and political life. However, more and more scholars have advocated for increased protection of the freedom of expression.[518] Disentangling the realisation of this right from pragmatic considerations, those scholars affirm the need to realise freedom of expression as a necessary step for the state to be legitimate.

These considerations echo liberal discourses. The influence of the Renaissance and Enlightenment thinking is visible and overtly acknowledged by scholars who developed those views. However, if we elaborate more on the way Chinese scholars understand the idea of 'human nature', from which they derive the basic characteristics of rights, we see that the concept is not coincident with the idea of human nature that grounds European and American thinking on rights. Human rights are not natural rights (*ziran quanli* 自然权利).[519] These focus on the individual understood as a monad, with original rights (life, liberty, equality). This individual is forced to join society in order to protect his natural rights (in Hobbes' account) and agrees to make a social contract (in Rousseau's account). The understanding of human nature is different in the Chinese theorisations.

In the Chinese theorisations under discussion, the fundamental premise is the relational and contextual nature of human beings. Every person is viewed as not just immersed in, but rather as being *constituted by* the net of his or her social relationships. In other words, humans are made of the relations they have with their family members and with other members of society. The theoretical premises of Chinese theories of human rights that resemble liberal discourses are

---

[518] Among others: Chen Zhonglin (2009) 'Several Basic Issues' supra note 195; Li Buyun (2004) 'On the Origin of Human Rights' (22-2) *Tribune of Political Science and Law* 11; Cheng Liaoyuan and Wang Renbo *Quan li lun* supra note 2.

[519] Liang Zhiping (1989) '"Fa ziran" yu "Ziran fa"' [Law of nature versus natural law] (2) *Zhonghuo shehui kexue* [Social Sciences in China] 209.

190

therefore based not only on the idea that human beings have a common nature, but also on the notion that human nature has an intrinsically relational aspect. The emphasis on the social and relational aspect of rights—which is seen as the common ground for the attribution of human rights—is a distinctive element of the Chinese discourse of rights. The intellectual roots of this conception may be traced back to Confucian views of the person as relational. Incidentally, these views are in line with the Marxist conception of humans as 'species beings.' It is therefore not surprising that most Chinese scholars generally reject the idea that human rights originate from natural rights, as, they argue, this account would deny the social character of rights.[520] As such, Chinese theorists of rights appear to engage critically with Western theories while elaborating their own. This critical engagement with both Marxist and Western theories is clear in the doctrines on the origin of human rights, a theoretical question that has been debated in the past two decades by Chinese scholars and that we turn now to describe, starting from the theories on their origin.

The Origin (*benyuan* 本原) of Human Rights and their Universal Nature (*pubian* 普遍)

In his article 'On the Origin of Human Rights', the renowned scholar Li Buyun[521] criticises some of the core tenets of Marxism, but also some claims of the Western theories of rights. In particular, Li Buyun rejects four views on the origin of human rights which are generally upheld by old school Chinese Marxist scholars.

The first view rejected by Li is the doctrine called the 'struggle for' human rights (*douzhengde lai shuo* 斗争得来说), supported by many scholars, including professor Zhang Guangbo,[522] which holds that citizens' human rights are derived from the people's struggle. Li attacks this doctrine, arguing that the struggle to obtain popular sovereignty is a means to obtain an effective protection of human rights rather than their source. Li also criticises the doctrine called *shangfu renquan shuo* (商赋人权说), that is, the idea that rights are

---

[520] Li Buyun 'On the Origin' supra note 516.

[521] Li Buyun is a member of the faculty of the Chinese Academy of Social Sciences and editor of *Studies in Law*.

[522] Zhang, Guangbo (1989) *Quanli yiwuyaolun* [A Concise Theory of Right and Duty] Changchun: Jilin daxue chubanshe.

'the product of the capitalist commodity economy'. Li considers this view as 'unscientific' because human rights existed long before the capitalist economy was introduced, in the West as in China. In particular, Li recalls that in the West the antecedents of the idea of human rights are found in the theories of natural rights.

However, Li finds the humanist tradition in China to be rich with examples of antecedents of human rights as well. Among them, the virtue of *ren* (仁), epitomised in the expression 'the benevolent person loves others' (*ren zhe ai ren* 仁者爱人);[523] the centrality of the human being, a core pillar of Confucian humanism: 'the human being is the most important thing between Heaven and Earth' (*tian di jian renwei gui* 天地间，人为贵);[524] the 'golden rule' which was allegedly formulated by Confucius: 'Never impose your preferences on other people in their own affairs' (*ji shuo bu yu wu shi yu ren* 己所不欲，勿施于人);[525] the idea of the benevolent government, according to which the emperor must care for the people otherwise his government is illegitimate: 'People are more important than the monarch' (*min gui jun qing* 民贵君轻); and, finally, the idea that 'The world is equally shared by all' (*tian xia wei gong* 天下为公).[526]

In Li's opinion, therefore:

> The doctrine of 'human rights as the product of the capitalist commodity economy' is incorrect because it only emphasises the economic conditions supporting modern human rights, while ignoring its inherent basis, ie human needs. China has implemented a highly centralised planned economy for a long time, and if the above doctrine were right, Chinese people could not enjoy any human rights under such an economic system, but that is not the case.[527]

The third view rejected by Li is the doctrine that human rights originated from social history (*shengchan fangshi* 生产方式). Li

---

[523] Li Buyun (2004) 'On the Origin' supra note 516.

[524] Ibid.

[525] Ibid.

[526] Ibid.

[527] Ibid.

criticises this view, considering the socio-economic structure as the external condition for the recognition and development of human rights rather than as their inner basis, which lies in human nature. In particular, in his view, 'some human rights are given by nature to the people, but their specific content and spirit will expand and change with the material system of civilisation, such as freedom and equality. Freedom of person and freedom of thought should be natural, but the freedom of speech, press and association is formed historically'.[528]

Lastly, Li Buyun opposes the doctrine that sees human rights as conferred by the state (*guofu renquan* 国赋人权). Quoting Milton, Locke and d'Holbach, Li points out the absurd consequences of such a theory, according to which the state can suspend, fail to protect, and even entirely deprive its citizens of human rights. Since this is an untenable position, the theory of the origin of human rights as state endowments must be rejected.

Other scholars have proposed different solutions to the question of the origin of human rights. Zheng Wenxian,[529] for instance, argues that basic human rights originate from man's natural attributes. In his view, these basic rights are directly relevant to man's survival, development and status as a subject, and they cannot be taken away or transferred. The basic rights of citizens provided for by the Constitution of China belong to the domain of basic human rights, even if basic human rights are not of course limited to these provisions. Ma Weilong[530] regards human rights as inborn. Nevertheless, he also argues that citizens should be able to have a say in political matters in order to actually exercise these rights. Unfortunately, in Ma's view, China is in a phase of 'immaturity of public opinion'. People's ideas are not taken into due consideration by the power holders, who, on the contrary, use autocratic means to suppress them. Ma believes that if and when public opinion grows in strength and becomes a force to oppose the autocratic government, a constitutional government will be installed.

---

[528] Ibid.

[529] Zhang Wenxian (2014) 'Human Rights Protection and Judicial Civilization' (2) *China Law Review*.

[530] Ma Weilong (1999) 'If the Citizens Want to Rid Themselves of the Evils of Autocracy, They Must Have Political Power' (31, 1) *Contemporary Chinese Thought* 44.

According to Qiu Xinglong,[531] the immature status of public opinion on the human rights issue is due to the absence of the deep-seated idea of human rights as inborn and inalienable, that cannot be renounced and that the state must respect. In his view, the very idea of the sacrosanct nature of human life is not commonly shared among Chinese citizens, and this constitutes a huge hindrance to the affirmation of human rights.

As one can appreciate by looking at the theories surveyed above, Chinese legal scholars criticise both Chinese Marxist and Western theories on the origin of human rights, and in their arguments they show their intellectual autonomy from both sides. A similar attitude can be found in the discussion concerning the universal nature of human rights or its denial in favour of the thesis of a class nature of rights.

Against the class nature of rights, reputable Chinese scholars[532] today advocate the universal nature of rights. After the horrors perpetrated by citizens and officials in the Cultural Revolution, Xu Bing,[533] in particular, stated that China should understand human rights 'afresh' and adopt a realistic attitude towards the issue. Xu Bing was among the first who, already in 1983, argued against the class nature of human rights, based on the idea that human rights are rights possessed by all human beings, so that their scope transcends social classes. Xu Bing and Li Buyun also criticise the orthodox Marxist position that sees human rights as coincident with citizens' rights. Li Buyun distinguishes between citizens' rights and human rights in many respects. He argues that the subject of human rights is universal: it includes citizens and non-citizens, such as foreigners, refugees and stateless persons. In his article 'On Three Forms of Human Rights', Li

---

[531] Qiu Xinglong (2005) 'The Morality of the Death Penalty' (36-3) *Contemporary Chinese Thought* 9; Chen Xingliang (2005) 'An Examination of the Death Penalty in China' (36-6) *Contemporary Chinese Thought* 35.

[532] Han Depei; Dong Yunhu and Li Wuping; Xu Bing (1989) 'The Origin and Historical Development of Human Rights Theory' (3) *Chinese Journal of Law*; Li Buyun (2007) 'Lun renquan de pubian xing he teshu xing' [On the universality and particularity of human rights] (6) *Huanqiu falu pinglun* [Global Law Review] 5.

[533] Xu Bing (1989) 'Renquan lilun de changsheng he lishi fazhan' [The Emergence and Historical Development of Human Rights Theory] (3) *Legal Studies* 1.

194

Buyun affirms that 'human rights' and 'fundamental rights' are not one and the same concept; instead, human rights are broader and include fundamental rights.[534] Li argues in opposition to the opinion by Zhang Guangbo, who instead considers that human rights do not encompass the whole content of citizens' rights but only 'fundamental or universal rights'.[535]

The Subjects of Human Rights: Individuals, Groups and Collectives

The prevailing Marxist position in the past considered individual rights as a consequence of the existence of collective rights, which were understood as the prototype of rights. Legal scholars[536] have recently criticised this position, arguing for the historical and conceptual priority of individual rights. The latter now seems to be the dominant view, although Chinese scholars do argue for the existence of collective human rights.

The critique of the idea of collective rights as the model of human rights, and of individual rights as bourgeois, was first raised by Zhang Wenxiang.[537] He supports this claim by referring to the constitutional provisions attributing rights to citizens, who are individuals and not collectives. Zhang holds that human rights arose historically as claims of individuals against the state, in order to get protection for their own person, properties and other legitimate interests, and that the holder of human rights in Chinese law is the individual and not the collective. Moreover, Zhang argues that while classical subjective rights are conferred upon individuals, legal persons and collective entities, human rights only pertain to individuals. According to Zhang, the subjective scope of legal rights in general is broader than that of human rights because the latter pertain only to individuals, while the former pertain to legal persons, collectives, etc. Zhang defends the thesis that an individual's human

---

[534] Li Buyun (1991) 'Lun renquan de sanzhong cunzai xingtai' [On Three Forms of Human Rights] in CASS Legal Institute (ed) (1992) *Dangdai renquan* (Contemporary Human Rights) Zhongguo shehui kexue chubanshe 3.

[535] Zhang, Guangbo *Quanli* supra note 520 at 10.

[536] See Li, Buyun (1994) 'Lun geren renquan yu jiti renquan' [On individual human rights and collective human rights] (6) *Zhongguo shehui kexueyuan yanjiusheng yuan xuebao* [Academic Journal Graduate School Chinese Academy of Social Sciences] 9; Zhang Wenxian (1992) 'On the Subject of Human Rights and Subjective Human Rights' in Legal Research Institute (ed) (2000) *Contemporary Human Rights*, Press of the Chinese Social Academy 36.

[537] Ibid.

rights are more concrete than collective human rights, as opposed to abstract (which is viewed as a defect). This thesis is the opposite of the old-school mainstream view, which regarded collective and social human rights as the only ones that are concrete.

Moreover, Zhang argues that by securing human rights, the public interest is secured and promoted as well, while Marxist socialist legal scholars attribute to the idea of rights the spread of egoism and self-interest to the detriment of collective good.[538] In Zhang's view, groups and collectives are the result of individual activities. Thus, in his view, guaranteeing human rights will support the good of the collective and not undermine it. A sign of the increased importance attributed to individual rights may be given by constituted by one of the most remarkable innovations introduced to support the shift to the quasi-capitalist market economy: the recognition of equal legal dignity to private individual property, alongside public ownership, which was definitely preeminent before the 1978 reforms.

Zhang's view is only one of the positions in the contemporary Chinese jurisprudential debate about the legal qualification of rights. The opposite one holds the view that human rights could be extended to legal persons and collectives as well. Li Buyun, in particular, considers individual human rights to be the basis of collective human rights, because collectives are constituted by individuals and because collective rights are also human rights. According to Li, the 'striving for and the obtaining of any collective human rights relies on the active and joint efforts of individuals who constitute the collective'. On the other hand, Li argues that even though human rights are primarily individual, collective human rights also exist, and they may constitute a guarantee for individual rights, in the domestic realm. This is due to the fact that: 'In any country, collective human rights require the state and the whole society to create various conditions for the protection and guarantee of individual human rights'.[539] Li uses three arguments against the superiority of collective human rights over individual rights.

---

[538] Chen, AHY 'Developing Theories' supra note 39 at 145.
[539] Li Buyun 'Lun geren' supra note 534 at 9.

The first argument is based on authority and offers a new interpretation of the works by Karl Marx. Li argues that the Marxist scholars who consider collective rights as superior to individual human rights do not understand Marx's doctrine of historical materialism very well. Quoting Marx, Li argues that 'individual existence is the prerequisite for collective and social existence, and individual activities and development are the basis for activities and development of the whole society'.[540] The second argument is based on the principle of equality, and it pivots on the assumption that the market economy requires the equal treatment of the subjects of rights, therefore the size of the subject (individual, group or collective) should not interfere with the equal enjoyment of rights.[541] The third argument is based on the distinction between the emphasis on individual human rights and the market, on the one hand, and individualism on the other hand. According to Li, in a market economy both collective and individual human rights should be given equal emphasis.[542]

In a similar vein, Ge Hongyi[543] argues for a theoretical link between the legal recognition of rights and individual, personal autonomy. The concept of a right, in his view, theoretically presupposes a distinction of the individual from an abstract totality. In his opinion, 'the interest of the totality or the collective interest is a concept constructed on the basis of the interest of individuals, and reflects the interest of the majority. The existence of any collective interest separated from the interest of individuals is unreal. If what is called the collective interest is in fact the special interest of certain individuals or classes', then 'raising the question of rights means confronting such collective interest'.[544]

Regarding the subject of rights, most Chinese contemporary scholarship considers that not only individuals but also collectives and groups can be entitled to rights. The theory of 'the special grouping of rights' considers the rights that some persons have in virtue of their membership of a particular group as 'collective rights'. These rights would be recognised at the domestic level and they would differ from individual rights from the point of view of both the subject and the content. In particular, the category 'group rights' was created by

---

[540] Ibid.
[541] Ibid.
[542] Ibid.
[543] Ge Hongyi (1991) 'Law, Rights and Rights-Orientation' (6) *Science of Law* 22.
[544] Cfr. Chen, AHY 'Developing Theories' supra note 39.

Chinese jurisprudence in order to protect vulnerable groups: women, children, and the elderly.[545] Some[546] consider that the subject entitled to collective rights is the special group. The members of this special group are entitled to rights both as individuals and as members of the collective. The guarantee of the rights of the special groups is provided through legal means (eg the rights of the minorities in the autonomous regions). Li indicates that collective or group rights which can be individual rights at the same time [547] include the rights of ethnic minorities, children, women, the elderly, the disabled, detainees, foreign nationals and refugees.

Chinese scholars differentiate the rights of the person (*renshen quan* 人身权) from the rights of the personality (*renge quan* 人格权), but both are included among basic human rights. They argue that human rights, namely those rights that should be equally enjoyed by all human beings, guaranteeing substantial and not just formal equality, are very few. They must be distinguished from the rights of the person, which are different for different groups of people, who have different needs and interests. In order to ascertain the content of human rights, the focus must be on the interests of people, individuated and understood by means of empirical research.[548] The community should meet the needs of each person. The interests of people are indeed relevant to determine both human rights and the rights of each individual. The difference is that human rights are common to all human beings, while the interests of the person can differ.

The Theory of Serving the People (*wei renmin fuwu* 为人民服务)
The doctrine of 'serving the people' was already discussed in Chapter Three as a possible foundation for placing limits on power. Li Buyun reinterprets the Mencian doctrine of 'serving the people' and

---

[545] Keith, R and Lin, Z *Law and Justice* supra note 263.

[546] Zhang Wenxian (1992) 'On the Subject' supra note 534.

[547] Li offers the examples of the 1992 Act of Protection of Women's Rights and the Ethnic Minority Regional Autonomy Act, which both provide for legal remedies when the rights are violated.

[548] These ideas resonate with the basic tenets of the Chinese communist principle regulating political action as for instance the principle of democratic centralism.

incorporates human rights in it. While in the traditional view individuals are seen as servants of state interests, in his interpretation of the theory Li Buyun dramatically changes the perspective and clearly affirms that the purpose of the state is to protect human rights. He argues that the protection of human rights constitutes at the same time: 1) the noble ideal of socialism; 2) the practical guarantee for realising the commandment 'Serve the People!'; 3) the fundamental purpose of making and implementing the laws of socialism; 4) the starting point as well as the end result of scientific development; 5) the common value pursued by the whole of humanity. Li's theorisation involves a significant shift in the representation of the relationships between the state and citizens.

The Mencian theory that the aim of the government is to care for the people was incorporated in past theorisations on the purpose of rights, but the emphasis was always on the duties of the subjects and on the power of the state to suspend or to withdraw protection and guarantees of rights from its subjects. The new theorisation by Li Buyun has a revolutionary momentum because for the first time it is stated with such clarity that human rights set limits on the power of the state. This idea is epitomised by the amendment to the Constitution which affirms that 'The state protects and safeguards human rights'. Li Buyun argues that the significance and value of the existence of state power is to 'serve the people', and serving the people means protecting human rights. Li Buyun's approach also entails a new perspective on the idea and place of 'development' with respect to human rights. His interpretation of the 'scientific approach to development' stresses that development is for the people (*fazhan wei renmin* 发展为人民) because the fruits of development should be enjoyed and shared by the people. Such fruits should be enjoyed equally for the realisation of the people's common prosperity.[549]

Orthodox Marxist theorisations on rights consistently held that the right to development is prior and paramount. In order to reach the goal of development, understood as a collective right, the argument by orthodox Marxist theories goes, it is possible to temporarily trump individual human rights. Li Buyun's thesis challenges this reasoning, holding that the people's rights are part and parcel of development,

---

[549] Li Buyun 'On the Origin' supra note 516 at 16. Social morality (*shehui gongde* 社会公德) is linked to the theory of the common principles of mankind: 'the pursuit of justice, equality, fraternity, and other values of all mankind is the ethical basis for the human rights that anyone should have'.

and should be respected and enjoyed equally by all. Other scholars agree that human rights are part of the development of human society, a view which in fact stems from Marx's theory of history as a line of progressive development. [550] In the words of Xu Bing, [551] 'the development of human civilisation and the development of human rights are inseparable. Human rights promote the development of human civilisation: human civilisation is manifested in human rights'.[552] Bearing this in mind, Li Buyun recognises history as a process of enlargement of human rights, in three areas: 1) rights of the human body and human dignity (life, health, personal freedom, spiritual freedom, personal dignity, freedom of correspondence, protection from intrusion into the home and privacy); 2) political rights and freedoms (the right to vote and to be elected, freedom of expression, freedom of the press, freedom of assembly, freedom of association, demonstration access to information and evidence supervision); 3) economic, social and cultural rights (property, employment, labour insurance, equal pay for equal work, holidays, education, family, membership of trade unions, social welfare).[553]

Ought-Rights and their Social Enforcement

As mentioned previously, one of the specific characteristics of the conceptions of rights in China is the common idea that rights are derived from the social nature of human beings. Drawing from this idea, in fact, Chinese scholars (Li Buyun, Zhang Wenxiang, Gong Pixiang) have elaborated the notion of 'ought-rights' (*yingyou quanli* 应有权利). This category of ought-rights includes socially derived rights, which reflect the characteristics of social relationships and exist independently of their legal recognition. The grounds or bases

---

[550] Zhang Wenxian 'On the Subject of Human Rights' supra note 534 at 29.

[551] Xu Bing wrote 'The Rise and Historical Development of Human Rights Theory' where he affirms that human rights promote the development of human civilisation and that human civilisation is manifested in human rights. Moreover, he encourages Chinese intellectuals to adopt a realistic attitude towards human rights in China (Xu Bing 'Renquan lilun' supra note 531.

[552] Chen, AH 'Developing Theories' supra note 39 at 131-132).

[553] Li Buyun (1996) 'On individual and collective human rights' in Baehr, PR (et al) (eds) (1996) *Human Rights: Chinese and Dutch perspectives* Martinus Bijhoff Publishers 119.

for ought-rights are the interests and needs of people, arising from their relationships and their interaction. This means that ought-rights are not abstract but concrete, and change when the structure of social relations changes. They are not dependent on their recognition by law, and 'can be violated, but someone will still recognise and respect them'.[554] Ought-rights are specified by external and internal causes. The internal causes are the natural and social attributes of persons, such as existing social relationships, which are in turn determined by the means of production. The external causes, in contrast, represent the material and spiritual level of development.

Examples of ought-rights are the rights and the corresponding duties which exist among family members (the parents' duty to support and educate children, the duty to support elderly parents). The guarantee of ought-rights, when they are not recognised by the law, is realised through social forces (custom, social conventions, habits, tradition, moral ideas and political consciousness). The Chinese idea of ought-rights is in line with traditional ideas in China, where social rules rather than legal ones protect the basic needs and interests of individuals within social entities such as the family.[555] After a short presentation of ought-rights theories we will see how the notion of ought-rights can potentially contribute to the broader global debate on human rights.

In particular, Li Buyun's category of ought-rights indicates a specific path for the protection of rights by society, besides and prior to their legal enforcement.[556] Ought-rights constitute a specific category of rights, along with legal rights and actual rights.[557] The second category, 'legal rights', are those rights provided by the law. The third category, 'actual rights', includes the rights actually enjoyed

---

[554] Chen, A 'Developing Theories' supra note 39 at 141.

[555] The idea that the law should not be the only means to protect human rights, and instead they should also be enforced by social norms, has recently been upheld by John Tasioulas: 'Another way in which the orthodox view has been elaborated so as to address concerns that inspire the political view is by emphasizing the idea—traceable to John Stuart Mill, but stretching much further back—that human rights are rights that should in some broad sense of "enforcement", be socially enforced, at least pro tanto. This view differs from standard political views in stopping short of conceptually privileging a specific mode of enforcement, such as legalization, or various forms of international intervention of "concern"' Tasioulas, J (2015) 'On the Foundations of Human Rights' in Cruft, R; Liao, M and Renzo, M (eds) (2015) *Philosophical Foundations of Human Rights* Oxford University Press 45 at 51.

[556] In this sense, ought-rights resemble 'moral rights'.

[557] Li Buyun 'Lun renquan' supra note 532 at 3-6.

by a particular individual. Legal rights become actual rights depending on the degree of rights consciousness and on social, economic and cultural conditions.

Among other classifications, Zhang Wenxiang, in particular, distinguishes ought-rights, legal rights, customary rights and actual rights. Ought-rights are defined as moral rights, and constitute standards to criticise legislation. They belong to human beings as such. The law and the Constitution provide legal rights. This category includes 'presumed rights' (*tuiding quanli* 推定权利), which are rights a citizen may presume to have when the law does not expressly command or prohibit the action that constitutes the object of the presumed rights. Customary rights are based on people's voluntary repetitive behaviour and depend on people's cultural tradition. Actual rights are rights that the holder actually practises and enjoys.

Zhang emphasises the importance of political rights, and considers economic and social rights as 'foundational' in the sense that they provide the foundation for the realisation and protection of political and civil rights. He quotes Marx and Engels to argue that, generally speaking, customary rights constitute the basis and limit of legal rights. For Zhang, the origin of basic human rights is 'man's natural attributes and social essence'; these rights are 'directly relevant to man's survival, development and status as a subject'.[558] Therefore, he considers basic rights as inalienable. Basic rights include the basic rights enshrined in the Constitution. According to Zhang Wenxian, economic, social and cultural rights are more basic than other rights, and in this respect he shares the Marxist view. Actual rights or subjective rights are those realised through the efforts of the subjects.[559]

Gong Pixiang[560] affirms that the idea of 法 *fa* represents the law as it ought to be, in contrast to the concept of 律 *lü*, which refers to the law as it is. Gong compares *fa* to the expressions *ius*, right, *diritto* and *recht,* as indicating the idea that law embodies justice and

---

[558] Zhang Wenxian (1991) 'On the Subject' supra note 548.
[559] Chen, A 'Developing Theories' supra note 39 at 145.
[560] Gong Pixiang (1992) 'A Value Analysis of the Phenomenon of Rights' (8) *Science of Law* 33; Gong Pixiang (1991) 'On the Realisation of Rights' (6) *Science of Law* 27.

202

rights, comparing *falu* (the law) to the law based on will. At the core of Gong Pixiang's theory of rights is the notion of 'ought-rights'. Since human beings are autonomous and creative agents, in their lives they use ought-rights to fulfil needs and interests, to realise their autonomy and express their value and dignity. Ought-rights are conceived as the means through which the value of the human being is expressed. The nature of rights is linked to human nature in that ought-rights are means to express and realise human autonomy and value in history. At the same time, they constitute ends or value goals in that they represent what the subject expects and demands in his life. The state, through legal provisions, elevates ought-rights into legal rights.

Having articulated the main theorisations concerning ought-rights, I now will briefly highlight how the process of critical engagement plays out with reference to this particular notion.

The category of ought-rights is an original element of the Chinese understanding of rights. With this elaboration they reject the notion of rights as attributions of the individual before and independent of society. It appears that Chinese scholars have engaged with and recovered Marx and Engels' idea of the social existence of human rights: (*renquan de shehui cunzai* 人权的社会存在). However, it is arguable that this category reflects also the specific idea of society as represented in the classical school of thought in China. According to this idea, society is not just a fact, an aggregation of free and equal beings. Instead, social relationships possess an intrinsic normative character. This intrinsic normativity grounds the moral rights and calls for their enforcement by society itself. Even if the prescriptive character of social relations (bonds) that are capable of generating duties and rights has been theorised by the classical Confucian school of thought, this influence is not explicitly recognised by Chinese scholars.

The theoretical premise on which the different theories of ought-rights just described are based is that human beings have a common nature, shared throughout history and by every person living in different countries: the fundamental and constitutive relational aspect of their being. From these social relationships emerge needs and interests, which provide the reasons for the attribution of human rights. These needs and interests of human beings are specified by the material, economic, and historical context in which the person is situated. Human rights derive from social relationships.

Because the needs and interests emerge from social relationships, it seems that the conception of the human being underlined by Chinese scholars is not the classic liberal representation of the autonomous and sovereign individual. On the contrary, every person is viewed as not just immersed in, but rather *constituted by* the net of his or her social relationships, which possess intrinsic normativity. Humans are made of the relations they have with their family and members of society. Another constitutive element is the context in which a person is situated, and the creative interaction with and responses to this particular context.

The concept of the 'social enforcement of rights' represents an original contribution of Chinese human rights theory to the global discourse on rights. Although it may be disputed, it seems that legal enforcement of rights may cause severe failures in the protection of basic human rights, that social enforcement might be able to correct.[561] However, theorisation of the scope, means and method of the social enforcement of rights is missing in the Chinese academic debate, and should be further developed.

The Justification of Rights
The justification of rights individuates the fundamental reasons for the attribution of a right broadly understood, ie a claim, power, immunity, or other similar subjective legal position to a person.[562] As such, the

---

[561] Especially when the violation of basic human rights is the result of complex phenomena, as for instance in the case of human trafficking, when the response of the law may come too late. More importantly, as in the phenomenon of trafficking, cooperation from social actors can make a difference in detecting, reporting and stopping severe violations. It seems also that these failures could be corrected by coupling the legal with the social enforcement of rights. In the case of human trafficking, for example, the cooperation of social actors is deemed necessary, because complex phenomena require complex answers.

[562] The philosophical discussion on legal rights is monumental and cannot be reconstructed here. However, the core elements of the debate can be found in the following references, which are by no means exhaustive but only essential, fundamental references to the relevant debate: Hohfeld, W N, (1919) *Fundamental Legal Conceptions as Applied in Judicial Reasoning*, in Cooke, WW (ed.), Yale University Press; Austin, J (1885) *Lectures on Jurisprudence, or the Philosophy of Positive Law*, 5th ed., Campbell R. (ed.), John Murray; Bentham, J (1970) [1782] *Of Laws in General*, H.L.A. Hart (ed.), Athlone Press; Hart, HLA (1983) 'Between

204

justification of rights applies to rights in general, including the category of human rights, defined as the rights a person has in virtue of being human. The justification is specified in relation to subjective individual rights. However, since human rights are enshrined by law, they are involved in this justification.

The justification of rights identifies a core element grounding the attribution or recognition of that subjective legal position. Even if the concept of rights does not fully coincide with their justification, the justification influences the conception of what a right is in practice. More specifically, different theoretical justifications are capable of influencing the scope and limits of the actual protection of a legal right. The question of the justification of rights is whether there is a central and focal sense of the concept of rights, which has a kind

Utility and Rights' (reprinted) in Hart, HLA, *Essays in Jurisprudence and Philosophy*, Clarendon Press, at 198; Hart, HLA(1982) 'Bentham on Legal Rights' (reprinted) in Hart, HLA, *Essays on Bentham. Studies in Jurisprudence and Political Theory*, Clarendon Press, at 162; Hart, HLA (1955) 'Are There any Natural Rights?', *Philosophical Review*, 64 at 175; Feinberg, J (1966) *Duties, Rights, and Claims*, in Feinberg, J (1980), *Rights, Justice and the Bounds of Liberty*, Princeton; Dworkin, R (1978) *Taking Rights Seriously*, (revised edition), Duckworth; Kramer, M H, Simmonds, N E, Steiner, H (1998) *A Debate over Rights. Philosophical Enquiries*, Clarendon Press; Kramer, M H, (2010) 'Refining the Interest Theory of Rights', *American Journal of Jurisprudence*, 55 at 31; Kramer, Matthew H, Simmonds, N E and Steiner, H, (1998) *A Debate Over Rights: Philosophical Enquiries*, Oxford University Press; Kramer, M and Steiner, H (2007) 'Theories of Rights: Is There a Third Way?', *Oxford Journal of Legal Studies*, 27, at 281; Kelsen, H (1946) *General Theory of Law and State*, Harvard University Press; MacCormick, N (1976) 'Children's Rights: A Test-Case for Theories of Rights', reprinted in MacCormick, N (1982) *Legal Right and Social Democracy: Essays in Legal and Political Philosophy*, Clarendon Press, at 154; MacCormick, N (1977) 'Rights in Legislation', in Hacker P.M.S., Raz J. (eds.), *Law, Morality and Society: Essays in Honour of HLA Hart*, Clarendon Press, at 189; Raz, J (1984) 'The Nature of Rights', reprinted in Raz, J (1986) *The Morality of Freedom*, Clarendon Press, at 165; Raz, J (1984) 'Legal Rights', reprinted in Raz, J (1994) *Ethics in the Public Domain: Essays in the Morality of Law and Politics*, Clarendon Press, at 238; Waldron, J, (1988) *The Right to Private Property*, Clarendon Press; P. M. S. Hacker, J. Raz (1977) *Law, Morality and Society*, Clarendon Press; MacCormick, N (1982) *Legal Right and Social Democracy*, Clarendon Press; Raz, J (1970) *The Morality of Freedom*, Clarendon Press; Raz, J (1996) *Ethics in the Public Domain*, Clarendon Press; Simmonds, N E (1986) *Central Issues in Jurisprudence. Justice, Law and Rights*, Sweet & Maxwell; Waldron, J (1993) *Liberal Rights*, Oxford University Press; Wellman, C (1977) *An Approach to Rights*, Kluwer. See, also, Celano, B (2002) 'I diritti nella jurisprudence anglosassone contemporanea. Da Hartz a Raz' in Comanducci, P and Guastini, R (eds) (2002) *Analisi e diritto* Torino 1.

of explanatory priority with respect to the others, and in virtue of which the rights are attributed to the subjects.

In this respect, the different justifications offered by contemporary Chinese scholars centre upon what each of them assumes to be the essential factor or key element of rights, called (*yaosu* 要素), that grounds their attribution to human beings. On this point, the scholars' views may be classified into five groups. The first group identifies the key element for the attribution of rights in the freedom of human beings (will or choice); the second group locates the key element in the interest; the third group, which upholds a mixed theory, finds the justification in both interest and freedom; the fourth group affirms that the key element for attributing rights is empowerment (or action);[563] finally, the fifth group identifies this element in the 'power of legality'.

The theories based on interest and will (or choice) represent two classical positions in Anglo-American and European jurisprudence. In Western legal thought, the first was famously affirmed by Jeremy Bentham as well as by Rudolf Jhering, and most recently by Raz, Kramer and others, and the second had two famous supporters in Hans Kelsen and H.L.A. Hart. The two theories respectively see the protection of an interest and of a choice as the core reasons for the attribution of a legal power, immunity, claim, and privilege to a person. Chinese theories of rights justify their attribution with reference to non-Chinese classical theories, from Marxist to liberal approaches to the law. However, the scholarly theorisations are becoming increasingly more sophisticated and present some original elements. In less apparent fashion, classical and traditional Chinese legal thinking has been also influential in the elaboration of contemporary justifications of rights, as the following analysis will show. The discussion will highlight the characteristics of the different theories on the justification of rights. Each one of these theories presents continuities and discontinuities with the Chinese tradition, the liberal, and the Marxist views, respectively, and thus represent instances of the process of critical engagement.

---

[563] Cheng Liaoyuan and Wang Renbo *Quan li lun* supra note 2 at 58.

Theory of Freedom

The theory of freedom (*ziyou shuo* 自由说) is the view that the justification of rights rests on the guarantee of individual liberty. The importance of these accounts rests on the circumstance that the emphasis has traditionally been on interests as the justification of rights. The theory of freedom or choice is a more recent acquisition in the Chinese internal debate. This theory focuses on freedom of choice, but the choice at issue consists in the capacity of a person to determine aspects of her and other people's conduct. It does not consist only in the legal power that a person has to decide whether another person should or should not perform an action on her behalf, just because she so wishes, as a sovereign does. Thus the Chinese perspective on rights as freedoms does not coincide with the view that a right only consists in the possibility of triggering a sanction against the person who violates a duty, as in Hans Kelsen's approach, or more generally in having control over other people's duties, as argued by H.L.A. Hart.[564] The Chinese justification of rights based on freedom seems rather to be grounded on a notion of the human being, which may be related on the one hand to Marxist premises, and on the other hand is more similar to ideas developed in Confucian times regarding the nature of human beings and their relationships with nature and society, as described in Chapter Two. The fundamental idea is that of a human being who is able to act and transform nature: the human being as a co-creator of the world and of history.

In general, as explained above, there is a certain criticism towards the idea of natural rights which places emphasis on freedom, as it would neglect the social aspect of the human being. However, there are some exceptions. The most important is the theory of the justification of rights by Zhou Fucheng. This intellectual espouses the theory of natural rights and, quoting Grotius, argues that the prototype of rights is freedom: 'Statutory rights, no matter whether they are private ones or public ones, which include national and municipal

---

[564] Jeremy Waldron synthesises Hart's approach with the thesis that 'control' over other people's duty is the point of attributing rights: 'To be a right holder is not necessarily to be in a position to benefit from another's duty but it is to be in a position of control over another's duty. X has a right against W, on this account only if it is for X to claim performance of the duty from X or to waive it. In other words it is for X to determine, by his choice, how W ought to act in this regard.' Waldron, J (1993) 'Can Commonal Goods Be Human Rights?' in Waldron, J (ed) (1993) *Liberal Rights. Collected Papers 1981-1991* Cambridge University Press 339 at 352.[564]

rights, are originally called "freedom"...the first true right is a kind of freedom'. [565]

For the majority, the legal provision of rights is meant to guarantee respect for rights by establishing the obligations of others towards the right holder. Wang Chunguo holds the view that a 'legal right, regulated by legislation, is a permission which allows people to act autonomously, (and require others to) perform or not to perform certain actions. Broadly speaking, it also includes the function and right, which are enjoyed by the state organs, social organisations and governmental officials',[566] who need to act in accordance with law. Chen Zhonglin individuates the point of rights in the fact that an individual who is entitled to a right 'can act according to his wishes without being interfered by others, or even request the other people to act in accordance with his wishes'. [567]

The accounts by Wang and Chen seem to be coincident with the classical accounts of the choice theory, according to which the capacity to control another person's duty is the only relevant characteristic in order to establish that someone has a right. Therefore, any right would entail a claim corresponding to someone else's duty, a power through which the person can control the performance of the duty and the liberty to decide whether to accept or to refuse the performance of the duty. The predicament of this theory is that by justifying subjective rights, including human rights, with the capacity to choose, this would exclude (in principle) the attribution of rights to subjects that cannot choose, such as babies or people who are severely ill.

However, there is another version of the theory of freedom, which diverges in part from the classical account of the choice or will theory. The point of the attribution of rights according to this account is the capacity of human beings to act freely to transform the world in which they live. Cheng Liaoyuan and Wang Renbo articulate the

---

[565] Zhou Fucheng (1966) *Selected Saying of the Bourgeois Philosophers and Political Thinkers from the Renaissance to the 19th century* The Commercial Press at 681.

[566] Wang Chunguo (1995) *Modern jurisprudence: History and Theory* Hunan Press at 223.

[567] Chen Zhonglin (2009) 'Guanyu renquan' supra note 491.

paradigmatic version of this theory, at the core of which is Marx's conception of freedom. The two authors recall that for Marx, freedom is 'the essence of the spiritual existence'. Men and women are able to come out from the natural condition by exercising 'free and conscious activities' (*ziyou zijue huo dong* 自由自觉活动) and, in their view, this is precisely the reason for the attribution of rights.[568] Humans are the only animals who are able to consciously transform nature through labour, in order to achieve their own ends. However, human beings are social animals and need society to be free. In this sense there is a necessary relationship between man and society. In society human beings can realise their freedom or be enslaved. The transformation of natural and social conditions is the process of 'materialisation' and requires human labour. The actual exercise of freedom, however, needs favourable conditions, the ability of people to transform reality is only potential, and it is enacted when people exchange their labour in society. According to Cheng and Wang: 'In order to actualise their ability to become free, people should first of all have the right to realise their ability'.[569]

Cheng and Wang's starting point is Marx's doctrine of historical materialism. They affirm that the inner nature of rights is constituted by 'free and conscious activities'. In fact, human beings become subjects by exercising the faculty of consciousness. The prerequisite of freedom is the fact that human subjects possess human abilities, which enable them to transform the reality. It is this capacity to transform nature, rather than adapt to it, that distinguishes human beings from animals. Among the abilities is the capacity to gain and create knowledge. However, in order to be actualised, human abilities need certain conditions of social development.

To indicate how important are social conditions for the actual exercise of freedom, Cheng and Wang refer to Copernicus, the scientist who elaborated the heliocentric theory. In fact, using his knowledge (ability) and research (labour), Copernicus discovered the truth: planet Earth revolves around the Sun, and not the opposite. But the truth he discovered was considered heretical and banned because of religious obscurantism, and Copernicus himself underwent trial and condemnation. Cheng and Wang also mention the case of 1930s Germany where people formally enjoyed freedom of association but there was only one party: the Nazi party. In this sense, Cheng and

---

[568] Cheng Liaoyuan and Wang Renbo *Quan li lun* supra note 2 at 166.
[569] Ibid.

Wang argue that social conditions are necessary for the exercise of the right of freedom. The two scholars advocate the modification of present social circumstances to enhance the actual enjoyment of the right to freedom:

> For an enlightened and sound social system, it is impossible to completely eliminate the alienation of people, but it is possible to reduce the cost of freedom to the largest possible extent. It is, on the one hand, in relation to economic, political and cultural development that the conditions for freedom are determined, such as the provision of rights for more subjects, the mobilisation of resources and guarantees for those rights; on the other hand, people's freedom and ability should be improved by allowing more people to participate in social management and in the practice of democracy. An enlightened and healthy society cannot eliminate the natural limits that freedom has, but it can make the limit 'reasonable'.[570]

For Cheng and Wang, 'the right of the subject depends on his choice of meaning among the range of meanings that the society can offer'.[571] The most important basis for the right is the freedom to choose one's behaviour in order to satisfy the people's needs determined by the natural and social conditions. There must be a range of meaningful alternatives for the subject to choose from in order to exercise the freedom of choice according to conscience.

In Cheng and Wang's view, the justification for the attribution of rights to individuals is the exercise of free choice between meaningful alternative options so that individuals can satisfy their subjective interests. The same justification is shared by Li Buyun. Li agrees that human beings are by nature free, and that the capacity to perform 'free and conscious activities' is the distinctive characteristic that distinguishes human beings from animals.[572]

This theory is influenced by Marxism: dialectical materialism and historical materialism are still part of its elaboration. In this sense, this theory apparently draws heavily from Marxist thought. But it is

---

[570] Cheng Liaoyuan and Wang Renbo (2014) *Quan li lun* supra note 2 at 126.

[571] Ibid at 161.

[572] Li Buyun (1991) 'On the three modes of existence of human rights' (4) *Studies in Law* 11.

arguable that it is also influenced by the intellectual tradition of the past. In particular, it is the idea of freedom as a process, that entails cognitive elements, a process restrained by the circumstances of the context, including social limitations, that resonates with the conceptualisation of human beings and society by some Confucian scholars. Here I recognise elements of the past intellectual tradition: the idea of humanity as an achievement concept; the virtue of *ren* 仁 which has an epistemic value and an ethical significance. These influences are indirect and implicit, therefore they are not acknowledged. Cheng Liaoyuan and Wang Renbo, who advocate freedom of expression and freedom of economic initiative, as fundamental rights, do that on the basis of a new interpretation of Marxist ideas. Even if they overtly reject the Chinese tradition of the past as detrimental to the affirmation of human rights, they are in fact still under its indirect influence.

Theory of Interest
The theories of interest upheld by Chinese scholars share the view that the justification of rights consists of the recognition of the importance of an interest, which deserves protection. The very word used to indicate 'rights' is *quanli* (权利). The second component of this word is the character *li* 利, which means interest or benefit. The view of rights as 'our legitimate benefits' or 'interests' is widely supported by Chinese jurisprudence.[573] This view is called the theory of interest (*liyi shuo* 利 益说). The Chinese doctrine considers 'needs' to be at the basis of social relationships, because humans can only satisfy their needs through cooperation with other human beings. Satisfaction of needs outside society would be impossible because of the inherent limitations of individuals: humans are vulnerable, mortal, fragile, and therefore need to get organised with other humans in order to survive and eventually flourish. This is the reason why contemporary Chinese doctrine defines a 'need' as something belonging to the individual and 'inalienable' (humans cannot get rid of it); moreover, the notion of interest can be deconstructed into multiple levels and aspects.

According to Cheng and Wang, the satisfaction of needs is represented by the realisation of the interest. In their view, the pursuit of human interests depends on material conditions: 'Marx's doctrine

---

[573] Angle, SC *Human Rights and Chinese Thought* supra note 2 at 29; Cfr. Tong Zhiwei (2018) *Right, Power and Faquanism. A Practical Legal Theory from Contemporary China* Brill at 27-28

has never denied the significance of political and spiritual needs, but it is only a dialectical explanation of the relationship between this kind of needs and material needs'.[574]

Some scholars acknowledge that people's interests are mutually conflicting.[575] The conflict is real and not apparent, as it was believed in Confucian times, and therefore the necessity to provide rights through legalisation arises. 'Legalisation' modifies the nature of the previous relationship of mutual help and cooperation and sets up a relationship based on rights and obligations in order to satisfy a certain interest. Only the conflict of interests recognised by the community can lead to the attribution of rights. The choice of the conduct prescribed to satisfy the interest is made by society and it is a crucial moment in determining the legalisation of rights.[576]

The theory of interest is upheld by Li Buyun and Xu Bing[577] who affirm that: 'Rights refer to certain interests of the citizens which the state law clearly defines and the state power guarantees'.[578] In a similar vein, Zhang Qingfu affirms that rights, including the constitutional ones, are provided for the interests of the right holder. Rights reflect, embody and protect substantial, spiritual and personal interests in the name of constitutional law and other regulations.[579] Among the scholars who find the key element for the attribution of rights in the protection of a human interest are Liang Zhiping, Qiu Hanping, and Yuan Kunxiang. In particular, Liang Zhiping explains how the concept of rights can be understood from two perspectives:

---

[574] Cheng Liaoyuan and Wang Renbo *Quan li lun* supra note 2 at 203.

[575] Liang Zhiping (1989) 'Explicating "Law": A Comparative Perspective of Chinese and Western Legal Culture' (3) *Journal of Chinese Law* 59; Liang, Zhiping (1995) 'Law and Fairness at a Time of Change' (2) *China Perspectives* 30; Liang, Zhiping *Fabian Zhongguo* supra note 316 at 64-67; Yu Keping (2002) 'Toward an Incremental Democracy and Governance: Chinese Theories and Assessment Criteria' (24) *New Political Science* 181; Yu Keping (2004) *From the Discourse of Sino-West to Globalisation: Chinese Perspectives on Globalisation* China Centre for Comparative Politics; Cheng Liaoyuan and Wang Renbo *Quan li lun* supra note 2.

[576] Ibid at 160-172.

[577] Tsinghua University Law School, KoGuan Research Centre executive director.

[578] Li Buyun and Xu Bing (1986) *Quanli yu yiwu* [Rights and Obligations], Remin Press at 1.

[579] Zhang Qingfu (1994) *Basic Theories of Constitutional law* Shehui kefawenxian chubanshe at 491.

on the one hand, rights manifest as a claim, a demand or a reasonable expectation; on the other hand, these subjective intentions are closely related to objective interests.[580] For Qiu Hanping, personal rights, as recognised by law, protect interests and also set limitations on power.[581] Yuan Kunxiang considers that rights, serving as an interest, are established and protected by the law, but cannot be exclusively enjoyed by a single person.[582]

When analysing the contemporary Chinese theories, it seems that the interest of the right holder is the main justification for the attribution of rights in the Chinese scholarly discourse. The view that justifies rights in virtue of the existence of a 'legitimate' benefit (or interest) implies that a benefit that is not legitimate should not be dignified as a right. Clearly, the qualification of the interest as legitimate is the most problematic point. In this sense, this justification for the protection of social interests differs from the interest theory of rights purported by liberal scholars. In fact, the view that justifies rights in virtue of the existence of a 'legitimate' benefit stresses that the interest must be recognised and qualified as one deserving protection. 'Legitimate interests' may include self-interest and exclude selfish interests. Moreover, the qualification of an interest as legitimate is normally operated directly or indirectly by the CCP. The question is therefore what interests are regarded as legitimate ones, and thus deserve recognition and protection, to be distinguished from those other interests whose satisfaction is not relevant or that may even be deemed as harmful for the realisation of more important public interests. However, the presence of different theorisations on these questions shows the degree of intellectual pluralism in Chinese academia. The plurality of accounts for the justification of rights pivoting on the protection of interests is a case in point.

Mixed Justifications, Theory of the Power of Legality, and Theory of Competence

Besides the theories of choice and interest, Chinese scholars advance other theories regarding the key element that justifies the attribution of rights to individuals. In this section we will make reference to three:

[580] Liang Zhiping (1997) *Xunqiu ziran zhixu zhong de hexie: Zhongguo chuantong falu wenhua yanjiu* [Seeking for the harmony in the natural order-A study on the Traditional Chinese legal culture] China University of Political Science and Law Publishing Press at 173.

[581] By Qiu Hanping (1935) *General Theory of Law* The Commercial Press at 91.

[582] Yuan Kunxiang (1980) *Introduction to Law* Sanmin Press at 121.

mixed justification, the theory of the power of legality and the theory of competence.

Let us start with the mixed justification theory. Some Chinese scholars consider the point of the attribution of rights to be the protection of both interests and freedoms. In a sense, the exercise of freedoms could be considered as a fundamental interest of human beings. So, any theory of choice could be considered as part of a theory of interest. If so, all the theories of choice would be 'mixed'. Normally, the objection that the theory of choice is part of the theory of interest is overcome by emphasising that the theory of choice focuses on the power or capacity of the right holder to control someone else's duty, rather than on the interest everybody has to have his freedom protected. Among the most prominent advocates of the mixed justification is Sun Guohua, who argues that a right is 'what its holder can use in order to satisfy his interests and enjoy his freedoms'.[583] In particular, the right allows to act[584], in the sense that a right 'is a permitted domain in which the right holder acts to satisfy his interest, where satisfaction of the interest is guaranteed by the legal obligation of the others'.[585]

According to Wu Buyun, another supporter of the mixed theory, a right is both a kind of freedom and a boundary for people in their social networks. The provision and enjoyment of rights, however, is constrained by the socio-economic structure and the development of culture. A 'right' means: 'the enthusiasm and creativity of human beings, and the enjoyment of substantial and spiritual interests'.[586]

The second group of theoreticians upholds the 'theory of the power of legality' (*falu shang de li shuo* 法律上的力说). The character *quan* 权 contained in the Chinese expressions 'right' (*quanli* 权利) and 'human right' (*renquan* 人权), means 'power'. The theory of the 'power of legality' holds that rights empower their holder to

---

[583] Sun Guohua (ed) *Basic Theory* supra note 465 at 348-349.
[584] Ibid.
[585] Ibid.
[586] Wu Buyun (1992) *Introduction to the Philosophy of Marxism* Shaanxi Renmin Press at 199-200.

214

engage in certain activities, including the institutional power to modify legal relationships. This power is attributed and guaranteed to the individuals by the state. According to this view, rights, guaranteed by the state's power, are the capacity or power that can enable people to engage in activities in the name of a certain interest, or to change legal relations. This power is 'legal' in nature, and allows the subject of the right to obtain or maintain specific interests with the permission of the law. According to Gao Weijun, a right is understood as a power enabling people to determine their own reasonable behaviour in the light of the law.[587] For Li Zhaowei, a 'right is due power, held with legitimacy by the subjects of the right'.[588] According to Zheng Yubo, a right is the power based on law.[589]

The last theory that is worth mentioning, although little has been written on it in China, is the theory of competence or qualification (*zige shuo* 资格说), which refers to the capacity or the ability to perform certain actions to realise the right. The defenders of this theory, such as Liu Jinguo and Zhang Guicheng, consider that in essence, a right is regulated by the state through law, and it is both a permission and a guarantee allowing people to perform certain acts.[590] Similarly, Chen Shouyi explains that the subject of the legal relationship has the capacity or capability to act (or not), or require others to act or not.[591] On the contrary, Yu Keping describes a right as the capability that individuals possess to perform proper actions without the intervention of others (including the government).[592]

---

[587] Gao Weijun (1943) *General introduction of law* National Institute for Compilation and Translation Press at 89.

[588] Li Zhaowei (1979) *Jurisprudence* at 273. MISSING EDITORIAL

[589] "Quanli zhe falu shang zhi liye" [Personal rights have their force in law]. Cfr Zheng Yubo 1981 *Introduction to law* Sanmin Press at 115.

[590] Liu Jinguo (1995) *Fa lixue* [Jurisprudence] Zhonguo zhengfa daxue chuban she at 164.

[591] Chen Shuoyi (1981) *Basic Theory of Law* Taxue Chubanshe at 350.

[592] Yu Keping (1988) *Communitarianism* China Social Sciences Press at 80.

CHAPTER NINE

Conclusion

The dynamic evolution of human rights discourses in China between the last decade of the 20th century and the first decade of the 21st century is the result of a plethora of different voices. The authorities, civil society, activists and human rights advocates working on the ground all propose their own ways to establish the protection of citizens' rights from violations and abuses of power. All these different Chinese voices advocate—in varied, often contrasting, ways—for a stronger recognition of freedom of expression, association, press, and thought. One of the most sophisticated contributions to this multivocal discussion is that of the intellectuals, and particularly of Chinese legal scholars: a vibrant group of intellectuals who have produced compelling theories of human rights and whose work has been practically ignored by Western observers.

As correctly observed by Cheng Liaoyuan,[593] contemporary Chinese jurisprudence in this period is characterised by two fundamental aspects: professional qualification and independence of thought. When contextualised historically, these two aspects appear as a Copernican revolution within Chinese scholarship. The jurisprudential debate in China, once engaged in only by philosophers and literati, became the domain of scholars and intellectuals trained in law. More importantly, Chinese scholars have abandoned the attitude of 'borrowing science from the West and making sure it comes to the East'. Following the age of reform inaugurated by Deng Xiaoping in the 1980s, scholars have attempted to develop an original system of thought. Doubtless, the contents of their reasoning still largely include Western elements: it would be enough to mention Marxism as this theory originated in 19th century Europe. However, Chinese scholars are now more autonomous in their relationship with foreign traditions.

---

[593] Cheng Liaoyuan 'The Discovery' supra note 82.

The theories examined in this book show that Chinese legal scholars did not simply accept Western discourses passively. Rather they have been engaging with them in an active and dynamic way, assessing, weighing and moulding them to produce new syntheses that are relevant for the Chinese context. This new attitude of critical engagement—which is particularly visible in the debate on human rights—demonstrates a regained maturity in theoretical speculation: a sign that the Chinese intelligentsia was on its way to overcoming the 'crisis of Chinese consciousness'. The party has not overlooked the power of scholarly theorisations and the use made of theories of rights coming from the European and the Anglo-Saxon schools of thought. The capacity of the new syntheses to influence the action of agents outside academia, especially in the legal field, and potentially legitimise movements to claim rights, must have scared the regime.

Moreover, the evolution of academic debates was contrary to the project of progressive and full sinicisation of beliefs carried out by Xi Jinping. This project involves every aspect of human theoretical and spiritual endeavour: philosophy, religion, science and law must be aligned with the 'Chinese identity', and possess 'Chinese characteristics'. According to the new party agenda, this means respecting the leadership of the CCP and conforming to its official ideology. Not only has religion been sinicised, but also law, and this increased control by the party over thought and conscience risks wiping out the most recent developments in the philosophy of law and legal scholarship when they are contrary to the party line. The fruitful two decades of law studies and the flourishing of theories of law and rights that have been examined in this book are now obscured by the strong censorship and the ideological agenda of the regime. Nevertheless, the significance of these theories for the internal Chinese debate must not be dismissed. These theories contributed to the advancement of Chinese consciousness, and truly provide a reasoned approach to human rights on which it would be possible to base a global consensus on human rights norms, if they were not silenced and marginalised by the regime. The call to recover 'Chinese identity' is answered much more in substance by the legal scholars who endeavour to harmonise Chinese culture with the human rights theories, than by the regime which proclaims a rigid adherence to the party line as the new Chinese identity. The dynamics of the mature use of concepts that originated in the West described in the book is a measure of the recovered Chinese identity. This identity, however, does not correspond to the wishes of the people in power because of its plurality, and because of the value attributed to law per se.

In shedding light on these dynamics, a specific choice was made. Instead of simply comparing Chinese theories of rights with American and European approaches, I have preferred to look at Chinese discourses on human rights in their own terms. The main methodological stance was the adoption of an internal perspective that takes into account the legal, philosophical, economic, cultural and political conditions of China. Of course, in considering the relationship between China and the West I have also made use of a cross-cultural approach, but only because Chinese scholars have a cross-cultural awareness, as shown by their critical engagement with Western discourses. Following Ruth Chang,[594] I argued that the choice between different interpretations of human rights, that is a choice between values, is ultimately the choice in favour of a specific identity. This is what Chinese intellectuals have in mind when they discuss human rights: the construction of a specific Chinese identity for their legal system, state and society. To better convey this point let me briefly summarise the main findings of my study.

Engaging with Tradition

To facilitate the discussion of such complex phenomena, I have grouped the most influential Chinese views on human rights under three broad headings: Marxism, liberalism and the Chinese tradition. This choice is not meant to essentialise these discourses; nor did it intend to deny that other influences might have shaped the debate. Rather this was a reflection of the conceptual coordinates that one can detect—or that are explicitly mentioned—in the work of Chinese scholars. A focus on these three theoretical strands also allowed me to illuminate some of the more interesting dynamics involved in the recent debate on human rights. Chinese theories have produced outcomes that differ from orthodox Marxist positions dominant in the 1980s and 1990s. Even the most Marxist-oriented approaches have incorporated views on personhood and society that are usually

---

[594] Chang, Ruth (1997) 'Introduction' in Chang, Ruth (ed) *Incommensurability, Incomparability, and Practical Reasons* Harvard University Press 1.

associated with liberalism, as well as concepts developed by early Confucian and Neo-Confucian thinkers.

This hybrid approach demonstrates, amongst other things, a process of recovery of the Chinese legal-philosophical tradition. This is testimony to a renewed attention to the Chinese past: a sign of the search for continuity with current jurisprudential investigation. In their quest for a theory of human rights, today's scholars undoubtedly reject a number of Confucian ideas, including the notion of a hierarchical society, the idea that relationships are organised according to fixed roles, and the moral practice of rites. Many contemporary mainland scholars do not even mention Confucian theorisations, and often prefer to make use of Marxist-Maoist ideas. However, in the work of these intellectuals one can detect, implicitly or explicitly, the desire to retrieve values (and ideas) from tradition, and to assess whether there are points of connection between these values (and ideas) and the modern idea of rights. This attitude, marked both by an appreciation of tradition and by the necessity to consider contemporary views of law, is evident in various aspects of these scholars' discourses.

As explained in Chapter Two, in classical Chinese philosophical texts the characters *quan* 权 and *li* 利, now composing the word 'right', had a derogative meaning. Significantly, in contemporary jurisprudential writings this pejorative meaning has been lost. This has to do with the fact that, following legal modernisation, the Confucian view that law is inherently intertwined with ethics—and that ethics is about abandoning selfish desires for the good of society—has been progressively abandoned. Even though the law still maintains a link with morality in several ways, with the CCP being the main actor in deciding what morality entails, an independent legal dimension has emerged, separate from the ethical domain. In this understanding of law, being entitled to rights and claiming them is no longer identified with having selfish motives. Even so, this separation between law and ethics is not necessarily an indication that Chinese scholars have embraced Westernised views of law completely.

The current debate on law and rights in China is still informed by Confucian ideas, particularly by the idea that common feelings and common reason are parameters to be taken into consideration in law making and in legal interpretation. These traits set Chinese discourses of human rights apart from the prevailing ideas in the Western legal traditions. In European reasoning since Aristotle, law has been regarded as being 'without passion': a 'cold' matter that should not be influenced by feelings. Only recently have Western scholars begun to reconsider the importance of emotions in law making and adjudication. [595] Bearing this in mind, Chinese theorisations of the relationship between human rights and common feelings stand out as an important contribution to the global discourse on law and rights.

Another important contribution that contemporary Chinese scholars can make concerns the role of mediation: a concept rooted in Chinese tradition that is now regarded as one of the most original elements of Chinese legal culture. Demonstrating their attitude of critical engagement, scholars have praised the traditional understanding of mediation but they have also expressed the need for it to be regulated by law. According to some of them, particularly Cheng and Huang, the institutions of extrajudicial mediation should be further rationalised and reformed in order to make them more capable of delivering justice, especially when disputes over rights arise. At the heart of this critical, but also appreciative, relationship with tradition lies the view that Confucian notions are compatible with the recognition of rights.

Beyond Western Discourses

Contemporary scholars often refer, directly or indirectly, to traditional views of society as being made of different groups, and to the Confucian idea that different responsibilities are attached to different social roles. In doing so, however, they tackle a specific principle behind these notions: the need to exercise rights in a way that takes into account the situation of different individuals belonging to social groups with significant characteristics. Chinese intellectuals argue that, particularly when it comes to vulnerable groups like women, children or the elderly, specific rights should be attributed in virtue of specific circumstances. This position is partly related to the tendency of contemporary Chinese intellectuals to substitute the Marxist notion of class with the more flexible one of group. On a deeper level, however, this focus on the needs of different social groups is based on a true situational anthropology of rights, which is in turn based a contextual view of personhood that comes from Chinese tradition.

---

[595] Corso, L 'Should Empathy' supra note 253 at 94.

The understanding of the individual that appears in the Mencian meta-ethical reflections, and that was adopted in Neo-Confucianism, is founded on the notion of *xing*, a term which is usually translated as 'human nature'. Nonetheless, in the Mencian interpretation, human nature is not strictly understood as nature—a given, pre-cultural endowment from birth—but rather as something that is achieved. *Xing* implies that one is not born human, but rather becomes truly human by cultivating humanity: a process that entails refining the self, and interacting with others. Undeniably, these views clash with the Western understanding of a person as the holder of inner prerogatives: a datum that explains why arguments based on inalienable human qualities have not in general been used as grounding for human rights discourses in China. The Confucian view of human nature, however, offers a valid alternative foundation for human rights that is different from that of dominant Western liberal discourses, but does resonate with communitarian views of rights.

In the Confucian ethics self-realisation depends on interacting with the socio-cultural environment. The environment in turn is based on relations with others, and relations depend on fulfilling duties towards other people, particularly family members. These duties—be it the need to act in a filial way with one's parents or the duty of being loyal to higher officials—are understood as part of one's self-refinement. This process stresses the importance of obligations and authority; but it also presents human relationships as an inherent part of one's personal cultivation and flourishing. It is on this second aspect that some contemporary Chinese scholars focus. This view of humanity, which sees personal edification as linked with the edification of others, illuminates the limitations of those liberal theories of rights that focus merely on the individual sphere and could potentially engage in a fruitful dialogue with communitarians' account of human rights.

Significantly, the relational understanding of personhood that comes from the Confucian tradition sheds light also on the shortcomings of Marxist views of rights. On a superficial level, one might say that the Confucian articulation of law and human nature is compatible with—and even similar to—those found in Marxist thought. Even though Marxism has produced different analytical approaches, a common feature that can be found in all Marxist thinkers, and certainly in Mao Zedong, is the idea that consciousness, and therefore humanity, is generated by specific material, historical and political conditions. In this perspective, very much like with

221

Chinese tradition, in the Marxist framework rights are not seen as inherent in human nature, but as created and attributed by the state through legal dispositions. Nonetheless, when the notion of *xing* is properly contextualised, one realises that it cannot be reduced to the premises of Marxist historical materialism.

Though focused on the idea that humanity is not given at birth, *xing* does not indicate that human nature is entirely dependent on historical circumstances. On the contrary, the concept implicitly indicates that every person has the innate potential to become human. Everyone possesses, one might say, the germ of humanity, and the capacity to become a sage who lives in harmony with his relationships and with her specific socio-cultural environment. Doubtless, in the traditional account not everyone is capable of fulfilling this potential, and it is precisely this aspect that has pushed contemporary scholars dealing with human rights not to rely fully on Confucian thought. However, *xing* does suggest that what defines a person as such is, amongst other things, that fact that she is born with the propensity to actualise her humanity. This aspect shows a difference with strictly Marxist views, and suggests that human rights discourses should include the need to protect one's propensity for human growth, cultivation, and self-realisation.

Searching for the Rule of Law

In striking a balance between Chinese tradition and Western discourses—and in critically engaging with them—Chinese scholars do not always distance themselves from Western notions. This is particularly evident in the recent scholarly debates on the Rule of Law. The principle of 'ruling the country according to the law' enshrined in the Chinese Constitution after the 1999 amendment appeared to affirm the prevalence of law over politics and the need to establish a form of governance based on the autonomy of law. However, the way in which this principle is framed suggests that this 'prevalence of law' can be used instrumentally by those in power to achieve their goals. Incidentally, this latter explanation recalls Chinese traditional views which define law as a 'tool' in the hands of the emperor. Chinese scholars have therefore looked for notions that might help them establish a true rule of law.

Even though some Chinese scholars have defended the Confucian idea of rule of man as a valid alternative to rule of law, others have distanced themselves from tradition and argued that Confucianism poses obstacles to the authority and autonomy of law. According to these intellectuals, Confucians have articulated very strong moral arguments to limit abuses by those in power—particularly the emperor—but these limits are only moral in nature. There is no indication of how these limitations can be actualised in law. In theory, the Confucian framework would expect the emperor to act according to the principles of harmony and preservation of relations. However, in the end, it provides no tool to ensure that, if the emperor does not conform to moral norms and abuses his power, the law can effectively counter this abuse.

Because of this perceived limitation in tradition, scholars have generally argued for the implementation of a new understanding of the primacy of law over politics. Intellectuals have noticed that, very much as in imperial times, nowadays China is in need of legal tools that prevent power-holders from trampling over the law to pursue their interests. Implementation of the rule of law thus seems to be the only effective antidote against this state of affairs, and the fact that many scholars advocate it shows once more that Chinese scholarship critically engages with tradition as much as it does with Western discourses. However, the interest in the rule of law is also a sign of a certain economic sensibility.

In their theorisations, Chinese scholars take into consideration China's current economic conditions and trajectory of development. With the recent reforms leading to the establishment of a socialist market economy, Chinese scholars have strived to reconcile the notion of rule of law with the need to maintain an efficient market that, though regulated by the state, follows capitalist principles at least to some extent. As I have shown, this conundrum has prompted a discussion on the very significance of efficiency as a parameter for law making. In dealing with this issue, Chinese scholarship has expressed the need to recalibrate the notion of efficiency by pairing it with the notion of fairness. In a way, this is an attempt to go beyond strictly liberal interpretations of the market, and to ensure that the need to maintain economic dynamism does not overshadow the importance of human rights. As Keith and Lin have also authoritatively argued, this is perhaps one of the biggest challenges faced by the current jurisprudential debate in China.

The need to maintain stability, understood in a rigid fashion, also represents a powerful hindrance for the affirmation of an idea of law as a regulatory framework to which every person, including the government, has to adhere. As demonstrated by Biddulph's powerful analysis, the stability imperative trumps the legitimate use of law to vindicate rights and to protect citizens from abuse. Rather than becoming the base of stability in a system grounded on the rule of law, legal norms, including those protecting rights, are disregarded whenever social stability is threatened and the primacy of party rule is questioned. As the previous pages show, the theorisations of academics regarding the law as having a value per se are regarded by the regime as having the potential to debase and erode the political dominance of the party and must therefore be silenced.

Current Relevance and Future Developments

The Chinese theorisation on rights possesses its own original voices, and comprises various elements. Bearing in mind the material I have analysed in the preceding Chapters, one might argue that these elements are still disjointed. Perhaps due to the heterogeneity of the discourses used by scholars, the various components that inform the Chinese legal debate do not form a specific 'Chinese theory of rights' that is clearly recognisable. Nevertheless, arguably, even in this embryonic state, these theorisations have the potential to enrich the global consensus on human rights. Like precious gems, they are valuable in themselves even though they are not yet linked together to compose a necklace: a fully-fledged theory of rights. The value of these theories also becomes apparent when one takes into account the context in which Chinese scholars work.

The capacity to articulate theories of rights in an autonomous manner still suffers heavily from limitations imposed by the elite in power. This is particularly true for the recent past, as since 2011 the government has tightened control over universities and higher education, as well as over legal research. In 2015 the head of state even issued guidance prohibiting the teaching and use of Western theories and values, including jurisprudence, and called on the scholars to adhere to dialectical materialism as a heuristic tool to foster 'scientific' development. These measures prevent scholars from fully expressing their innovative insights. Their agency, however, is not completely nullified. Chinese scholarship, particularly when it deals with human rights, has created strategies that allow it not to be entirely limited by the watchful eye of censorship. The further question to explore is whether and how they are going to survive after the tightening of control and censorship in the current phase of authoritarian resilience.

In the two decades between the 1990s and the early 21st century, contemporary Chinese scholars devised rhetorical devices to communicate their ideas, and were able to exercise some influence both on the political debate and on the reforms introduced by the state. This might be a sign that, though somewhat disjointed and subject to control by the state, Chinese jurisprudential theorisations had acquired at least some degree of strength and authoritativeness. The leverage of Chinese scholarship on politics also showed that the relationship between scholars and political power could not be reduced to one of complete submission. The rapport between the two has been more nuanced, and could be described as a relationship of reciprocal, though ultimately asymmetrical, influence. It is in this context that the Chinese intelligentsia was undertaking the task of elaborating new theoretical constructions to effectively integrate the human rights discourse into the Chinese legal system. This trajectory of evolution, however, has been curtailed in the recent past by the elite in power, which claims to be the only repository of scientific method and wishes to dictate the content of orthodox thinking in a monopolistic regime.

Scholars still have a long way to go in their quest to establish the protection of human rights and freedoms as the ultimate justification of government by law. However, the confidence of legal scholars has increased remarkably when compared with the past. Together with the more mature attitude scholars have developed towards the West, this newfound sense of assertiveness is a sign that Chinese intellectuals were overcoming the crisis that affected their country in the past century. Since the late 1980s China has been through a promising phase of transition, and human rights discourses have been a fundamental aspect of this vibrant process.

As the general level of people's education increases, human rights awareness has progressively spread among Chinese citizens. Human rights lawyers strenuously worked in the face of persecution, and people in general, including citizens living in rural areas, have been developing a stronger consciousness of their rights, and, consequently, they increasingly demand that their rights are respected.

It is therefore likely that the call for the establishment of state protection of human rights will become louder. However, this tendency is harshly repressed and powerfully countered by the party. Legal scholars' important role in this process has not been overlooked. Theirs has been a task of rationalisation and vision. Their theories attempted to harmonise individualistic and collectivist perspectives, cosmopolitan aspects of human rights and national identity. These voices risk being silenced by the regime. Given the growing geopolitical and economic importance of China, it is crucial to give voice to the theorisations that differ from the official interpretation of rights sponsored by the Chinese government, and, perhaps for this reason, are less able to reach out to academic discussion outside China.

Bibliography

Alford, WP (1993) 'Double-Edged Swords Cut Both Ways: Law and Legitimacy in the PRC' (122) *Daedalus* 45.

Alston, P (1988) 'Making Space for New Human Rights: The Case of the Right to Development' (1) *Harvard Human Rights Y.B.* 3.

Ames, RT (1991) 'The Mencian Conception of Ren Xing: Does It mean "Human Nature"?' in Rosemont, HJ (ed) (2003) *Chinese Texts and Philosophical Contexts: Essays Dedicated to Angus C. Graham* Open Court 143.

Angle, SC (2000) 'Should We All Be More English? Liang Qichao, Rudolf von Jhering, and Rights' (61) *J. of the History of Ideas* 241.

Angle, SC (2002) *Human Rights and Chinese Thought: A Cross-Cultural Inquiry* Cambridge University Press.

Angle, SC and Svensson, M (eds) (2001) *The Chinese Human Rights Reader: Documents and Commentary 1900-2000* Routledge.

Angle, SC and Weatherley, R (2000) 'Review of the Discourse of Human Rights in China: Historical and Ideological Perspectives' (59) *The Journal of Asian Studies* 719.

Anonymous (2003) 'Chung-yung' [The Doctrine of the Mean] in Plaks, A (trans) (2003) *Ta Hsüeh and Chung Yung: The Highest Order of Cultivation and On the Practice of the Mean* Penguin 21.

Bauer, JR and Bell, DA (eds) (1999) *The East Asian Challenge for Human Rights* Cambridge University Press.

Balme, S (2016) *Chine, le visages de la justice ordinaire. Entre faits et droit* Les Presses de Sciences Po.

Barth, F (1987) *Cosmologies in the Making: A Generative Approach to Cultural Variation in Inner New Guinea* Cambridge University Press.

Beitz, Charles R (2011) *The Idea of Human Rights* Oxford University Press 2011.

Berman, HJ (1993) *Faith and Order. The Reconciliation of Law and Religion* Wm. B. Eerdman Publishing.

Biddulph, S (2015) *The Stability Imperative: Human Rights and law in China* UBC Press.

Bingham, T (2010) *The Rule of Law* Allen Lane.

Bobbio, N (1991) *The Age of Rights* Wiley.

Bobbio, N (1999) *Teoria generale della politica* Einaudi.

Broadman, HG (1996) 'Reform of China's State-Owned Enterprises' in Schoepfle, GK (ed) *Changes in China's Labor Market: Implications for the Future* U.S. Department of Labor, Bureau of International Labor Affairs 4.

Buckley, C (2015) 'China Warns Against 'Western Values' in Imported Textbooks' *New York Times* January 30 2016 available at <https://cn.nytimes.com/china/20150130/c02textbook/en-us/>.

Callahan, WA (2004) 'National insecurities: Humiliation, salvation, and Chinese nationalism' (29, 2) *Alternatives* 199.

Caney, S (2005) *Justice Beyond Borders. A Global Political Theory* Oxford University Press.

Cao, T (ed) (2005) *The Chinese Model of Modern Development* Routledge.

Cao Siyuan (2007) 'Hibernation and the Revival of China's Privately Owned Economy' (40) *Chinese Law and Government* 89.

Cao Siyuan (2007) 'The Homogenization and Decline of China's State-Owned Economy' (40) *Chinese Law and Government* 22.

Cao Siyuan (2007) 'The Ownership System Reform of State-Owned Entrerprises' (40) *Chinese Law and Government* 71.

Carty, A (2007) *Philosophy of International Law* Edinburgh University Press at 204.

Castellucci, Ignazio (2007) 'Rule of Law with Chinese Characteristics' (13) Annual Survey of International and Comparative Law 35.

Catá Backer, L (2006-2007) 'The Rule of Law, The Chinese Communist Party, and Ideological Campaigns: *Sange Daibiao* (The Three Represents) Socialist Rule of Law and Modern Chinese

Constitutionalism' (16) *Transnational Law and Contemporary Problems* 29.

Cardinale, V and Rinella, A (2010) 'La costituzione economica' in Rinella, A and Piccinini, I (eds) *La Costituzione* supra note 285.

Cavalieri, R (1999) *La legge e il rito. Lineamenti di storia del diritto cinese* Milano.

Cavalieri, R (2018) 'La revisione della Costituzione della Repubblica Popolare Cinese e l'istituzionalizzazione del "socialismo dalle caratteristiche cinesi per una nuova era"' (34-1) *Diritto Pubblico Comparato ed Europeo* 307.

Celano, B (2002) 'I diritti nella jurisprudence anglosassone contemporanea. Da Hartz a Raz' in Comanducci, P and Guastini, R (eds) (2002) *Analisi e diritto* Torino 1.

Celano, B (2011) 'Liberal Multiculturalism, neutrality and the Rule of Law' in (11) *Diritto e Questioni Pubbliche* 559.

Celano, B (2013) 'Publicity and the Rule of Law' in Green, BLL (ed) *Oxford Studies in Philosophy of Law: Volume 2* Oxford University Press 122.

Clarke, DC and Feinerman, JV (1996) 'Antagonistic Contradictions: Criminal Law and Human Rights' in Lubman, S (ed) (1996) *China's Legal Reforms* Oxford University Press.

Chan, J (1999) 'A Confucian Perspective on Human Rights for Contemporary China' in Bauer, J (1999) *The East Asian Challenge for Human Rights* Cambridge University Press 212.

Chan, KW (2019) 'China's Hukou System at 60: Continuity and Reform' in Ray Yep; Jun Wang and Johnson, T (eds) (2019) *Edward Elgar Handbook on Urban Development in China* Edward Elgar 59.

Chang Jian and Liu Kun (2004) 'On Equal and Special Protection of Human Rights' (4) *Human Rights* 20-23.

Cheek, T (ed) (2002) *Mao Zedong and China's Revolution: A Brief History with Documents* Palgrave Macmillan.

Chang, Ruth (1997) 'Introduction' in Chang, Ruth (ed) *Incommensurability, Incomparability, and Practical Reasons* Harvard University Press 1.

Chang, W (1986) 'Traditional Chinese Attitudes Toward Law and Authority' Paper presented at the Symposium on Chinese and European Concepts of Law, University of Hong Kong (20-25 Mar).

Chang, W (2012) 'Classical Chinese Jurisprudence and the Development of the Chinese Legal System' (2) *Tsinghua China Law Review* 207.

Chase, MS (2002) *You've got dissent! Chinese dissident use of the internet and Bejing's counter-strategies* Rand.

Chen, AHY (1993) 'Developing Theories of Rights and Human Rights in China' in Wachs, R (ed) (1993) *Hong Kong, China and 1997: Essays in Legal Theory* Hong Kong University Press 123.

Chen, AHY (1996) 'The Developing Theory of Law and Market Economy in Contemporary China' in Wang, G and Wei, Z (eds) (1996) *Legal Developments in China. Market Economy and Law* Sweet and Maxwell in collaboration with [the] Centre for Chinese and Comparative Law, City University of Hong Kong 3.

Chen, AHY (2000) 'Toward A Legal Enlightenment: Discussion in Contemporary China on the Rule of Law' in The Mansfield Center For Pacific Affairs (2010) *The Rule of Law: Perspectives from the Pacific Rim* The Mansfield Center For Pacific Affairs 13.

Chen, AHY (2004) *An introduction to the legal system of the PRC* (3rd ed) Lexis/Nexis.

Chen, AHY (2004) 'Socio-legal Thought and Legal Modernization in Contemporary China: A Case Study of the Jurisprudence of Zhu Suli' in Doeker-Mach, G and Ziegert, KA (eds) *Law, Legal Culture and Politics in the Twenty First Century* Franz Steiner Verlag 227.

Chen, AHY (2006) 'Conclusion: Comparative Reflections on Human Rights in Asia' in Peerenboom, R; Petersen, CJ and Chen, AHY (eds) (2006) *Human Rights in Asia. A Comparative Legal Study of Twelve Asian Jurisdictions, France and the USA* Routledge 487.

Chen, AHY (2016) 'China's Long March Towards the Rule of Law or Chinese Turn Against Law?' (4) *The Chinese Journal of Comparative Law* 1.

Chen, J (2004) 'To have a Cake and Eat it Too?: China and the Rule of Law' in Doeker-Mach, G and Ziegert, KA (eds) (2004) *Law, Legal Culture and Politics in the Twenty First Century* Franz Steiner Verlag 250.

Chen, J (1999) *Chinese Law: Towards an Understanding of Chinese Law, its Nature and Development* Kluwer Law International.

Chen, J (2004) 'The Revision of the Constitution in the PRC. A Great Leap Forward or a Symbolic Gesture' (33) *China Perspectives* 250.

Chen, J (2015) *Chinese Law: Context and Transformation. Revised and Expanded Edition* Nijhof.

Chen, J; Li, Y and Otto, JM (eds) (2002) *Implementation of Law in the PRC* Kluwer Law International.

Cheng Lixian (1999) 'Lun shehui gongzheng, pingdeng yu xiaolu' [On Social Justice, Equality and Efficiency] (9) *Zhexue dongtai* [Philosophical Trends] 3.

Chen Shuoyi (1981) *Basic Theory of Law* Taxue Chubanshe.

Chen Xingliang (2005) 'An Examination of the Death Penalty in China' (36-6) *Contemporary Chinese Thought* 35.

Chen, Zhonglin (2007) *Xingfa zong lun* [General theories of criminal law] Gaodeng jiaoyu chuban she.

Chen Zhonglin (2009) 'Guanyu renquan gainian de ji ge jiben wenti' [Several Basic Issues on the Concept of Human Right] unpublished article on file with the author, trans. by Ma Xiao-wei.

Chen Zhonglin (2009) '"E fa" fei fa. Dui chuantong faxue lilun defansi' [The "Evil Law" is Illegal. Theoretical Reflection from Traditional Jurisprudence] (142) *Social Scientist* 9.

Cheng, CY (2006) 'Toward Constructing a Dialectics of Harmonization: Harmony and Conflict in Chinese Philosophy' (33) *Journal of Chinese Philosophy* 25.

Cheng Liaoyuan (1999) *Cong fazhi dao fazhi* [From Legal System to Rule of Law] Falu chubanshe.

Cheng Liaoyuan (2008) 'Zhongguo jindai fa lixue, falu zhexue mingci kao shu' [The terms of Jurisprudence and Legal Philosophy in modern China] (30) *Xiandai Fashue* [Modern Law Science] 144.

Cheng Liaoyuan (2009) 'Zhongguo fa lixue de faxian. Zhongguo fa lixue shi zai jindai de chuangjian' ['The Discovery of Chinese Jurisprudence. The Establishment of Chinese Jurisprudence History in Modern Times] (3) *Fazhi yu shehui fazhan* [Law and Society Journal] 87.

Cheng Liaoyuan and Wang Renbo (1989) *Fa zhi lun* [Rule of Law] Shandong People's Publishing House.

Cheng Liaoyuan and Wang Renbo (2014) *Quanli Lun* [On Rights] Guilin Shi Guangxi shi fan da xue chu ban she.

Cheung, ASY (2007) 'Public Opinion Supervision: A Case Study of Media Freedom in China' (20) *Columbia Journal of Asian Law* 357.

Cheung, LKC (2001) 'The Way of the Xunzi' (28, 3) *Journal of Chinese Philosophy* 301.

China Daily (2013) 'Reform of hukou system' available at <http://usa.chinadaily.com.cn/opinion/2013-03/08/content_16290371.htm>.

Choukroune, L (2006) 'Justiciability of Economic, Social, and Cultural Rights: The UN Committee on Economic, Social and Cultural Rights Review of China's First Periodic Report on the Implementation of the International Covenant of Economic, Social and Cultural Rights' (19) *Colum. J. Asian L.* 30.

Clarke, DC (2003) 'Economic Development and the Rights Hypothesis: The China Problem' (51) *The American Journal of Comparative Law* 89.

Clarke, DC (2007) 'China: Creating a Legal System for a Market Economy' available at <https://ssrn.com/abstract=1097587>.

Cohen, JA and Lange, JE (1997) 'The Chinese Legal System: A Primer for Investors' (17) *New York Law School Journal of International and Comparative Law* 345.

Cohler, A; Miller, C and Stone, H (eds) Cambridge University Press.

Cass, R (2004) 'Property Rights Systems and the Rule of Law' in Colombatto, E (ed) (2004) *The Elgar Companion to the Economics of Property Right* Edward Elgar Publications 131.

Collotti Pischel, E (1979) *Le origini ideologiche della rivoluzione cinese* Einaudi.

Consiglio, E (2015) 'Early Confucian Legal Thought: A Theory of Natural Law?' (4) *Rivista di Filosofia del Diritto* 359.

Consiglio, E (2018) 'Ipotesi Concorrenti sulla Futura Sostenibilità del Sistema Politico Cinese' (49) *Giornale di Bordo* 86.

Corso, L (2014) 'Should Empathy Play Any Role in the Interpretation of Constitutional Rights?' (27-1) *Ratio Juris* 94.

Crespi RG (1999) 'Verso il mercato e lo Stato di diritto: recenti riforme costituzionali in Cina' (2) *Diritto pubblico comparato ed europeo* 485.

Csordas, TJ (1997) *The Sacred Self: A Cultural Phenomenology of Charismatic Healing* University of California Press.

Cua, AS (2005) *Human Nature, Ritual, and History: Studies in Xunzi and Chinese Philosophy* The Catholic University of America Press.

Dam, KW (2006) *China as a Test Case: Is the Rule of Law Essential for Economic Growth?* Law and economics working paper 275.

Dam, KW (2006) *The Law-growth Nexus: The Rule of Law and Economic Development* Brookings Institution Press.

Davis, KE and Trebilcock, MJ (2008) 'The Relationship between Law and Development: Optimists versus Sceptics' (56) *American Journal of Comparative Law* 895.

Davis, MC (1995) 'Chinese Perspectives on the Bangkok Declaration and the Development of Human Rights in Asia' (89) *Am. Soc'y Int'l L. Proc.* 157.

Delmas-Matry, M (2003) 'Present Day China and the Rule of Law: Progress and Resistance' (2) *Chinese J. Int'l L.* 11.

De Bary, WT (1983) *The Liberal Tradition in China* The Chinese University Press.

De Bary, WT, and Tu Weiming (eds) (1998) *Confucianism and Human Rights* Columbia University Press.

Edwards, RR (1980) 'Ch'ing Legal Jurisdiction Over Foreigners' in Cohen, J (et al) (eds) (1980) *Essays on China's Legal Tradition* Princeton University Press 222.

Delury, J (2008) 'Harmonious in China' (148) *Policy Review* 35.

Edwards, RR; Henkin, L and Natan, AJ (1986) *Human Rights in Contemporary China* Columbia University Press.

Deng Yungcheng, Hu Xiyan (2012) 'An Empirical Analysis of Students' Scientific Research Stimulated by Existing Scholarship System in China' (7) *Legal Education Research* 267.

Dernberger, RF (1991) 'China's Mixed Economic System: Properties and Consequences' in The Joint Economic Committee, Congress of the United States (ed) (1991) *China's Economic Dilemmas in the 1990s: The Problems of Reforms, Modernization, and Interdependence* Government Printing Office 89.

Diamond, L (2003) 'The Rule of Law as Transition to Democracy in China' (12) *Journal of Contemporary China* 319.

Diciotti, E (2006) *Il Mercato delle Libertà* Il Mulino.

Dowdle, MW (2002-2003) 'Of Parliaments, Pragmatism and the Dynamics of Constitutional Development: The Curious Case of China' (35) *New York University Journal of International Law and Politics* 1.

Dworkin, R (1985) *A Matter of Principle* Oxford University Press.

Edward, E (1998) 'Codification of Civil Law in the PRC: Form and Substance in the Reception of Concepts and Elements of Western Private Law' 32 *U. Brit. Colum. L. Rev.* 153.

Epstein, EJ (1989) 'The Theoretical System of Property Rights in China's General Principles of Civil Law: Theoretical Controversy in the Drafting Process and Beyond' (52) *Law and Contemporary Problems* 177.

Ehr-Soon Tay, A (1984) 'China and Legal Pluralism' (8) *Bull. Austl. Soc. Leg. Phil.* 23.

Erh-Soon Tay, A and Kamenka E (1985) 'Elevating Law in the PRC' (9) *Bull. Austl. Soc. Leg. Phil.* 69.

Elster, J (2000) 'Arguing and Bargaining in Two Constituent Assemblies' (2) *U. Pa. J. Const. L.* 345 available at <https://scholarship.law.upenn.edu/jcl/vol2/iss2/1>.

Elster, J (2000) *Ulisses Unbound. Studies in Rationality, Precommitment and Constraints* Cambridge University Press

Fabre, C (1998) 'Constitutionalising Social Rights' (6, 3) *The Journal of Political Philosophy* 263.

Faundez, J (2000) 'Legal Reform in Developing and Transition Countries: Making Haste Slowly' in Faundez, J; Footer, M and Norton, J (eds) (2000) *Governance, Development and Globalization* Blackstone 396.

Feinberg, J (1966) *Duties, Rights, and Claims,* in Feinberg, J (1980), *Rights, Justice and the Bounds of Liberty,* Princeton University Press.

Foust, A (2017) *Confucianism and American Philosophy* SUNY Press.

Fox, A (1995) 'The Aesthetics of Justice: Harmony and Order in Chinese Thought' (14) *Legal Studies Forum* 43.

Forti S (2005) *Il Totalitarismo* Laterza.

Frankfurt, H (1971) 'Freedom of the will and the concept of a person', *Journal of Philosophy*, 68, 5–20.

Frankfurt, H (1999) 'On caring', in *Necessity, Volition, and Love*, Cambridge University Press, at 155–180.

Friedman, LM (1997) 'The Concept of Legal Culture: A Reply' in Nelken, D (ed) (1997) *Comparing Legal Cultures* Dartmouth 33.

Fu, H and Palmer, M (2017) *Mediation in Contemporary China* Wildy, Simmonds and Hill Publishing.

Fuller, LL (1969) *The Morality of Law: Revised Edition* Yale University Press.

Fuller, LL (1976) *Anatomy of the Law* Greenwood Press.

Gao, HS (2018) 'The WTO transparency obligations and China' (12, 2) *Journal of Comparative Law* 329.

Gao Wei and Chang Xuemei (2015) 'Xi Jinping: Persist in Applying the Dialectical Materialism World Outlook Methodology to Improve the Basic Problems of China's Reform and Development' *People's Daily Online* available at <http://cpc.people.com.cn/n/2015/0125/c64094-26445123.html>.

Gao Weijun (1943) *General introduction of law* National Institute for Compilation and Translation Press.

Gellhorn, W (1987) 'China's Quest for Legal Modernity' (1) *Journal of Chinese Law* 1.

Gillespie, J (2006) 'Evolving Concepts of Human Rights in Vietnam' in Peerenboom, R; Petersen, CJ and Chen, AHY (eds) (2006) *Human Rights in Asia: A Comparative Legal Study of Twelve Asian Jurisdictions, France and the USA* Routledge 452.

Gong Pixiang (1992) 'A Value Analysis of the Phenomenon of Rights' (8) *Science of Law* 33.

Gong Pixiang (1991) 'On the Realisation of Rights' (6) *Science of Law* 27.

Goody, J (1977) *The Domestication of the Savage Mind* Cambridge University Press.

Gu, EX (1999) 'Cultural Intellectuals and the Politics of the Cultural Public Space in Communist China (1979-1989): A Case Study of Three Intellectual Groups' (58) *The Journal of Asian Studies* 389.

Goldstein, J and Martin, L (2000) 'Legalization, Trade Liberalization and Domestic Politics: A Cautionary Note' (54) *International Organization* 603.

Guo Daohui (2009) 'Renquan de Guojia Baozhang Yiwu' [State Responsibility for Human Rights Protection] (27, 8) *Hebei Faxue* 10

Guo Xuezhi (2001) 'Dimensions of *Guanxi* in Chinese Elite Politics' (46) *The China Journal* 69.

Guthrie, D (1998) 'The Declining significance of *Guanxi* in China's Economic Transition' (154) *China Quarterly* 254.

Graham, AC (1967) 'The Background of the Mencian Theory of Human Nature' (6) *Tsing Hua Journal of Chinese Studies* 215.

Graham, AC *Studies in Chinese philosophy and philosophical literature* State University of New York Press.

Gramsci, A (1974) [1921-1922] *Socialismo e Fascismo: L'Ordine Nuovo 1921-22* Einaudi.

Gries, PH (2004) *China's New Nationalism: Pride, Politics, and Diplomacy* University of California Press.

Han Depei (ed) (1995) *Renquan de Lilun Yu Shijian* [The theory and practice of Human Rights] Wuhan University Publishing House.

Han Depei; Dong Yunhu and Li Wuping; Xu Bing (1989) 'The Origin and Historical Development of Human Rights Theory' (3) *Chinese Journal of Law*

Hall, DL and Ames, RT (1991) *Thinking through Confucius* State University of New York Press.

Hall, DL and Ames, RT (1995) *Anticipating China: Thinking through the Narratives of Chinese and Western Culture* State University of New York Press.

Hall, DR and Ames, RT (1998) *Thinking From the Han: Self, Truth, and Transcendence in Chinese and Western Culture* State University of New York Press.

Hart, HLA, *Essays in Jurisprudence and Philosophy*, Clarendon Press.

Hart, HLA(1982) 'Bentham on Legal Rights' (reprinted) in Hart, HLA, *Essays on Bentham. Studies in Jurisprudence and Political Theory*, Clarendon Press.

Hart, HLA (1955) 'Are There any Natural Rights?', *Philosophical Review*, 64.

Hayek, F (1973) *Law, Legislation, and Liberty* University of Chicago Press.

Hayek, F (1976) The Mirage of Social Justice University of Chicago Press.

Hayek, F (1979) *The Political Order of a Free People* University of Chicago Press.

He Weifang (1999) *Juti Fazhi* [The Specific Rule of Law] Falü Chubanshe.

He Weifang (1999) 'The Judicial System and Governance in Traditional China' in The Mansfield Center for Pacific Affairs (2019) *The Rule of Law, Perspective from the Pacific Rim* The Mansfield Center for Pacific Affairs 91.

He Weifang (1999) 'Realizing social justice through the judicial system: A perspective on Chinese judges situation' in Yong Xia (ed) (1999) *Toward an age of rights* China University of Political Sciences and Law Press 179.

He Weifang (2005-2006) 'China's Legal Profession: The Nascence and Growing Pains of a Professionalized Legal Class' (19) *Columbia Journal of Asian Law* 138.

He Weifang (2010) 'He Bin, He Weifang deng Beijing faxue mingjia yantao Li Zhuangan' [Discussion on Li Zhuang case by He Weifang, He Bin and other Beijing famous jurists] available at <http://news.mylegist.com/1605/2010-01-05/18658_2.html>.

He Weifang (2012) *In the Name of Justice: Striving for the Rule of Law in China* Brookings Institution Press.

Hermann, M (2007) 'A Critical Evaluation of Fang Dongmei's Philosophy of Comprehensive Harmony' *Journal of Chinese Philosophy* 59.

Hobbes, T (2017) [1651] *Leviathan* Penguin.

Hohfeld, WN (1913) 'Some Fundamental Legal Conceptions as Applied in Judicial Reasoning' (23) *Yale L. J.* 16.

Hoque, A (2015) 'Does the Law Work in a Village Like Gulapbari? An Anthropological Insight' (1) *University of Asia Pacific Journal of Law and Policy* 33.

Howard, R (1983) 'The Fully-Belly Thesis: Should Economic Rights Take Priority Over Civil and Political Rights? Evidence from Sub-Saharian Africa' (5) *Hum. Rts. Q.* 467.

Hu Angang (2000) *Jingji xiaolu yu shehui gongping hu angang* [Economy efficiency and social fairness, Society and Development] Zhejiang People's Publishing House.

Hu Jian and Shen Guang (1993) 'Lue lun shichang jingji zhong de pingdeng yu xiaolu' [A Brief Discussion on Equality and Efficiency in Market Economy] (4) *Renwen zazhi* [The Journal of Humanities] 50.

Hsu, SC (ed) (2003) *Understanding China's Legal System: Essays in Honor of Jerome A. Cohen* New York University.

Huang, PCC (2010) *Chinese Civil Justice, Past and Present* Rowman and Littlefield; Huang, PCC and Yuan Gao (2015) "Should Social Science and Jurisprudence Imitate Natural Science?" (41-2) *Modern China* 131.

Huang, PC (2015) 'Morality and Law in China Past and Present' (41, 1) *Modern China* 39.

Huang, Y (1986) 'Foreign Investment in China – the Legal Requirements' (27) *South China Morning Post*.

Humphrey, C and Laidlaw, J (1994) *The Archetypal Actions of Ritual: A Theory of Ritual Illustrated by the Jain Rite of Worship* Clarendon Press.

Huwitch, J and Hui Li (2013) 'China eyes residence permits to replace divisive hukou system' available at <http://www.reuters.com/article/2013/03/06/us-china-parliament-urbanisation-idUSBRE92509020130306>.

Information Office of the State Council of the PRC (1991) 'White Paper on Human Rights in China' available at <http://www.china.org.cn/e-white/7/index.htm>.

Information Office of the State Council of the PRC (2016) 'National Human Rights Plan of China (2016-2020)' available at <http://english.gov.cn/archive/publications/2016/09/29/content_28147 5454482622.htm>.

Information Office of the State Council of the PRC (1995) *The Progress of Human Rights in China* available at <http://www.china.org.cn/e-white/phumanrights19/index.htm>.

Hsu, BFC and Arner, D (2007) 'WTO accession, financial reform and the rule of law in China' (7) *China Review: An Interdisciplinary Journal on Greater China* Hong Kong 53.

Jhering, R (1915) [1872] *The Struggle for Law* Lalor, JJ (trans) Callaghan and Company.

Ivanhoe, PJ (2000) *Confucian Moral Self Cultivation* Hacket Publishing.

Ivanhoe, PJ (2002) *Ethics in the Confucian Tradition: The Thought of Mengzi and Wang Yangming* Hacket Publishing.

Jacobson, L (2004) 'Local Government, Village and Township Direct Election' in Howell, J (ed) (2004) *Governance in China* Rowman and Littlefield 97.

Jayasuriya, K (ed) (1999) *Law, Capitalism and Power in Asia: The Rule of Law and Legal Institutions* Routledge.

Jiang Qing; Bell, DA and Ruiping, F (eds) (2013) *A Confucian Constitutional Order, How China's Ancient Past Can Shape Its Political Future* Princeton University Press.

Kang Xinhai (2009) 'Qian xi pingdeng yu xiaolu de guanxi ji qi chuli duice' [Analysis of the Relationship between Equality and Efficiency and Its Countermeasures] (1) *Zhongxiao qiye guanli yu keji* [Management and Technology of SME] 80.

Ke, Wei (2007) *Foundations of the Main Body of Rule of Law in Contemporary China: Study on Public Consciousness of Rule of Law* Falu Chubanshe.

Kim, HI (1981) *Fundamental Legal Concepts of China and the West: A Comparative Study* Kennikat Press.

Keith, RC (1991) 'Chinese Politics and the New Theory of "Rule of Law"' (125) *The China Quarterly* 109.

Keith, RC (1994) *China's Struggle for the Rule of Law* St. Martin's Press.

Keith, RC (1997) 'Legislating Women's and Children's Rights and Interests in the PRC' (149) *The China Quarterly* 29.

Keith, RC and Lin, Z (2001) *Law and Justice in China's New Marketplace* Palgrave.

Keith, RC and Lin, Z (2005) *New Crime in China. Public Order and Human Rights* London.

Keith, RC (1998) 'Post-Deng Jurisprudence: Justice and Efficiency in a 'Rule of Law Economy' (45) *Problems of Post-Communism* 48.

Kelsen, H (1946) *General Theory of Law and State*, Harvard University Press.

Kent, A (1993) *Between Freedom and Subsistence. China and Human Rights* Oxford University Press.

Kramer, M H, Simmonds, N E, Steiner, H (1998) *A Debate over Rights. Philosophical Enquiries*, Clarendon Press.

Kramer, M H, (2010) 'Refining the Interest Theory of Rights', *American Journal of Jurisprudence*, 55.

Kramer, Matthew H, Simmonds, N E and Steiner, H, (1998) *A Debate Over Rights: Philosophical Enquiries*, Oxford University Press.

Kramer, M and Steiner, H (2007) 'Theories of Rights: Is There a Third Way?', *Oxford Journal of Legal Studies*, 27.

Lai, KL (2006) *Learning from Chinese Philosophies. Ethics of Interdependent and Contextualised Self*, Ashgate.

Lau, DC (1970) *Mencius* Penguin.

Lau, DC (2003) *Mencius* (New Bilingual Edition) Chinese University Press.

Lau, AKL and Young, A (2009) *In Search of Chinese Jurisprudence: Does Chinese Legal Tradition Have a Place in China's Future?* Hong Kong Baptist University School of Business.

Lee, DC (2000) 'Legal Reform in China: A Role for Nongovernmental Organizations' (25) *Yale J. Int'l L.* 363.

Lei Chen and van Rhee, CH (eds) (2012) *Towards a Chinese Civil Code: Comparative and Historical Perspective* Martinus Nijhoff.

Lei, D (2005) '*Guanxi* and its Influence on Chinese Business Practices' (5-2) *Harvard China Review* 81.

Lenin, VI (2013) [1902] *What is to be done?* Martino Fine Books.

Li Buyun and Xu Bing (1986) *Quanli yu yiwu* [Rights and Obligations], Remin Press.

Li Buyun (1991) 'Lun renquan de sanzhong cunzai xingtai' [On Three Forms of Human Rights] in CASS Legal Institute (ed) (1992) *Dangdai renquan* (Contemporary Human Rights) Zhongguo shehui kexue chubanshe 3.

Li Buyun (1991) 'On the three modes of existence of human rights' (4) *Studies in Law* 11.

Li, Buyun (1994) 'Lun geren renquan yu jiti renquan' [On individual human rights and collective human rights] (6) *Zhongguo shehui kexueyuan yanjiusheng yuan xuebao* [Academic Journal Graduate School Chinese Academy of Social Sciences] 9.

Li Buyun (1996) 'On individual and collective human rights' in Baehr, PR (et al) (eds) (1996) *Human Rights: Chinese and Dutch perspectives* Martinus Bijhoff Publishers 119.

Li Buyun (2004) 'On the Origin of Human Rights' (22-2) *Tribune of Political Science and Law* 11.

Li Buyun (2004) *New Constitutionalism in China* Falu Chubanshe.

Li Buyun (2007) 'Lun renquan de pubian xing he teshu xing' [On the universality and particularity of human rights] (6) *Huanqiu falu pinglun* [Global Law Review] 5.

Li Buyun (2008) *Lun Fazhi* She hui ke xue wen xian chu ban she.

Li Buyun, (2006) *Xianzheng Yu Zhongguo* [Constitutionalism and China] Falu Chubanshe, reprinted in Yu Keping (ed) (2010) *Democracy and the Rule of Law in China* Brill 197.

Li, L (2001) 'Towards a More Civil Society: Mingong and Expanding Social Space in Reform-Era China' (33) *Columbia Human Rights Law Review* 149.

Li Songling (1993) 'Lun shichang jingji de pingdeng yu xiaolu' ['On the equality and efficiency of market economy'] (5) *Qiusuo* [Seeking] 3.

Li Yining (1997) *Ethical Issues in Economics* Peiking University Publishing House.

Li, Z (2004) 'NPC: The Rule of Law' (47) *Beijing Review* 10.

Liang Zhiping (1989) 'Explicating "Law": A Comparative Perspective of Chinese and Western Legal Culture' (3) *Journal of Chinese Law* 59

Liang Zhiping (1989) '"Fa ziran" yu "Ziran fa"' [Law of nature versus natural law] (2) *Zhonghuo shehui kexue* [Social Sciences in China] 209.

Liang, Zhiping (1995) 'Law and Fairness at a Time of Change' (2) *China Perspectives* 30.

Liang Zhiping (1997) *Xunqiu ziran zhixu zhong de hexie: Zhongguo chuantong falu wenhua yanjiu* [Seeking for the harmony in the natural order-A study on the Traditional Chinese legal culture] China University of Political Science and Law Publishing Press.

Liang Zhiping (2002) *Fabian Zhongguo Fade Guoqu, Xianzai yu Weilai* [The Difference of Law: Chinese Law Past, Present and Future] Zhongguo zhengfa dazue chubanshe.

Liang Zhiping (2006) 'Mingyu quan yu yanlun ziyou: Xuan ke an zhong de shifei yu qingzhong' [Reputation Right and Freedom of Speech: the Right and Wrong in Xuan Ke Case] (2) *Zhongguo Faxue* [China Legal Science] 143.

Lichtenstein, NG (1987) 'Legal Implications of China's Economic Reforms' (1) *ICSID Review – Foreign Investment Law Journal* 289.

Lieberthal, K and Oksenberg, M (1998) *Policy Making in China: Leaders, Structures and Processes* Princeton University Press.

Liebman, BL (2005) 'Watchdog or Demagogue? The Media in the Chinese Legal System' (105) *Columbia Law Review* 1.

Liu Hainian, Li Buyun and Li Lin (eds) (1996) *Yifa Zhiguo Jianshe Shehuizhuyi Fazhi Guojia* [Ruling the Country According to the Law Establishing a Socialist Nation Ruled According to Law] Zhongguo Fazhi Chubanshe.

Liu Meng, Yanhong Hu and Minli Liao (2009) 'Traveling theory in China: contextualization, compromise and combination' (9, 4) *Global Networks* 529.

Liang Zhiping (1999) *Cong lizhi dao fazhi* [From rule of *li* to rule of law] (126) *Kaifang shidai* 78.

Lidija, R and Basta, F (eds) (2000) *Rule of Law and Organisation of the State in Asia: The Multicultural Challenge* Helbing et Lichtenhahn.

Liebman, BL (2008) 'China's courts: Restricted reform' (21) *Columbia Journal of Asian Law* 2.

Lien Sheng Yang (1957) 'The Concept of Pao as a Basis for Social Relations in China' in Fairbank, JK (ed) (1957) *Chinese Thought and Institutions* University of Chicago Press 291.

Lin, G (2004) 'Leadership Transition, Intra-Party Democracy, and Institution Building' (44) *China Asian Survey* 255.

Lin Yu-Sheng (1979) *The Crisis of Chinese Consciousness: Radical Antitraditionalism in the May Fourth Era* University of Wisconsin Press.

Ling Li (2016) 'The Chinese Communist Party and People's Courts: Judicial Dependence in China' (64) *American Journal of Comparative Law* 6.

Liu, Y (1998) *Origins of Chinese Law, Penal and Administrative Law in its Early Development* Oxford University Press.

Linz, JJ (2000) *Totalitarian and Authoritarian Regimes* Lynne Rienner Publishers.

Liu, H (2008) 'International Human Rights Law and the Establishment of Rule of Law in China' in Li, HW; Feng, J; Wang, M; Wu, Y; Zhang, G and Zou, H (eds) (2008) *The China Legal development Yearbook I* Brill 209.

Liu, H (2009) 'Protection of Human Rights and the Establishment of Rule of Law in China' in Li, L (ed) (2009) *The China Legal Development Yearbook II* Brill, 279.

Liu Jinguo (1995) *Fa lixue* [Jurisprudence] Zhonguo zhengfa daxue chuban she.

Liu Yuli (2004) *The Unity of Rule and Virtue: A Critique of a Supposed Parallel Between Confucian Ethics and Virtue Ethics* Eastern Universities Press.

Litwack, EB (2015) 'Totalitarianism' *Internet Encyclopedia of Philosophy* available at <https://www.iep.utm.edu/totalita/>.

Locke, J (1988) [1689] *Two Treaties on Government* Cambridge University Press.

Lubman, SB (1999) *Bird in a Cage: Legal Reform in China after Mao* Stanford University Press.

Luo, Haocai (2008) 'China Embarks a Road towards Human Rights Progress with Chinese Characteristics' (3) *Human Rights* 2.

Ma Weilong (1999) 'If the Citizens Want to Rid Themselves of the Evils of Autocracy, They Must Have Political Power' (31, 1) *Contemporary Chinese Thought* 44.

MacCormack, G (1996) *The Spirit of Traditional Chinese Law* University of Georgia Press.

MacCormick, N (1976) 'Children's Rights: A Test-Case for Theories of Rights', reprinted in MacCormick, N (1982) *Legal Right and Social Democracy: Essays in Legal and Political Philosophy*, Clarendon Press, at 154;

MacCormick, N (1977) 'Rights in Legislation', in Hacker P.M.S., Raz J. (eds.), *Law, Morality and Society: Essays in Honour of HLA Hart*, Clarendon Press.

MacCormick, N (1982) *Legal Right and Social Democracy,* Clarendon Press.

Manion, M (2000) 'Chinese Democratization in Perspective: Electorates and Selectorates at the Township Level' (163) *The China Quarterly* 764.

Marmor, A (2007) *Law in the Age of Pluralism* Oxford University Press.

Marks, S (2004) 'The Human Right to Development: Between Rhetoric and Reality' (17) *Harvard Human Rights J.* 137.

Martines, J (2016) 'Despite Policy Reforms, Barriers to Obtaining Hukou Persist' *The Diplomat* available at

<https://thediplomat.com/2016/02/despite-policy-reforms-barriers-to-obtaining-hukou-persist/>.

Marx, K (1973) [1857] *Grundrisse: Foundations of the Critique of Political Economy* Penguin Books.

Marx, K and Engels, F (1970) [1845] *The German Ideology. Part One with selections from Parts Two and Three, together with Marx's Introduction to a Critique of Political Economy* International Publishers.

Marx, K and Engels, F (1996) *Collected Works Vol. 35* International Publishers.

Massad, J (2015) 'Orientalism as Occidentalism' (5) *History of the Present* 83.

McConville, M and Pils, E (2013) *Comparative Perspectives on Criminal Justice in China* Edward Elgar Publishing.

Miller, HL (1999) 'Xu Liangying and He Zuoxiu: Divergent Responses to Physics and Politics in the Post-Mao Period' (30) *Historical Studies in the Physical and Biological Sciences* 89.

Metzger, TA (1996) *Transcending the West: Mao's Vision of Socialism and the Legitimization of Teng Hsiao-ping's Modernization Program* Hoover Institution on War, Revolution and Peace, Stanford University.

Montesquieu, C (1989) [1748] *The Spirit of the Laws* Penguin.

Morlino, L and Palombella, G 2010 *Rule of Law and Democracy: Inquiries into Internal and External Issues* Brill.

Mou, B (ed) (2009) History of Chinese Philosophy vol. 3 of History of World Philosophies Routledge.
Nan Shi (1974) *The History of the Southern Dynasties* Zhonghua shuju.

Munro, DJ (2008) *Ethics in Action. Workable Guidelines for Public and Private Choices* The Chinese University Press.

National People's Congress of the PRC (2018) *Zhonghua renmin gongheguo xianfa xiuzheng an* [Peoples Republic of China

Constitutional Amendment] available at <http://www.npc.gov.cn/npc/xinwen/2018-03/12/content_2046540.htm>.

Nathan, AJ (2003) 'China's Changing of the Guard. Authoritarian Resilience' (14) *Journal of Democracy* 1.

Nathan AJ (1986) 'Sources of Chinese Rights Thinking' in Edwards, RR; Henkin, L and Natan, AJ (eds) (1986) *Human Rights in Contemporary China* Columbia University Press 125.

Nozick, R (1974) *Anarchy, State and Utopia* Basic Books.

Office of The State Council of the People's Republic of China (2014) *Guowuyuan guanyu jìnyibu huji gaige de yijian* [State's Council Opinions on Further Promoting Reform of the Household Registration System] People's Press.

Office of The State Council of the People's Republic of China (2015) *Guowuyuan bangong ting guanyu jiejue wu hukou renyuan. Dengji hukou wenti de yijian* [The General Office of the State Council on the settlement of non-*hukou* personnel. Opinions on the problem of *hukou* registration] available at <http://www.gov.cn/zhengce/content/2016-01/14/content_10595.htm>.

Palmer, M (1987) 'The Revival of Mediation in the PRC: (1) Extra-Judicial Mediation' in Butler, WE (ed) (1987) *Yearbook on Socialist Legal Systems* 143.

Palmer, M (2006-2007) 'Controlling the State? Mediation in Administrative Litigation in the PRC' (16) *Transnational Law and Contemporary Problems* 165.

Palmer, M; Fu, H, and Zhang X (eds) (2019) *Transparency Challenges Facing China* Wildy, Simmonds and Hill Publishing.

Palombella, G (2009) 'Rule of Law. Argomenti di una teoria giuridica istituzionale' (1) *Sociologia del diritto* 27.

Peerenboom, RP (1990) 'Confucian Jurisprudence: Beyond Natural Law' (36) *Asian Culture Quarterly* 12.

Peerenboom, RP (1993) *Law and Morality in Ancient China: The Silk Manuscripts of Huang-Lao* State University of New York Press.

Peerenboom, RP (1993) 'What's Wrong with Chinese Rights? Toward a Theory of Rights with Chinese Characteristics' (6) *Harvard Human Rights J.* 29.

Peerenboom, RP (2001) 'Globalization, Path Dependency and the Limits of Law: Administrative Law Reform and the Rule of Law in the PRC' (19) *Berkeley Journal of International Law* 161.

Peerenboom, RP (2002) *China's Long March toward Rule of Law* Cambridge University Press.

Peerenboom, RP (ed) (2004) *Asian Discourses of Rule of Law: Theories and Implementation of Rule of Law in Twelve Asian Countries, France and the U.S.* Routledge Curzon.

Peerenboom, RP (2006) 'A Government of Laws. Democracy, Rule of Law, and Administrative Law Reform in China' in Zhao, S (ed) *Debating Political Reform in China. Rule of Law vs. Democratisation* Routledge 58.

Peerenboom, RP (2006) 'What Have We Learned About Law and Development? Describing, Predicting, and Assessing Legal Reforms in China' (27) *Mich. J. Int'l L.* 823.

Perry, EJ (2007) 'Studying Chinese Politics: Farewell to Revolution?' (57) *The China Journal* 1.

Pils, E (2008) 'China's Troubled Legal Profession' *Far Eastern Economic Review* available at: <https://ssrn.com/abstract=1563922 >.

Pils, E (2015) *China's Human Rights Lawyers: Advocacy and Resistance* Routledge.

Pils, EM (2016) 'If Anything Happens…:' Meeting the Now-detained Human Rights Lawyers' *China Change* available at <https://chinachange.org/2016/01/10/if-anything-happens-meeting-the-now-detained-human-rights-lawyers/>

Pils, E (2018) *Human Rights in China. A Social Practice in the Shadows of Authoritarianism* Wiley.

Potter, PB (1992) 'The Legal Framework for Security Markets in China: The Challenge of Maintaining State Control, and Inducing Investor's Confidence' (7) *China Law Reporter* 61.

Potter, PB (2003) *From Leninist Discipline to Socialist Legalism: Peng Zhen on Law and Political Authority in the PRC* Stanford University Press.

Potter, PB (2006) 'Selective adaptation and institutional capacity: Perspectives on Human Rights in China' (61, 2) *International Journal* 389.

Potter, PB (2013) *China's Legal System* Polity Press.

Qin Xuan (2003) 'Pingdeng yu xiaolu: Shehui zhuyi de liang da jiazhi mubiao' [Equality and Efficiency: Two Values of Socialism] (1) *Wenshi zhe* [Journal of Literature, History & Philosophy] 152.

Qiu Hanping (1935) *General Theory of Law* The Commercial Press

Qiu Xinglong (2005) 'The Morality of the Death Penalty' (36-3) *Contemporary Chinese Thought* 9.

Rawls, J (1971) *A Theory of Justice* Oxford University Press.

Rawls, J (1993) *Political Liberalism* Columbia University Press.

Raz J (1975) *Practical Reason and Norms* Hutchinson.

Raz, J (1975) 'Reasons for Action, Decisions and Norms' (84) *Mind* 481.

Raz, J (1979) 'The Rule of Law and Its Virtue' in *The Authority of Law. Essays on Law and Morality* Clarendon Press 211.

Raz, J (1985) 'Authority and Justification' (14) *Philosophy and Public Affairs* 3.

Raz, J (1984) 'The Nature of Rights', reprinted in Raz, J (1986) *The Morality of Freedom*, Clarendon Press, at 165.

Raz, J (1984) 'Legal Rights', reprinted in Raz, J (1994) *Ethics in the Public Domain: Essays in the Morality of Law and Politics*, Clarendon Press.

Raz, J (1970) *The Morality of Freedom,* Clarendon Press.

Raz, J (1996) *Ethics in the Public Domain,* Clarendon Press.
Simmonds, N E (1986) *Central Issues in Jurisprudence. Justice, Law and Rights,* Sweet & Maxwell.

Rinella, A and Piccinini, I (eds) (2010) *La Costituzione economica cinese* Il Mulino.

Roberston, R (1994) 'Measuring State Compliance with the Obligation to Devote the "Maximum Available Resources" to Realising Economic, Social and Cultural Rights' (16) *Human Rights Quarterly* 693.

Rosemont, HJ (2004) 'Whose Democracy? Which Rights? A Confucian Critique' in Kwong-loi Shun and David B. Wong (2004) *Confucian Ethics: A Comparative Study of Self, Autonomy, and Community* Cambridge University Press 49.

Rousseau, JJ (2012) [1762] *Of the Social Contract and Other Political Writings* Penguin.

Said, EW (1978) *Orientalism* Pantheon Books.

Santangelo, P. (1992) *Emozioni e desideri in Cina. La riflessione neoconfuciana dalla metà del XIV alla metà XIX secolo* Laterza.

Sen, A (1997) 'Human Rights and Asian Values' *Sixteenth Morgenthau Memorial Lecture on Ethics and Foreign Policy* Carnegie Council on Ethics and International Affairs.

Sen, A (2004) 'Elements of a Theory of Human Rights' (32, 4) *Philosophy and Public Affairs* 315.

Seppänen, S (2016) *Ideological Conflict and the Rule of Law in Contemporary China: Useful Paradoxes* Cambridge University Press.

Sethi, JD (1981) 'Human Rights and Development. Symposium South Asian Perspectives on Human Rights' (3) *Human Rights Quarterly* 11.

Scarpari, M (2015) *Ritorno a Confucio, La Cina di oggi tra Tradizione e Mercato* Il Mulino.

Schall, JV (1987) 'Human Rights as an Ideological Project' (32) *Am. J. Juris.* 47.

Schiavello, A (2000) 'Principio di eguaglianza: breve analisi a livello concettuale e filosofico politico' (14) *Ragion Pratica* 65.

Schwartz, BI (1965) 'Modernization and the Maoist Vision – Some Reflections on Chinese Communist Goal' (21) *China Quarterly* 51.

Sen, A (1993) *Markets and Freedoms* Oxford Economic Papers.

Shahid, Y; Kaoru, M and Dwight, P (1994) *Under New Ownership Privatizing China's State-owned Enterprises* Stanford University Press and The World Bank.

Sharma, A (2006) *Are Human Rights Western? A Contribution to the Dialogue of Civilizations* Oxford University Press.

Shavell, S and Kaplow, L (2000-2001) 'Fairness versus Welfare' (114) *Harv. L. Rev.* 961.

Shen Zhonglin (1996) 'Ruling the Country According to the Law, Constructing a Socialist Legal System State' (6) *Beijingdaxue Xuebao Zhesheban* 4.

Shen Zhonglin (1991) 'Human Rights: Rights in Which Sense?' (5) *Chinese Legal Science* 22.

Shih, CY (1993) 'Contending Theories of Human Rights with Chinese Characteristics' (29) *Issues and Studies* 42.

Svensson, M (2002) *Debating Human Rights in China: A Conceptual and Political History* Rowman and Littlefield.

Silverstain, G (2003) Globalization and the Rule of Law: 'A machine that runs of itself?' (1-3) *ICON* 427.

Stawar, A (1973) *Liberi Saggi Marxisti* La Nuova Italia.

Strauss, Leo (1952) *Persecution and the Art of Writing* Free Press.

Sun Guo Hua (ed) (1998) *Basic Theory of Law* Tianjin Renmin Chubanshe.

Supreme People's Court of the PRC (2012) 'Intellectual Property Protection by Chinese Courts in 2012' available at <http://www.court.gov.cn/zscq/bhcg/201304/t20130426_183662.html>.

Tamanaha, BZ (2006) *Law as a Means to an End: Threat to the Rule of Law* Cambridge University Press.

Tambiah, SJ (1985) *Culture, Thought, and Social Action* Harvard University Press.

Tasioulas, J (2015) 'On the Foundations of Human Rights' in Cruft, R; Liao, M and Renzo, M (eds) (2015) *Philosophical Foundations of Human Rights* Oxford University Press 45.

Tarello, G (1988) *Cultura giuridica e politica del diritto* Il Mulino.

Taylor, C (1999) 'Conditions for an Unforced Consensus on Human Rights' in Bell, D and Bauer, JR (ed) (1999) *The East Asian Challenge for Human Rights* Cambridge University Press 124.

Teng Biao (2013) 'The Sun Zhigang incident and the Future of Constitutionalism: Does the Chinese Constitution Have a Future?' Centre for Rights and Justice Occasional Paper available at <https://www.law.cuhk.edu.hk/en/research/crj/download/papers/2013-tb-szg-constitutionalism.pdf>.

Teng Jianhua (1997) 'How to balance the relationship between efficiency and equality in social market economy' (1) *Academic Exchange* 6.

Tong Zhiwei (2018) *Right, Power and Faquanism. A Practical Legal Theory from Contemporary China* Brill.

Trotsky, L (1979) [1904] *Our Political Tasks* New Park Publications.

Trubek, DM (1972) 'Toward a Social Theory of Law: An Essay on the Study of Law and Development' (821) *The Yale Law Journal* 1.

Trujillo (2000) 'La Questione dei Diritti Sociali' (14) *Ragion Pratica* 43.

Tsu-Ch'u Tung (1961) *Law and society in traditional China* Mouton.

Tu Weiming (1989) *Centrality and commonality: An essay on Confucian religiousness* State University of New York Press.

Trujillo, I and Viola, F (2016) *What Human Rights Are Not (or Not Only): A Negative Path to Human Rights Practice* Nova Science Publishers.

UN World Conference on Human Rights (1993) 'Final Declaration of the Regional Meeting for Asia of the World Conference on Human Rights' (1993) available at: <https://www.ru.nl/publish/pages/688605/bangkok-eng.pdf>.

Viola, F (2000) *Etica e metaetica dei diritti umani* Gisppichelli.

Walder, A (2004) 'The Party Elite and China's Trajectory of Change' (2, 2) *China: An International Journal* 189.

Waldron, J (ed) (1993) *Liberal Rights. Collected Papers 1981-1991* Cambridge University Press 339.

Waldron, J (2008) 'The Concept and the Rule of Law' (43) *Georgia Law Review*, 59.

Waldron, J (1993) *Liberal Rights,* Oxford University Press.

Waldron, J (1988) *The Right to Private Property*, Clarendon Press.

Walzer, M (1981) 'The theory of tyranny, the tyranny of theory. Totalitarianism vs. Authoritarianism' (185) *The New Republic* 21.

Wang Chunguo (1995) *Modern jurisprudence: History and Theory* Hunan Press.

Wang, J (2004) 'The Rule of Law in China: a Realistic View of the Jurisprudence, the Impact of the WTO and the Prospects for Future Development' *Singapore Journal of Legal Studies* 347.

Wang, J; Hainian, L and Li Buyun (1989) 'Lun Fazhi Gaige' [On the Reform of the Legal System] (8) *Faxue Yanjiu* [Studies in Law] 1.

Wang, N (1997) 'Orientalism versus Occidentalism?' (28) *New Literary History* 57.

Weatherley, R (1999) *The Discourse of Human Rights in China. Historical and Ideological Perspectives* Palgrave Macmillan.

Wei Y (2006) 'Zhongguo gu dai de he xie zhi lu' ['The Ways of Harmony in Ancient China'] in Xian, Y (ed) (2006) *Falü wenhua yanjiu* [Research in Legal Culture] Zhongguo renmin chubanshe.

Wellman, C (1977) *An Approach to Rights*, Kluwer.

Weiss, L (2007) 'Guiding Globalization in East Asia: New Roles for Old Developmental States' in Weiss, L (ed) *States in the Global Economy* Cambridge University Press.

Wu Buyun (1992) Introduction to the Philosophy of Marxism Shaanxi Renmin Press.

Xia Yong (1992) *Renuquan Gainian Qiyuan* [The Origin of the Theory of Human Rights] China University of Politics and Law Printing House.

Xia Yong (2007) *Zou xiang quanli de shidai. Zhongguo gongmin quanli fa zhan yan jiu* [Toward an Age of Rights—A Research of the Civil Rights Development in China] Shehui kexue wenxian chubanshe [Social Sciences Academic Press] at 319.

Xie Hui (1994) 'On Legal Instrumentalism' (1) *Zhongguo Faxue* 50.

Xu Bing (1989) 'Renquan lilun de changsheng he lishi fazhan' [The Emergence and Historical Development of Human Rights Theory] (3) *Legal Studies* 1.

Xu Xianming (1996) 'The Main Constitutive Elements of the Rule of Law-And Some Rule of Law Principles and Concepts' (5) *Chinese Journal of Chinese Law*.

Xu Xianming (2006) 'The Right to Harmony: Human Rights of the Fourth Generation' (3) *Human Rights* 20.

Xu Xianming (2008) *Principles of Human Rights Law* China University of Political Science and Law Press.

Xu Xianming (2008) 'The Development of Human Rights in The World and the Progress of Human Rights in China. A Theoretical Reflection on the History of Human Rights Law' (12) Journal of the Party School of the Central Committee of the C.P.C. 30.

Xu Xianming and Qi Yongpin (2007) 'Practicality, Questions, and Characteristics of Chinese Jurisprudence' (1) *Chinese Jurisprudence* 111.

Xunzi (2006) *The Great Learning and the Doctrine of the Mean* available at <http://www.indiana.edu/~p374/Daxue-Zhongyong_(Eno-2016).pdf>

Xunzi (2016) 'The Way to be a Lord' in Hutton, EL (trans) (2016) *Xunzi: The Complete Text* Princeton University Press 117.

Yin Jicheng and Song Rufeng (2003) 'Shichang jingji xia de xiaolu yu gongping ji qi shixian jili' [The Efficiency and Equity in Market Economy and its Mechanism of Realization] (1) *Jinan daxue xuebao* [Journal of Jinan University] 52.

Yu Keping (1988) *Communitarianism* China Social Sciences Press.

Yu Keping (2002) 'Toward an Incremental Democracy and Governance: Chinese Theories and Assessment Criteria' (24) *New Political Science* 181.

Yu Keping (2004) *From the Discourse of Sino-West to Globalisation: Chinese Perspectives on Globalisation* China Centre for Comparative Politics.

Yuan Kunxiang (1980) *Introduction to Law* Sanmin Press.

Zolo, D (2004) *Globalizzazione. Una mappa dei problemi* Laterza.

Zhang, Guangbo (1989) *Quanli yiwuyaolun* [A Concise Theory of Right and Duty] Changchun: Jilin daxue chubanshe.

Zhang Guangbo (1990) 'Jianchi makesi zhuyi de renquan guan' [Adhere to the Marxist View of Human Rights] (4) *Zhongguo faxue* [Chinese Law] 10.

Zhang Qingfu (1994) Basic Theories of Constitutional law Shehui kefawenxian chubanshe.

Zhang Renshou (1994) 'Lun shichang jingji zhong de pingdeng yu xiaolu' [On equality and efficiency in market economy] (6) *Guancha yu sikao* [Observation and Ponderation] 7.

Zhang Wenxian (1992) 'On the Subject of Human Rights and Subjective Human Rights' in Legal Research Institute (ed) (2000) *Contemporary Human Rights,* Press of the Chinese Social Academy 36.

Zhang Wenxian (2014) 'Fazhi yu guojia zhili xiandaihua' [The Rule of Law and the Modernization of State Administration] (4) *Zhonguo Faxue* [China Legal Science].

Zhang Wenxian (2014) 'Human Rights Protection and Judicial Civilization' (2) *China Law Review.*

Zhang Wenxian (2014) 'Quanmian tuijin fazhi gaige, jiakuai fazhi zhongguo jianshe - Shiba jie san zhong quanhui jingshen de faxue jiedu' [Promoting Legal Reform in an All-round Way and

Accelerating the Construction of the Rule of Law in China - A Legal Interpretation of the Spirit of the Third Plenary Session of the 18th CPC Central Committee] (1) *Fazhi yu shehui fazhan* [Law and Social Development].

Zhang Xiangwen (trans) (1905) *Wanfa Jingli.* Shanghai: Wenming shuju.

Zhang, X (2005) *Implementation of the WTO Agreements in China* Wildy, Simmonds and Hill Publishing.

Zhao Zhenjiang (1994) 'On the principle of efficiency and equality in market economy context and its legal solution' (5) *Peking University Law Journal.*

Zheng Chenglian (1996) 'The Essence of the Jurisprudence of Ruling the Country According to Law' in Liu, H et al (eds) (1996) *Yifa Zhiguo jianshe zhuyi fazhi guojia* [Ruling the Country According to Law, Constructing a Socialist Rule-of-Law State] Zhongguo fa zhi chu ban she 126.

Zheng Chengliang (2000) 'On Legal Consciousness and Law-Based Mentality' (4) *Jilin University Journal Social Science Edition.*

Zheng Yubo 1981 *Introduction to law* Sanmin Press.

Zhenghui, L and Zhenmin, W (2002) 'Diritti dell'uomo e Stato di diritto nella teoria e nella pratica della Cina contemporanea' in Costa P, Zolo D (eds) *Lo Stato di diritto. Storia, teoria e critica,* Feltrinelli available at <https://www.juragentium.org/topics/rol/it/wang.htm>.

Zhou Fucheng (1966) *Selected Saying of the Bourgeois Philosophers and Political Thinkers from the Renaissance to the 19th century* The Commercial Press

Zhu Suli (1999) *Fazhi jiqi bentu ziyuan* [Rule of Law and its Local Resources] Zhongguo zhengfa daxue chubanshe.

Zhu Suli (2004) *Daolu tongxiang chengshi - zhuanxing zhongguo de fazhi* [All Roads Lead to Cities - Rule of Law in China's Transformation] Falu chubanshe.

Zhu, M (2004) 'Stability and Democracy' (4) *Human Rights* 1.

Zhu Jingwen (2004) 'Contradictions in the rule of Law' in Xia Yong (ed) *The Rule of Law and the 21st Century* Social Science Documentation Publishing House.

Lightning Source UK Ltd.
Milton Keynes UK
UKHW021137050321
379837UK00008B/1364